NEWS

# New Presidential Candidate Arrives in Haven.

## Corrup Judge

**Reporter: Alex Bay**

A parade will be held this coming Saturday to celebrate the coming of a new Presidential candidate, David Harrison, to Haven.

Main Street will be blocked off from 10am with crowds gathered around the city with the aid of police.

has promised to be the political savior of Haven, cleaning up the streets and putting a stop to rumoured corruption within the city.

to power in his party were found to be believe that the judge of a rival political party, but as accusations have as yet been made.

Gang Warfare Claims Two Lives.

Murder
Bribery

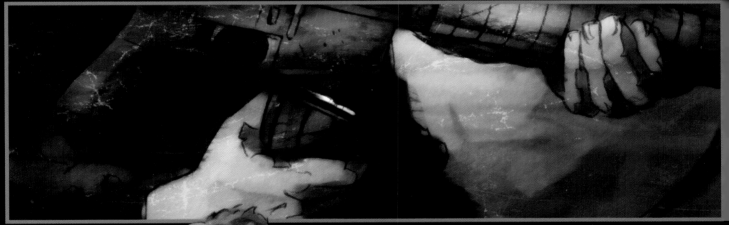

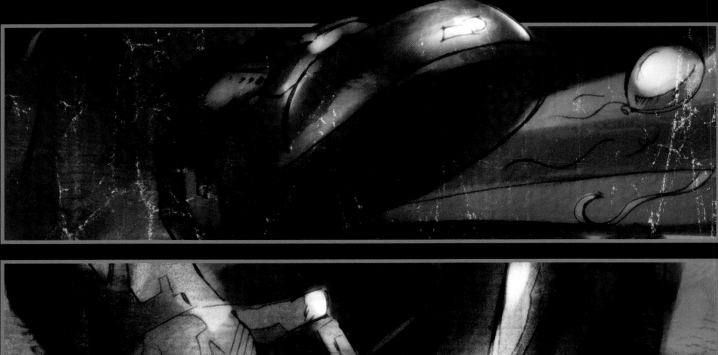

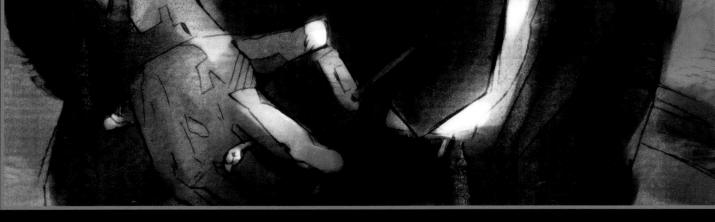

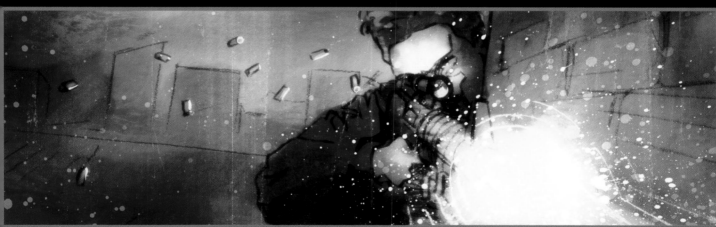

"The Future holds nothing ...
but confrontation"
- Public Enemy -

I know who you are

# HAVEN:

# A ROLE-PLAYING GAME

# CITY OF VIOLENCE

# OF MODERN VIOLENCE

# MY PERSONAL STATEMENT ON

**If there are any parents who are reading this and feel that the subject matter of this game is not appropriate for their children, THEN PLEASE TAKE IT AWAY FROM THEM**

When I first started working on this game, I wanted to make a game similar to the old TSR role-playing Game of the early 80's, Top Secret. I loved that game. The concept of spies and secret agents made me incredibly happy. The system was somewhat simple and the classmates I played with were all somewhat "normal" - whatever that means. We would play a game that had a lot of action combined with a lot of gunplay, espionage and fast cars. We loved it.

But, the funny thing at the time was when we were playing these games, there was a group of people coming out and blaming TSR's most popular game, Dungeon and Dragons, for everything that was bad in the world. If kids committed a crime and happened to play Dungeon and Dragons once, then it was Dungeon and Dragons fault, not the kids. If a kid committed suicide and played Dungeon and Dragons, then it was Dungeon and Dragons fault

Now before I go on I must tell you a little bit about myself. My full name is Louis M. Porter, Jr. I am an African-American male born right outside Chicago, Illinois on August 26, 1970. I am the youngest son of two boys; my brother Reginald is seven years older than I am and married. My father has been a vice president of human resources at a major corporation, with a Masters in Business Administration, while my mother has been an elementary school teacher for nearly 40 years. My parents have been married nearly 40 years and are very active in the Baptist religious faith. Both of my parents were born and raised in Mississippi during the 40s through 60s. In my life, I have lived in Rochester, NY, Danbury CT, Vienna, VA, Dallas, TX, Baltimore, MD, Indianapolis, IN, and FT. Lauderdale, FL and have traveled throughout America, Canada and Europe. I have a bachelor's degree in Political Science with a minor in American History. Several of my hobbies include movies, graphic design, martial arts, writing, video games and computers. I am currently employed and a graphic designer for a large international corporation in Florida, and dating a girl of Trinidad descent, who just received her Masters degree in Psychology in family therapy.

As you can tell, I am a very diverse and somewhat educated person. Now the reason I wrote all this about me is to give you a little understanding on how I see the world at large, in general and specifically. I am very sure that some time in the future, someone caught while committing a crime will try to use this game I created as a "scapegoat" to defend their actions. There will be people who will blame me for causing certain individuals to be pushed over the edge, or for playing out some type of anti-social behavior. Let me inform you on my personal feelings, my company's feelings and make a statement about this issue as follows: EVERYONE IS RESPON-SIBLE FOR THEIR OWN ACTIONS. That is right.

# HAVEN: CITY OF VIOLENCE

Any and all things that go on in my life, except for an act of God, I am responsible for. If I commit a crime, I did it and there is no one else to blame. If you go out and commit a crime, you are the one responsible, not the devil, not your mother, not little green men, not any of that other stuff, YOU ARE. In the last few decades in the United States of America, certain individuals have managed to convince many people that nothing is anyone's fault any more. The concept of self-responsibility has all but disappeared. Anyone over the age of ten has at least a basic understanding of what is right and wrong. The problem is, that in the United States we need to place blame on someone or something, other than ourselves, when it all goes wrong. One school kid kills another school kid with a gun and who do the people blame? The parents? The gun manufacturer? The school? What the hell happened to making the person who performed the act responsible for their actions?

The reason I wrote this game was to show the darker elements of the human mind and to play them out in a setting where everything takes place in a modern fantasy world. I like action movies and television shows from Jean Claude Van Damme to Chow Yun Fat to John Woo to Jet Li to Wesley Snipes. I like the action they bring to the big screen or to television and I wanted to bring that experience in to role-playing games, period. That is the reason I wrote this game. I did not do it to corrupt the morals of children or to help Satan gather souls. I did it because I like the genre of Action-Adventure.

This next part is for any parent who may be taking an active role in their child's development by seeing and reading whatever their children are involved with. If there are any parents who are reading this and feel that the subject matter of this game is not appropriate for their children, THEN PLEASE TAKE IT AWAY FROM THEM. Exercise your rights as a parent and do what is necessary. I am personally grateful for parents who act like parents instead of passing the responsibility off to anyone else. I am also thankful for any parent who gets directly involved with what-ever games or other activities their child is involved with, instead of just dropping their children off at whatever activity they do and leaving, like so many of the ones I have seen while playing role-playing games in the last twenty or more years. We need more good parents, instead of adult baby sitters.

This paragraph is for those who need to blame something or someone for their actions or the actions of another. STOP IT. I don't know what type of environment you grew up in, but I was taught that one stands up for the actions they have done, whether good or bad, and does not shirk away from the responsibility of those actions, good or bad. There will be people who will say that I am glorifying violence with this game. What I am glorifying with this game is the ability for individuals to make choices, whether they are positive or negative, good or bad, right or wrong. Once again, I will say it: EVERYONE IS RESPONSIBLE FOR THEIR OWN ACTIONS. I just wish some of you would act like that.

I must say as someone who enjoys role-playing games that I feel bad that I HAD TO PLACE THIS TYPE OF STATEMENT IN MY GAME. Please take this game in the context it is intended, as a peaceful way to interact with others of a similar interest. I created this game to promote having fun. I hope you enjoy it as much as I did creating it.

Peace

Louis Porter, Jr.
Owner and Chief Executive Officer
Louis Porter, Jr. Design

# TABLE OF CONTENTS

# HAVEN
## CITY OF VIOLENCE

**DESIGNED BY**
Louis Porter, Jr.

**ADDITIONAL DEVELOPMENT**
Brent Dragoo, Steven S. Long, Angus McNicholl,
and Simon Rocquette

**EDITING**
Angus McNicholl, Chris Negelein

**GRAPHIC DESIGN, LAYOUT & LOGO:**
Louis Porter, Jr Design

**COVER**
Rowan Dodds

**INTERIOR ART**
Rowan Dodds and Jason Walton

**SPECIAL THANKS**
Brian and Keith C. Dalrymple, Scott Kurkel,
Steven S. Long, and John Wick

**QUALITY ASSURANCE, PLAYTESTING AND ADVICE**
Christopher Boyd, George "Monkey" Cabeca, Chris Canary, Dan Creel,
Brent Dragoo, Chris Fraker, Stephen Gillispie, Jeremy Heller, Edwyn Kumar,
Luis Matos, Jessica Miller, Christopher Nelson, Rick Radcliffe, Jared
Robertson, Joe Sanzone, Dan Spaid, Shane Stafford, Jordan Stowe

Haven: City of Violence created by Louis Porter, Jr.

Louis Porter, Jr Design
350 NW 87th Terrace
Plantation, FL 33324
HavenGod@lpjdesign.com
www.lpjdesign.com

Dedicated to:
My mother and father for everything that they did for me ... thank you.

# WHAT THE HELL HAVE YOU GOTTEN YOURSELF INTO?

By picking up this book and opening its cover, you have commenced on an adventure of excitement, of right and wrong and the world that stands in between. All of these events will come about when discovering the power of creating a world with your imagination. You have chosen to open your mind in a new and unique way that may be the beginning of a lifetime of fun and entertainment. Welcome to the world of which we call role-playing.

Role-playing games do not require a board or pieces like many other types of traditional games you may be familiar with. Role-playing can be considered to be more like a book or story that is told by a group with everyone interacting with the story and the other storytellers. Quite often, you and your friends will take on the role of the main characters of the story, performing heroic tasks and undertaking epic quests. One of the players, however, assumes the responsibility of narrating the story, describing the scene, laying out the plot, and controlling the actions of all the other characters you will encounter during your adventures. This individual is called the Game Operation Director, G.O.D. for short. All the other people who partake in the game are known as Player Characters, PC for short. Any person in the adventure who is not controlled by a player is considered to be a Non-Player Character or NPC for short.

In the Haven: City of Violence Role Playing Game system, or Haven: COV as it is better known, one of the participants will act as the referee or G.O.D., designing exciting events and the environments in which they will be performed. The environment may be anywhere from the general public areas, such as quiet parks or bustling malls, to deserted streets or trash strewn back alleyways. With the use of dice, information, and events from the G.O.D., players randomly determine the characteristics and actions of their characters. Players will act out the role of the character they have created. While adventuring, characters gain experience, which can be used to increase the abilities and skills of the characters. A

long running or interconnected series of such role-playing game sessions is called a campaign. Some gaming campaigns will last a few sessions of role-playing, while others can last years. The G.O.D. and players will work together to create a story, or as it is better known, an adventure. Within this adventure the players assume the roles of characters, detailed personalities with a history completely separate for each player, who can seem as real as the player who controls him. All the important information including attributes, special abilities, and skills are kept track of on a sheet of paper, which will represent the character. The number and rating of a character will often determine the character's general effectiveness in a specific action or area.

However, the character's persona does not exist solely on paper. The player defines a character's actions and thoughts themselves, while staying true to the character's background and history. The best way to describe what a player is doing is acting in a movie or play with the difference being that the script is created and developed within the minds of the players and G.O.D. In a perfect setting, all the players and G.O.D. will work together to create a story that will be fun for all.

The players determine the reasoning for a character themselves. The player character is no more or less than what the person playing the character brings to it. Most people in the real world would, quite sensibly, run for cover and call the police if someone was shooting at them. In this game, however, this is an extremely rare occurrence. Many times the natural reaction of the character is to return fire to those who shoot at them while some others might still run for cover. Persons who have tried other role-playing games will be familiar with this concept. Haven: COV features campaigns similar to other games. The rules provide nearly endless possibilities for adventures. The adventure can move in any direction that the G.O.D. and the players may wish it to go.

The G.O.D. is one of the most active participants in gaming due to the fact he or she must do most of the initial work before the gaming ever starts. The G.O.D. must provide the labor of completing the game environment. As this game takes place almost entirely within the mind, the G.O.D. should have a good imagination with which to develop and "color" the adventure so that it will seem more realistic to the players. Being the G.O.D. requires a general sense of fair play and creativity carefully balanced with rewards for the circumstances designed. Remember the object of the game is to have fun.

All beginning characters are considered to be relatively weak and extremely inexperienced. The challenges characters will face increase in difficulty as their skill improves. The G.O.D. should plan to present fewer risks and correspondingly modest rewards at the initial start of the gaming campaigns and expand the risks and rewards as the player characters become more powerful and experienced.

The players cannot begin the game until the G.O.D. has concluded his or her design work. Once the G.O.D. has made the essential preparations, the players create their game personae called Player Characters, or PC for short, as described under the section called Character Creation. After a player character has been established, the player is respon-

sible for keeping records of his or her character's attributes and possessions, as well as notes and maps concerning areas which that character has explored. Much of this information can be conveniently recorded on a photocopy of the Haven: COV character sheets provided in the back of this book.

Unlike many games, the players will not necessarily be competing against one another but often against a common enemy. While the G.O.D. must play the role of the various people, the G.O.D. should remain completely neutral. The G.O.D. is not playing against the characters, but is in charge of running the world and environment the characters live and interact in. There is no player that will be declared a winner at the end of an adventure or campaign. Rather, anyone who survives to go on to the next adventure wins by being able to play another day!

The format of the Haven: COV allows for two different (but related) styles of play: running a pre-planned adventure from a module (a pre-created adventure) or letting the G.O.D. design his or her own scenario. It is a good idea for each G.O.D. to

play an adventure module before designing their own. Starting with a module will help the G.O.D. with the feel and play of the game. A pre-made module will provide the G.O.D. with good examples of how to run the game, how to design the environment and vital elements of play, types of non-player characters to populate the environment with, and so forth.

## USING THE DICE

The reader of this book may or may not have used the polyhedral dice system before. The dice will appear strange at first, but they are actually easy to understand. Dice come in various types. The types of die that are need for Haven: COV are 4-sided, or D4; 6-sided, or D6; 8-sided, or D8; 10-sided, or D10; 12-sided, or D12; and 20-sided, or D20. These dice will be numbered one to a specific number with a number belonging to a corresponding side. So if a

die has 10 numbers then it is a 10-sided die. The 10-sided die, however, is numbered 0 through 9, with 0 counting as the 10.

## ADDITIONAL EQUIPMENT

The G.O.D. will find that graph paper, normally with 4 lines per inch, will be one of the most useful items in designing floor plans of buildings the characters will enter, or even a section of a city that the character must search for something. Sheet protectors for often-used maps and notebooks or briefcases to keep all important papers and records together are options the G.O.D. may want to consider. Plenty of paper and pencils should always be handy.

## NUMBER OF PLAYERS

Unlike many other types of role-playing games, adventures in the Haven: COV system work best with a smaller number of players: 2 to 6 players and the G.O.D. Smaller adventuring groups emphasize more varied interaction between the players and the G.O.D.

# GLOSSARY

### Abilities
A broad reference to the aptitudes a character is capable of, including skills and attributes. Often abilities will be followed by a number, which ranks the character's effectiveness.

### Benefits
A special ability, or quirk, that a character possesses. Assets may enhance other abilities, including an attribute, or add a totally new element to game play.

### Campaign
A series of scenarios linked to each other.

### Character
A created identity or persona who is controlled by a player who exists in the Haven: COV system world. Normally this refers to a player character. Also see Player Character

### Character Points (CPs)
An amount given to initial characters to determine their successfulness in particular acts and endeavors.

### Character Sheet
A sheet of paper that is used to record abilities, statistics and equipment of the player character.

### Combat
A situation that develops in which the characters use violence, physical or otherwise, in order to resolve a problem.

### Drawbacks
A disadvantage, either mental or physical, that is possessed by a character. Liabilities often make it more difficult for a character to use an attribute or skill, or in some other way hinder the character.

### Experience points (XPs)
An artificial means of determining a character's level of experience. All characters begin play with a particular number of XPs, which are used to determine professions and skills. Additional XPs will be earned as the game progresses.

### Game Operations Director (G.O.D.)
A person who operates and controls the game and the general outcome of actions among the player characters and non-player characters.

### Game Setting
Imaginary places where all adventures and scenarios take place. In the Haven: COV system, the game world is the city of Haven.

### Non-Player Character (NPC)
A character that is controlled by the Game Operations Director during the course of the game. They are treated exactly the same way as normal characters, but the game does not concentrate on them. They are just people who the characters can meet.

### Player
The person who controls the player character.

### Player Characters (PC)
A character or persona who the player uses as his or her direct interface into the gaming setting.

### Primary Abilities
A general attribute that determines the level of success and which is common to all people. Primary Abilities in Haven: COV are STRENGTH (STR), WILL (WILL), AGILITY (AGI), STAMINA (STA), INTELLIGENCE (INT), and PERCEPTION (PER).

### Role-Playing Game (RPG)
Taking on a role, or persona, of a character set within an adventure setting. Role-playing is a lot like acting out a part in a movie or play, where a player must act, react, and think as he or she feels the character would.

### Scenario
An independent adventure or specific part of a campaign adventure. The average campaign will normally last a few sessions of gaming.

### Secondary Abilities
Secondary abilities are specific abilities that define

the character's general health and well being.

## Session

A meeting between a group of role-playing gamers to play out an adventure. Each gaming scenario or campaign typically takes several sessions to complete and play.

## Skills

Inclination that characters may possess used to perform a specialized ability, such as chemistry, at a specific moment, such as identifying a chemical compound.

## Special Abilities

Special abilities are specific abilities that are unique to specific characters. They can be said to be almost magical in nature. These abilities will normally defy the normal rules of play in the game.

# ENTERTAINMENT SOURCE REFERNCE GUIDE

Here is a list of books, films, music, and television shows that provide the correct mood, attitude, setting, behavior and general feeling for Haven: City of Violence-A Role Playing Game of Modern Violence. Some of these movies may be considered to be in the vein of Science Fiction and Horror but they possess the specific attitude for Haven: City Of Violence. Plus, some of these items are just too damn cool to miss.

# BOOKS

### Written by Octavia Butler

Clay's Ark
Parable of the Sower
Parable of the Talents
Xenogenesis Trilogy

### Written by Tom Clancy

Clear and Present Danger
Debt of Honour

Executive Orders
Patriot Games
Rainbow Six
The Cardinal of the Kremlin
The Hunt for Red October
The Sum of All Fears
Without Remorse

### Written by James Ellroy

American Tabloid
Black Dahlia, The
Big Nowhere, The
L.A. Confidential
White Jazz

### Written by William Gibson

Count Zero
Mona Lisa Overdrive
Neuromancer

### Written by David Morrell

Brotherhood of the Rose
Covenant of the Flame, The
Fifth Profession, The
Fraternity of the Stone, The
League Of Night and Fog, The

### Written by John Sanford

Certain Prey
Easy Prey
Eyes of Prey
Mind Prey
Night Prey
Rules of Prey
Secret Prey
Shadow Prey
Silent Prey
Sudden Prey
Winter Prey

### Written by Neal Stephenson

Snow Crash
Diamond Age, The
Crytonomicon

### Written By Andrew Vachss

Blossom

## COMIC BOOKS

Hellblazer, from DC Comics
Human Target, from DC Comics
Jinx, from Image Comics
Jon Sable: Freelance, from First Comics
Kabuki, from Image Comics
Long Hot Summer, from DC Comics/Milestone
Media
Maverick, from Marvel Comics
Moon Knight, from Marvel Comics
Nightwing, from DC Comics
Ninjak, from Acclaim/Valiant Comics
Punisher, from Marvel Comics
Robin, from DC Comics
Shi, from Crusade Comics
Sin City, from Darkhorse Comics
Skull & Bones, from DC Comics
Torso, from Image Comics
War Machine, from Max Comics/Marvel Comics
Wolverine, from Marvel Comics
Zero, from DC Comics

# FILMS

15 Minutes
187
A Better Tomorrow 1 & 2
Akira
Along Come A Spider
Asphalt Jungle
Assassins
Bad Company
Ballistic
Basic Instinct
Basketball Diaries, The
Billy Bathgate
Big Hit, The
Black Cat 1 & 2
Black Rain
Blade 1 & 2
Blade Runner
Boondock Saints
Bound
Bourne Identity. The
Boyz in the Hood
Brother
Bullet in the Head
B.U.S.T.E.D.

Carlito's Way
Casino
City of Industry
City on Fire
Clockers
Copland
Corruptor, The
Crow, The
Crying Freeman
Dead Pool, The
Deep Cover
Desperado
Die Hard 1, 2 & 3
Dirty Harry
Drugstore Cowboy
El Mariachi
Enemy of The State
Enforcer, The
Entrapment
Escape from New York
Escape from L.A.
Exit Wounds
Extreme Prejudice
Face Off
Fear
Fight Club
Fled
Formula 51
Fortress
French Connection
Full Alert
Fugitive, The
Full Contact (Hong Kong version)
Gang Related
Getaway, The
Ghost Dog: Way of the Samurai
Ghost in the Shell
Godfather 1, 2 & 3
Grosse Point Blank
Gun Crazy
Hannibal
Hard-Boiled
Hard Eight
Hard Target
Harley Davidson and the Marlboro Man
Heat
Johnny Handsome

Run Lola Run
Running Man, The
Scarface
School on Fire
Shaft
Siege, The
Set It Off
Seven
Silence of the Lambs, The
Snatch
State of Grace
Strange Days
Streets of Fire
Surviving the Game
Swordfish
Tango & Cash
Taxi Driver
Terminator 1 & 2
Thick as Thieves
Things to do in Denver when You're Dead
Time and Tide
To Live and Die in L.A.
Traffic
Training Day
Transporter, The
Trespass
True Romance
Truth or Consequences, NM
Untouchables, The
US Marshals
Usual Suspects, The
Warriors, The
Way of the Gun, The
Whiteboys
White Heat
Wicked City (Hong Kong and Anime version)
XXX
Year of the Dragon

# MUSIC

311
A Tribe Called Quest
Bauhaus
Chemical Brothers
Coal Chamber
Crystal Method

Deftones
Diggable Planets
Download
DMX
Dr. Dre
Fear Factory
Fluke
Front Line Assembly
Gravity Kills
Helmet
Ice Cube
Ice-T
Joy Division
Korn
Limp Bizkit
Linkin Park
Method Man
N.E.R.D.
Nine Inch Nails
Notorious B.I.G.
N.W.A.
P.O.D.
Papa Roach
Phosphorescence
Prodigy
Public Enemy
Puff Daddy
Rage Against the Machine
Skinny Puppy
Slipknot
Stuck Mojo
Tool
X-ecutioners
Wu Tang

Equalizer, The
Fastlane
Freedom
Homicide: Life on the Street
Investigative Reports
Johnny Quest
Jon Sable: Freelance
John Woo's: Blackjack
John Woo's: Once a Thief
La Femme Nikita
Law & Order
Law & Order: Special Victims Unit
Law & Order: Criminal Intent
Miami Vice
Millennium
New York Undercover
NYPD Blue
OZ
Profiler
Profit
Shield, The
Silk Stalkings
Sins of the City
Stingray
Solder of Fortune, Inc./SOF: Special Ops Force
Sopranos, The
Spenser for Hire
Twenty-Four
UC: Undercover
Vengeance Unlimited
Wire, The
Wiseguy

## TELEVISION

Alias
American Justice
Batman Beyond
Batman: The Animated Series
City Confidential
Crime Story
Corner, The
Cops
Cowboy BeBop
CSI: Crime Scene Investigations

## Did It Again

He set me up again. I do not know why or how he did it, but he did. He didn't give a fuck about me or you or what we planned. The plan was perfect. Go in the bank, hit the cash drawers and stay away from the time burning vault. Make sure the tellers give you the cash from the right drawer. The left ones have red dye paint bombs. We should have been out of there in less than a minute. With this job, we would have had enough cash to keep us happy for months, but betrayal stepped in. I should have known, by the way he was acting.

He was always glaring and undressing you with his eyes. He was the best man for this job as far as talent, but I should have never trusted him. He shot me in the back while we were leaving the bank. I think the bullet hit my spine because I can't feel my legs right now.

I can't feel much pain at all. The only thing that hurt was the way you looked at me after it happened.

You were standing there and laughing at me. Telling me what kind of fool I was. How you both had this planned from the beginning. Just another life lesson I guess. Funny thing is, I still love you and want us to be together. It's easy to ignore all kinds of shit when you're in love.

# CHAPTER:1

## HISTORY OF HAVEN

*The Devil tempts men to be wicked that he may punish them for being so.*

*Samuel Bulter*

I knew that this was a fucking bad idea. However, I have never been known as one who lives what others call a "safe or normal life". All of this started simple enough.

Out of the dark silence came a damn noise, an electronic howl. The phone's early morning jingle broke apart my peaceful, restful sleep. I barely opened my eyes, trying to scan my room for the phone. My blurry eyes finally came into focus and I grasped at the phone unsuccessfully, several times, trying to reach it without shedding the warm comfort of the bed. Pulling myself from the sheets, my flailing hand finally flopped onto the smooth plastic of the receiver. I coughed out a sound into the phone that resembled speech and said "Hello". The rough, gravely sounding voice on the other side of the phone came back across like a clap of thunder.

"Hey, you awake?" the voice was harsh from a lifetime of cigarettes and booze. It was Johnny Delluci, the Santucci family's main enforcer and Haven's favorite drunk on the line. Even over the phone, I smelled the liquor soaking his breath like it was filling a thirsty sponge.

"What the hell are you calling me this early for?" I barked back to Johnny in my best "I just woke up" voice. "What are you some kind of fucking idiot?"

"I'm sorry about that man, but I got a job for you, if you're looking?" Johnny replied.

"You know I'm trying to get out of that lifestyle, Johnny - not get dragged back into it," I said.

"No man, it's nothing like that," he said. "We are just looking for someone to give us a little background assistance on a business proposition we are conducting down in Little Saigon."

"Any time you call it's never for just a little business. It's for someone who can handle waste removal of all types," I replied. I reached for my smokes then started to sit up in bed.

"Hey man, I know that you are dead broke. So, cut the macho, tough guy bullshit," Johnny snarled. "I just thought you might be looking to earn some extra money to help pay those gambling debts you have with the Carlucci Family." For once in my life, Johnny had truly surprised me

"How do you know about that?" I said. "Nobody knew about that!"

"Hey, like they say, you can't keep a secret in Haven without everyone knowing what's going on." replied Johnny. I could almost see that damn grin creeping across his ugly mug shot.

I milled over the offer in my mind for a few seconds before answering. If I didn't pay back the Carlucci Family the twenty-five thousand dollars I owed them, they'd remove my favorite anatomical parts. There wasn't really a decision to make. I paused as if to give the matter my full think over, but we both already knew that I would. I mean, what choice did I have? The Carlucci Family would be looking for their cash in less than a week and I wasn't going to raise funds any other fucking way.

"OK, Johnny… if your looking for a cleaner, then I'm your man." I said, sounding resigned to the idea.

"Good man! I knew that you wouldn't let us down," he said. "Meet us over at the house. Take the train to the Crystal City station at Golden Heights at around 7:00 p.m. That will at least give you a few hours to get cleaned up and over here on time." The more Johnny spoke, the more it had a commanding tone creep into it. His last line was an order, not small talk.

"Yeah," I replied, then I hung up the phone.

I scratched my three-day old unshaven chin. My skin felt more like worn sandpaper, as I thought over and over to myself "What have I gotten myself into?" I was going back to hell once again. God, I knew that this was not where I wanted to be. Nevertheless, I had to do what I had to do, just to survive. I peered over at the clock and it read 9:54 am. Well, at least I could get some well deserved and needed rest before I go back down the road to hell. God, it is great to be alive.

I awoke at 4:28 p.m., with more than enough time to

eat, shower, shave, find my piece and get into my best suit to wear over to the Santucci compound. The entire time while I was getting ready, I kept thinking to myself. This job seemed excessively good to be true. By now, I already learned that all that glitters ain't always gold. I caught the 6:10 subway from the Waterfront station in Haven City to Crystal City station out in Golden Heights. The monstrous, metallic beast rolled to a stop and the doors hissed like a snake, opening to the station. I stepped off the subway car on to the station platform. Unlike the other subway stations of Haven, which reeked with the fumes of piss, crap and vomit, the Crystal City station gently wafted with the aroma of a warm spring day, even though it was the dead of winter. The black and gray chiseled granite walls shone like a mirror. I scanned the crowd, sizing up the surrounding persons as potential victim or target. The old ways die-hard. Through the crowd on the platform I caught sight of two men, rather large, olive skinned men, dressed immaculately in five hundred dollar silk suits with two hundred and fifty-dollar eel skin Italian dress loafers. I rather figured they might be for me.

They both walked up to me, moving like a pack of bull elephants. As they got closer, I recognized the person up in front. It was Carlos Devita, one of Haven's best "waste removal" experts. He wasn't in the same class as me, but dangerously fucking talented nonetheless. People in the business say he's got the blood of more than 47 people on his manicured and moisturized hands. You would think after killing so many people that it would be hard to hide all those bodies. I guess it pays that the Santucci Family own several meat packing plants all over Haven. It also pays that I am a vegetarian in this town. I know I would really hate to bite into a hot dog and find a couple of gold teeth inside it.

Even though they are wearing sunglasses, I felt their eyes sizing me up, visually checking out any lumps or odd lines in my suit that might reveal a concealed weapon. I paid them the same courtesy, of course. I picked out the tell tale signs that both men were packing automatics, probably 9mm, but the designer suits were cut to conceal them. We stared at each other, hoping to make the other one feel uncomfort-

able. After a few minutes of silence, I decided to end this game the easiest way I know how.

"So how long are we going to stand here and fucking stare at each other?" I said, my voice firm, but relaxed, careful not to betray any sense of my wariness.

The larger of the two slowly took off his sunglasses to reveal his crystal blue colored eyes.

"Sorry," The huge son of bitch said. "We just have never met a fucking legend up this close and not on the business end of a shotgun. Johnny Delluci sent us to escort you to the Santucci Compound " his voice equally neutral with just enough respect.

"Lead the way to the car," I replied with a hand motion, indicating for them to move ahead of me. I could tell they hated the idea of their back to me. Fuck them.

We all walked from the pristine, baroque subway and train station across the street towards a jet black Range Rover. The car rocked slightly on its suspension as one after the other of us large men all got in. The engine purred like a tiger. The car was new; I inhaled the new car smell as we sped through the streets of Golden Heights, heading for the Santucci Compound.

The journey was short, about twenty minutes and then a pair of familiar gates came into view. The large and foreboding steel blue iron gates of the Santucci's compound surrounded several acres of estate with a complete security and privacy from the outside world. We drove though the gates and into another world.

We emerged from the Range Rover to have the smell of freshly cut grass and honeysuckle invaded my senses. It took me back to when I was a young boy and my father would bring me to the compound when he would talk business with Gino Santucci, Sr. I used to sit on a patio and eat a bowl of ice cream while the old man got his orders. Those days of my childhood are long gone, now I am the man coming to do the talking. No fucking ice cream for me. Now I am a man who is not only feared for my skills, but also respected for my personal "code of conduct".

We walked towards the enormous oak front doors of the mansion.

They seem to open on queue at the exact moment we reached them. Through the doorway, I could see the aged face and slender frame of the most trusted of all the Santucci employees, Mr. Carlito "The Scarecrow" Gambruno.

To the average and unsuspecting person, Mr. Gambruno seemed to be only a "mere" well-dressed butler, but to all those involved in our business, he was a god among men. Mr. Gambruno was known to be the most effective killer in Haven during his career. It had been said that in his lifetime, he had killed at least a thousand people and many felt that was a very conservative estimate. It did not matter if it was with guns, knives, or a bare-knuckle fight Mr. Gambruno was the best. Many of those that studied under him had gone on to gain wealth and respect with the skills he taught. I must admit that I am very proud to be part of such an elite group of men. Even though, I wasn't his best student, I had always hoped that he knew how much I appreciated his training and expert experience and unique training.

"Well, well, well the prodigal son does return again," said Mr. Gambruno, his voice still powerful and commanding despite his apparent age.

"I thought you considered me to be more of a man in self-imposed exile than a prodigal son", I countered him.

"I consider you to be a true pain in the ass and a professional idiot but that doesn't mean I don't like you", Mr. Gambruno sneered, with a wickedly evil smile of false teeth in his face.

The door opened wider as he waved me into the mansion. Though he was at a smaller physical stature compared to other men, Mr. Gambruno stood spiritually taller than any other man I had met. He had saved my life on more occasions than I could remember or even hope to remember. Mr. Gambruno escorted us in to the main foyer, beautifully covered in white marble pillars and Old Italian sculptures and paintings art.

From the foyer, we entered the main living room where the true power of the organization resided. In

the living room stood Antonio Santucci, Jr., Antonio Santucci, Sr., and Johnny Delluci. Antonio Santucci, Sr. was the old establishment of the Santucci organization.

The three well-dressed men turn toward me and smiled. "Now that we are all here we can begin." Antonio, Sr. speaks. "The meeting we are having tonight will be one of the most important in the history of the City of Haven."

"What is going on tonight?" I asked.

With a sinister smile on Antonio, Sr.'s face he speaks, "Tonight were are going to Armistad to meet with the Red Wing Tong to form a alliance with them and to split the city in half."

Despite my well-practiced poker face, I could not hold back the look of surprise that appeared on my face and just as quickly, it vanished again. They were trying to bring back the old Coalition, an alliance of "business" that we all remembered as the good old days for us in Haven. In truth, any real success would probably spark another round of bloody street wars and crazy problems for all the organizations, all of which are good for my line of work.

"We are going to this meeting with only one thing in our minds. We are going to make a lasting peace with the Red Wing Tong. They are a powerful group and they'll make the best allies." Antonio, Sr. said as he slowly gazed around to be sure we all understood that, before he continued.

"We need to think about the future and as long as we have the Carlucci family slowly picking us off, we can not grow as an organization and a business. We are dying a slow death"

"Dad, you have to be fucking kidding me! Those chink bastards have been muscling in on our drug revenues for the last six months. Those jerk-offs have to sliced into our profits at Haven and Acadia proper.," blurted out Antonio, Jr. The sound of disbelief undisguised in his tone.

"If the Red Wing Tong is looking to make a bold move to enter into Carlucci controlled territories they will become strong enough to be the new number one players in this city. With that, I have a strong feeling that if we do not become partners with the Tong, then we will be in their sights sooner rather than later." commented Antonio, Sr.

"We need to destroy those little shits, not make them our allies." The callous and brash Antonio, Jr. said, as he took another puff from his Cuban cigar.

Antonio Sr. looked over to me with that trademark sly grin on his face as replies. "Just like youth, they believe everything is a power play instead of a simple game of chess, like where you sacrifice a pawn to capture the king."

"A head out assault on the Red Wing Tong will cost us too dearly in lives and revenue and if the Tong respond with an alliance to the Sangre or that nigger Nation, we will be fighting a brutal war on two fronts. Those battles are never winnable." Antonio Sr. states

"He's right." I said as I leaned closer to the three of them. "The Red Wing Tong are not only powerful and resourceful, but they are ruthless. If you start a war with them then you better be ready to fight to the last man, because they will."

Antonio Jr. walks over to me, face to face. I could smell the $200 cologne long before his bad breath. "Listen, I know that you are some type of legend to the old guys here, but get it straight, what you did in the past is past. Frankly, I think your rep is all hype and you don't look like shit to me."

Antonio Jr. was doing his best to look "hard" for Antonio Sr. but everyone in this room knew I could break the little shit in half without even working up a sweat. I decided to let the little bastard live just for a little longer. It's not good business to permanently cripple you boss's son on the first day of work.

I pulled out a cigarette, lit it, and took a deep drag. I blew the smoke right into the little shit's face. He was doing his best, trying to not look disgusted or nauseous from the smoke in his face. He failed, which meant points for me.

"What ever you say, junior." I answered back.

I walked past him, "accidentally" knocking into him as I moved closer to Antonio, Sr. The old man smiled at me, knowing that I let his son get away from becoming the newest corpse to show up at the Waterfront in downtown Haven City, this time.

"Trust me, Junior. I know what I am doing. The Tong will make great allies. Now we must be moving, we don't want to be late for our historic meeting." said Antonio Sr. as he rose from his comfortable arm chair and straightened the line of his suit jacket.

We all loaded up into the car and I took one quick look over everyone. They all looked slightly nervous, as they should, all except for Antonio Jr. who looked completely at ease. That kid must be a total idiot, thinking that this is going to be a cake-walk. How do I get myself into these things? I checked front and back, we had extra security a car in front and one behind.

We drove all the way from the clean and sparkling streets of Golden Heights, through the busy streets and seedy back alleys of downtown Haven City to the modern day steel hell of Armistad. The meeting was scheduled to be at Lao Hung Chinese restaurant in Little Saigon. The Lao Hung Chinese restaurant was not the greatest place in Armistad to get Chinese food. It was a hell of a place, however, if you wanted to meet the real people who ran Armistad, the Red Wing Tong.

The Red Wing Tong is the American version of the Crimson Eagle Triad, based out of Hong Kong. These Chinese sons of bitches are into everything from heroin smuggling to white slavery to -- my personal favorite -- murder for hire. They don't give a shit; if it makes money, then they want a piece of it. You can forget about trying to get some under-cover asshole into the Red Wing Tong. There aren't any hon chews; "bananas", yellow on the outside and white on the inside; that live long enough to report back to the Haven Police Department. The Red Wing Tong are some cold-blooded mother fuckers, and I had to wonder, in the back of my mind, why would they want to have a meeting with us. We arrive at the Lao Hung Chinese restaurant. The tension in the car is so thick you can cut it with a goddamn knife and that is not good at all.

The door to the car opened like breaking the seal on

an airtight container, I heard the rubber seal peel away from the car as the door opened. The smells of ginger and exotic spices smothered us as we exited the vehicle. The drivers stay with the cars, plus we have a couple of goons for extra protection. This place was not Golden Heights in the least bit. The old buildings were made of clay tile and wood trim that seemed to grow out of the street like some monstrous flower. I looked over the street, examining everything going on around us. I saw everything from the old man selling noodles on the corner, to the three young kids who just stole a few apples from the front most street stall of the Korean market, to the transvestite hooker making a sale of his "goods" to the two young Navy sailors fresh off the boat. I think those two sailors are in for a "big surprise" of the completely wrong type tonight.

I take one last look over our crew before we entered the den of the Asian beast; Antonio, Jr., Antonio, Sr., Johnny Delluci, three men for security and myself all going in. On the outside, we have three drivers and another two thugs watching the street. I gave the security team a stern look.

"Everybody stay frosty. I don't want any fucking screw ups here," I snarled to them

"Don't worry, sir. We know what we are doing here." the youngest looking member of the security team tries to come over all laid back, like he's had a world of fucking experience.

"If you assholes knew what you were doing, then I wouldn't have to be here," I said. "So shut your god damn pie-hole, open your fucking eyes and pay attention to the shit that is going on here and if you're lucky, you might survive this meeting and get a raise." I glared at him and he shuffled out from under my stare. That kind of guy only ends up one way, with a bullet hole in head and his brains on the street.

We strolled across the street to the restaurant. The neon glow of the storefront businesses illuminated the coal black night sky. The uneven cobble stone streets are symbolic of the uneven development of this city. The well to do European immigrants settled and thrived in the lush lands of Golden Heights, while the newest immigrants were banished to the decaying, dilapidated and neglected land of

Armistad. Life really is a bitch and don't I know that.

We reached the double plate glass door of the restaurant. I entered first to set the tone of this meeting and surveyed the restaurant for any potential danger. Golden Chinese symbols decorated the crimson red painted walls as well as exotic ornaments and classic art prints. The restaurant should have been bustling with waiters serving food and filled with the noise of patrons talking and eating as they soaked in the ethnic experience. But today, the restaurant is nearly empty, except for a few oversized bus boys cleaning tables and those we are meeting with. I didn't realize how important this meeting was to the Santucci Family and the Red Wing Tong. They told me that this would be an important meeting, but I did not know that we would be graced with the presence of Leland Tsai, third in command of the Red Wing Tong.

"Leland, it is so good to see you again." Antonio, Sr. said with a smile that looked like it was painted on.

Leland was dressed in only the finest, from the top of his Ralph Loren glasses to his imported Italian black leather Gucci loafers. For such a man of young age, Leland had become quite an impressive force in the Red Wing Tong. I can remember, like yesterday, when he was just an up and coming lieutenant on the streets of Armistad selling vials of rock cocaine for twenty dollars.

The times were changing, too bad I don't.

"It is my honor to have such individuals gracing this small restaurant. I see that you have brought the best that money can buy for this little meeting of ours." Leland hissed out of his teeth as he glares over in my direction.

It is amazing how many friends and enemies switch sides in this business. Leland and I have had several little "run-ins" in the past. Several of them were quite violent. I wondered if he has forgiven me for shooting off his index and ring fingers on his left hand. Oh well, I guess he is glad that he is right handed.

We sat at the large black round wooden table with our esteemed host. The Tong had some of their best men in for this little party of ours. One of them was Chow Pai, better known as the Steel Butcher because he liked to kill with a kitchen butcher's knife. Another was Kenny Ho, the top sharp shooter from Steel City in Armistad. People said that Kenny is such a good shooter that he always shoots out his victim's eyes. I could tell now that this was not going to be a simple little sit-down dinner.

"Well enough with the banter, gentlemen, If you please." Leland raised his voice so that it carried easily around the interior of the restaurant. He waved his hand towards an immaculately covered table laid out with all manner of dishes. The aroma was right from the mainland of China. Well it should, the people who made it were right off the boat from Mainland China. Their little trip to the United States, however, came with a thirty thousand dollar bill that had to be paid by working as a bus boy, drug bag man or prostitute, take your pick, for the next million plus years.

We moved over to the table while I scanned the room again for any potential problems I might see. I looked over Leland, and he seemed cool as did his bodyguards. I looked over the "little old mother" sitting over in the corner overseeing the bus boys cleaning the table and she seemed ordinary. I watched one of the bus boys and I notice something.

One of them had a tattoo on his arm. The bus boy coat covered the majority of it but it looked quite intricate. I glanced over at another bus boy and I saw a tattoo near his neck, just like the other bus boy's tattoo. It was very professionally done and very intricate. I scanned over the rest of the bus boys and I noticed that all of them had similar intricate tattoo patterns that were hidden by their clothing. There are no coincidences, then it hit me like a damn jolt of bad whiskey.

"IT'S A FUCKING SET UP!" I screamed out and all hell broke loose.

I should have known better. I didn't follow my natural instincts. You are either the hunter or the prey. Don't trust anyone I have always said. That is the easiest way to live and stay safe, but now, I got stupid. I let myself believe that there was honor among thieves, but, among murderers and killers, honor is a lost concept and friendship is an idea that can cost you your life. The mistake I made was going to cost me a little more than I thought. I should have known something was up when they wanted to meet at the Lao Hung Chinese restaurant in Little Saigon. This area was totally outside the Santucci Family sphere of influence. The Red Wing Tong never place themselves at a disadvantage, and the Santucci Family always thinks that they are at an advantage.

The next sound I heard goes off like an explosion next to my ear. My head felt as if someone was using a large mallet to drive a sleek ice-cold spike into my skull. The explosive pain in my shoulder struck like the sting of a million wasps. My shoulder began to burn like an inferno, with the nerves in my arm aching out in sheer agony. My arm goes dead and it drops as if it was made out of lead. In a brief moment that seems to last for infinity plus a day, I saw the worst thing in the world. I dropped my fucking gun.

I screamed out as if my soul was being ripped apart, piece by piece. The double cross started but I was too late and too stupid to realize it. At that moment, the place split from a 100 percent family restaurant into 50 percent East Los Angeles and 50 percent Beirut. No soul was safe and I was at the top of every limp dick's list as one of those that had to die. My eyes flickered as if I was sending off a SOS to anyone who could see. My body felt as light as a feather, almost angelic in stature floating above the ground, then gravity came back on and I went slamming into the ground. My eyes shut for the briefest of moments, and in the calm peacefulness of all that darkness, the world broke out into the sound of gunfire.

My eyes opened and closed, while I got small glimpses of the world around me. I reached over to where I feel the pain in my arm. The explosive pain started at the top of my arm and worked its way down to my fingers. Shaking like a detoxing crack addict, I finally brought myself to look at my shoulder wound. I covered the wound with my hand hoping to stop the flow of blood rushing out of the wound. The smell of gunpowder and sweat mixed in with a hint of blood filled the air. I rolled over on

my back and just over my head I saw the rain of bullet fire streaking above me like a flock of lethal humming birds.

I finally realized what my body had already known, I had been shot. The wound was bad, I could tell there was a good chance I would pass out again. The pain throbbed in my hand as if I was holding a ball of lightning. My eyes fluttered and finally buckled one last time as I felt myself enter into a cold and black embrace of darkness.

Just before the darkness enveloped me, I saw a sight that would haunt my remaining time left. It was Antonio, Jr. raising up a pistol and firing it into the back of his father's head. Antonio, Sr.'s head exploded like an overripe watermelon. The red juices of life spurted out of his mouth like a water fountain turned on high.

My mind raced to make the connections, trying to focus on something to keep the darkness at bay. That bastard Antonio, Jr. couldn't not wait for his father to retire. He wanted control of the family and killed us all for it. He must have made a deal with the White Rose Yakuza that he could get their two greatest rivals in one place. Antonio, Jr. killed his father and I bet the White Rose Yakuza would kill the leaders of the Red Wind Tong. With both of the main rivals, out of the way the two could form a new and more powerful alliance between the Santucci crime family and White Rose Yakuza. I had to admit, it was good business. With that type of alliance formed, they should have enough strength to displace the Carlucci crime family as the most powerful organized criminal syndicate in all of Haven. I knew I should have stayed in fucking bed today…

*Many might go to heaven with half the labor they go to hell.*

*Samuel Johnson*

# WELCOME TO HAVEN

*All the adventures for Haven: City of Violence gaming system takes place in the fictional metropolitan city known as Haven.*

# THE CITY OF HAVEN

Haven is one of the most populous cities in the eastern seaboard of the United States.  In addition to Haven's large population, it also boasts the third largest seaport in the nation.  Haven resides directly on the eastern coast of the United States next to the Atlantic Ocean, roughly 45 miles north of the city of Baltimore.  As one of the world's leading financial, commercial and cultural centers, Haven is subdivided into six boroughs that exist within the Haven City limits making it the city itself.  They are, in alphabetical order, the boroughs are Arcadia, Armistad, Freeman Hill, Golden Heights, Haven City and Rome Island.  Each borough possesses its own unique atmosphere, personality, social and economical structure.  As Calverton Churchill, former mayor of Haven discovered and announced during a speech, "Haven is unlike any place in the world that has been seen or experienced before."

Haven's six boroughs are said to be as diverse as the whole of America all rolled into one and no less dangerous.  The bright lights and large buildings of Arcadia will remind the most common type of visitor of the original "Sin City", Las Vegas.  Arcadia was created with one thing in mind, fun and entertainment for you and all.  The combination of burnt out buildings, abandoned car production plants and the smell of decaying meat from the numerous meat processing plants infest Armistad like a plague.  Armistad is the "Detroit" of Haven.  While in contrast to the rest of Haven, Freeman Hill appears as if this area had been frozen in time from the 1950's.  The people of Freeman Hill are not too busy to say "Hi" as they walk past.  It feels like the "good old days".  The ultimate utopian society of Haven is

the borough of Golden Heights. This area of Haven only produces the upper most crust of polite and wealthy society. If New York City has a twin then Haven City is it. The combination of a large city and the urban setting is what Haven City is. The complete opposite of Golden Heights is Rome Island. The quintessential slum ghetto and the worst of the "wrong side of the track". If there is a hell and a devil, then Rome Island must be purgatory.

One of the most interesting aspects of the city of Haven is its development of organized crime and corruption. In Haven, unlike many major metropolitan cities, crime and corruption begins at the top, with the Mayor's office and then drips all the way down to the back alleys and the dank city sewers. Haven can be described as New York City during a blackout and in the middle of a race riot that has lasted for 25 years without a reprieve. Even though, the majority of citizens of Haven have wished for the city to return to a earlier more simplistic time, when criminal corruption was only behind closed doors and not on every street corner. The grand return to those "Old Glory Days" of Haven seem almost impossible to most in this morally corrupted and socially bankrupt society. The only true future that is left for the city of Haven is a truly bleak one.

## POPULATION

The city of Haven's population has reached an all time high of 5,459,082 as recorded by last year's Census Bureau. Haven is noted as having one of the largest urban populations in the United States, as well as being one of the most racially and ethnically diverse cities on the eastern seaboard. Further data from the Census Bureau, Whites consist of 40.6 percent Haven's population; African-American were 23.2 percent; Hispanics were 17.7 percent; Asians were 13.5 percent with the remaining 5 percent to consist of all other various races and ethnicities.

Haven's population and ethnic diversity gives the City a "mish mash" feel, it is a melting pot that possess every racial group or cultural identity is boiled down to its most basic form. This City is a simmering cauldron of humanity where every lifestyle, religion or community can be found, if you have the time and the money to search for what you want. Haven is so many different things that it hard to draw an average across the whole lot, though this hasn't stopped the various Censuses' from trying. According to one recent study conducted by 'Economist Today Magazine' the average income for a family in Haven is $28, 064, while the average family size is up from last year number of 4.6 to a total of 5.3 people.

## ECONOMY

Haven was originally a blue-collar working seaport city, but over the last century has developed and evolved into a major financial, commercial, manufacturing empire. The only industry that seems to stall in Haven is tourism. Despite the Haven Convention and Visitors Bureau allegedly pouring millions of dollars into marketing aimed at tourists, the town still seems to have a reputation that keeps the city's small beaches empty during season. Haven is a national central area for road, rail, sea, and air transportation. The city also contains the headquarters of several major national and international businesses and corporations.

The heart of Haven's financial district is located in the borough of Haven City, centered on the corner of Justice Street and Harmony Avenue, better known as "Money Row" to the citizens of Haven. This includes the Haven Stock and Mercantile Exchange, initially founded over 125 years ago, the Haven Federal Reserve Bank of the United States, founded over 50 years ago, and many other important banking, brokerage, and financial institutions. Much of the city's domestic and international trade is conducted in Haven City's downtown executive offices, including those in the McHaverty Building, directly connected to the International Haven City Center.

All of Haven's seaport and airport transportation facilities are located in Haven City and Armistad. The largest seaport of the city is the Armistad Port Administration of Haven. The city's two major international airports, the Tsuji International Airport and the Michael S. Carboni National Airport, both located in Armistad's "Steel City", are major air-

cargo terminals with large amounts of freight passing through them every year.

Wholesale and retail trade shops are vitally important to the success and health of Haven's growing economy. Haven is particularly noted for its many retail outlets and several large department store chains, including Wellmen's & Taft, Portal Department stores and Williams of Haven as well as various types of specialty consumer shops. The most well known area for consumer and retail stores is the area called Alphabet City, located in the heart of downtown Haven City. The Waterfront area, located on the eastern waterfront property of Haven City, is especially famous and adored for their fine upscale boutiques and stores. Of the few tourists to the city, many are the rich and famous come to Haven just to shop in this area - with bodyguards in tow.

As a manufacturing center, Haven is falling far behind as a national leader. Haven may well be losing the fight in the manufacturing industries, but it has evolved its specialized service areas. In this area, Haven seems always to remain on top of its game. Haven has matured itself into an important center of the world financial industry in both the areas of advertising and communications industries. Both of these types of business have taken an incredible interest in the city of Haven in comparison to other employment sectors. Haven currently leads the nation in the development of new television stations. Several radio networks have headquartered themselves in the city. Haven also boasts a large number of prominent book and magazine publishers. The city's largest daily newspaper, the Haven Chronicles, is considered one of the United States best daily newspapers. It seems though that employment in this industry has a higher average of job-related deaths and suicides compared to the national average.

Tourism and trade show conventions does play a significant role in the economy in the boroughs of Arcadia and Haven City. As a direct consequence of which, numerous hotel facilities have emerged in the city of Haven. Many of the most interesting and exotic hotel locations include Riegero Manor, located in Haven City; the Parker Lane Hotel and the Rogers Inn, both located in Arcadia.

## POINTS OF INTEREST

The city of Haven, in particular Haven City and Arcadia, boasts many distinguished architectural masterpieces. Dozens of skyscrapers pierce the skyline; the Atlec Building, erected nearly 60 years ago, was one of the first permanently constructed high-rise executive suites in the city. Others include West Street Skyscraper, which was constructed over 30 years ago, the Nagota Towers constructed over 15 year ago, the Hope Building erected over 25 years ago and the Osirus Towers built 5 years ago. Many of the older architectural structures include the St. Anthony's Triumph Church of Arcadia first constructed nearly 150 years ago, then rebuilt in the aftermath of a massive fire 20 years ago, the South King Street Elementary school was built over 115 year ago and finally closed down roughly 40 years ago. It still stands today, boarded up and a refuge for the homeless and more.

Haven is home to several professional sports teams who play for the city. The Haven Angels baseball team just relocated to Haven City within the last five years and currently plays at the newly constructed Kimbrose Stadium in Arcadia. While in Freeman Hill, Haven's original hometown baseball team, the Freeman All-Stars, have played out of Old Soldier Stadium for nearly four decades.

Other major sports facilities of Haven include the Haven City Downtown Sports Complex located in downtown Haven City. This complex is a combination basketball court and hockey ice ring. This is home of the Haven Inferno basketball team and Haven Polar Bears ice hockey team. The Haven Polar Bears ice hockey team originally played hockey at the nearby Armistad Skating Complex, but with completion of the newer facilities, they have relocated. The greatest and most profitable sport in Haven is football. The Haven Titans football team has been playing to sell out crowds for the last two decades at Titan Stadium in Arcadia.

## EDUCATIONAL AND CULTURAL INSTITUTIONS

Like many larger cities there are many fine institutions of higher learning and education throughout the six boroughs that include University of Haven, Haven City University and Corel University. All of these universities are located in the metropolitan area of Haven City. State University and Freeman Hill College are located in Freeman Hill. Winston Military Academy, Lincoln College, York University and Arcadia College are located in Arcadia.

As one of the undisputed cultural centers of the United States, the city of Haven contains many museums, art galleries and performing arts organizations. Among the leading art museums in Haven are the Mechanic Museum located in Arcadia; the Livingstone Museum and Haven City Museum, both located in Haven City; Armistad Railroad Museum is located in Armistad and the Golden Heights hosts the Golden Heights Science and Technology Museum. The city's major libraries include the Haven Public Library, with some 6 million volumes, the libraries of the University of Haven, Corel University and York University.

Haven boasts one of the leading centers for medical research, technology and care. The University of Haven Medical School and Cartright Medical School, both located in Haven City and Crystal City Hospital, located in Golden Heights, is one of the leading researchers and developers in genetic manipulation and research. Rome Island Hospital in Rome Island and Cifier General Hospital in Arcadia are considered two of the best shock trauma and emergency rooms on the eastern seaboard. Other hospitals and medical centers include St. Helen's Memorial Hospital in Haven City; Mercy Memorial Center, Freeman Hill Hospital and Order of Saints Medical Center all located in Freeman Hill and Taft Medical Hospital located in Arcadia.

Haven contains the sixth largest center for theater production in the United States. In Haven City lie the two largest theaters in all of the city. The Dover Theater and Lindenburg Theater are both located in the direct center hub of the city's theater district.

There are more than 20 legitimate smaller theaters here presenting all types of plays from dramas, comedies, and musicals. Near the waterfront of Haven City is the Haven State Theater, where the Haven Ballet and Opera Company perform just about every night. The Kurkel Theater located on Mikal Avenue is home of the Dance Company of Haven which is more commonly referred to as the 'Haven Company'.

## HOW TO LIVE, DIE AND SURVIVE IN HAVEN

The city of Haven is the epitome of what is wrong in today's society. Consequently, it is a very dangerous place to live. The city is decaying both physically and spiritually. The city government and police forces are corrupt. The organized crime syndicates control any dark dealings that go on within the city limits. The people that stay here often live like hostages in their own homes. Drug dealers are at every corner looking to sell the latest new hit or fix to their next victim. Hit men and assassins almost take out billboards looking for work. Prostitutes and whores walk the street day and night to keep their masters and pimps in their expensive cars. The schools are like training grounds for the next generation of Haven citizens. Just about every child brings a gun or blade to settle any disputes that might arise.

## LIFE AND DEATH IN HAVEN

Life in Haven City is not easy and holding on to your life is often a lot harder than making a living. Every day there is a good chance that it may be your last one. It does not take much for a person to get killed. An argument, a miss placed word, an unwanted look is all it may take. Tempers flair easily and attitudes are hot. In one brief moment, a person can be pushed too far. In the next moment, the air explodes with the smell of sulfur and gunpowder.

## SURVIVAL IN HAVEN

The way to survive in Haven is to remember the golden rule: You, above all else. No one will care about you more than you will. If there is any question of you or the other guy, think yourself, because the other guy definitely is thinking that way.

## THOSE WHO HAVE POWER WILL CONTROL

True power in Haven is not about who has the most money or who has the biggest guns. It is about who has the most influence in the city. The real power in Haven is the power of influence. To really get things done in Haven one must know who to talk to, where to go to get it, and most important of all how to keep it when they have it. An individual can become lord and master of all they survey in a single day with only gumption, tenacity and an iron will. The next day, however, they will be just another corpse in a back alley by morning if they didn't posses the right connections, favors and dirt on the opposition. Influence can get one anything his or her heart desires, but it can cost, power is a web and everyone who has power is caught in that web. Remember, the friends you make today, are the enemies you may have to destroy tomorrow.

# carlucci family

The Carlucci Organized Crime Family is one of the oldest and the most powerful criminal organizations existing in the city of Haven. The Carlucci Family first came to power roughly 65 years ago, with the marriage of Theresa Avandondo and Vito Carlucci. This formed a union of the two families. Over the next 60 years, the Carlucci Family began to place themselves into several influential areas in the city from construction all the way to waste management. The Carlucci Family is directly responsible for the construction and development of Golden Heights and Arcadia. During this prosperous time for the Carlucci Family several other problems arose. For some reason that both sides want to keep it quiet, the Santucci Family and the Carlucci Family have been bitter rivals over the control of Haven. Several of these conflicts have spilled out into the streets of Haven. This also includes the now infamous bombing of the Haven Memorial Bridge two years ago. The bombing caused the death of 73 Haven citizens including Michael and Sarah Carlucci, son and daughter of Dominic Carlucci, leader of the Carlucci Family. Even though the Santucci organization never claimed responsibility for, nor were convicted of this act, this has given both sides an excuse to escalate the level of violence between the two organizations.

| STR | WILL | AGI | STA | INT | PER | HEA-C |
|-----|------|-----|-----|-----|-----|-------|
| 15 | 16 | 13 | 15 | 16 | 17 | 46 |
| INF | MV | ACC | FV | SUB | CM | HEA-L |
| 17 | 15 | 15 | 16 | 17 | 15 | 15 |

## SKILLS:

Finance +1, History (Organized Crime) +1, Law +1, Streetwise +1, Thievery +1

## LANGUAGES:

English (Native) 16, Italian 14, Latin 13, Spanish 11

## BENEFITS:

Connection (Carlucci Family), Sex Appeal, Status (Carlucci Family Member), Wealthy

## DRAWBACKS:

Braggart, Hatred (Santucci Family), Power Hungry, Pursued (Haven Police Department), Pursuing (Santucci Family) Reputation (Organized Crime Organization)

## SPECIAL ABILITIES:

Tough As Nails

## QUOTE:

This is our thing and we control Haven

carlucci family

haven police dept.

Power corrupts. Absolute power corrupts absolutely. The Haven Police Department outwardly appears as if it has no control of the city and what goes on in it, but the "real persons in control" know what is actually going on. The Haven Police Department has decided that it is in its best interest to not really stop crime, but to just make sure the really intense violence does not pour out on to the streets of Haven, due to them being outgunned and undermanned. The City of Haven Police Department does its best to solve crimes and protect the city, but this is like trying to hold back the entire ocean with a straw broom. There will always be various crimes committed on the streets of Haven, but the Haven Police Department does its best to make sure that none of the "everyday" people of Haven will be directly hurt or harmed by the actions of the criminal organizations. The Haven Police Department has taken the roll of "peace keepers" in their own city but they are weak and getting weaker by the minute. The Haven Police Department is sitting on top of a powder keg hoping that nothing explodes.

| STR | WILL | AGI | STA | INT | PER | HEA-C |
|-----|------|-----|-----|-----|-----|-------|
| 13 | 14 | 16 | 15 | 12 | 16 | 42 |

| INF | MV | ACC | FV | SUB | CM | HEA-L |
|-----|-----|-----|-----|-----|-----|-------|
| 15 | 14 | 16 | 13 | 14 | 14 | 14 |

### SKILLS:
Law +1, Law-Enforcement +2, Streetwise +2, Thievery +1

### LANGUAGES:
English (Native) 14, Spanish 9

### BENEFITS:
Connection (Haven Police Department), Eagle Eyes, Marksman, Rapid Fire, Status (Haven Police Department), Soothing Voice

### DRAWBACKS:
Braggart, Foolhardy, Hatred (Organized Criminals), Personal Constraint (Police Officer Code), Pursuing (Organized Criminals), Reputation (Corrupt), Secret (Corruption)

### SPECIAL ABILITIES:
Anti-Hero

### QUOTE:
We are the law in Haven and what we say goes, so don't even think about getting on our bad side.

haven police dept.

③

# Independent

The name alone is a symbol of weakness in Haven. Everything in Haven is connected to something else. Independents are not connected. They have no connection. They have no one to back them up. They have no one to save them if they get in over their head. Independent, Freelance, Individual, Autonomous, Detached, Ronin, these are synonymous with the word, death. In Haven, not having "right connections" to the all the "right people" can be dangerous, but there are a small few that do it and survive. They are able to defy the odds and do what many have failed horribly to do. They stand alone with no need of additional support. This not only makes these people impressive but it makes them highly dangerous and ruthless. As dangerous as the other organizations are, the independents are still the ones you really need to watch out for.

| STR | WILL | AGI | STA | INT | PER | HEA-C |
|-----|------|-----|-----|-----|-----|-------|
| 13 | 11 | 12 | 13 | 14 | 15 | 37 |

| INF | MV | ACC | FV | SUB | CM | HEA-L |
|-----|-----|-----|-----|-----|-----|-------|
| 13 | 13 | 14 | 14 | 15 | 13 | 12 |

### SKILLS:
Acrobatics +1, First Aid +1, Law-Enforcement +2, Military Science +2, Streetwise +1

### LANGUAGES:
English (Native) 17, French 14, Spanish 12

### BENEFITS:
Direction Sense, Eagle Eyes, Fast Draw, Marksman, Night Vision, Rapid Fire, True Sight

### DRAWBACKS:
Foolhardy, Hatred (Various Criminal Organizations), Loner, Reputation (Not Trustworthy), Pursued (Various Criminal Organizations), Pursuing (Various Criminal Organizations), Rivalry (Other Independents),

### SPECIAL ABILITIES:
Anti-Hero

### QUOTE:
Freedom is not a four-letter word.

# nubian nation

While one of the youngest and most inexperienced of the criminal underworld organizations, the Nubian Nation has made an impressive impact on the city. Their leader, Syrus, has proved to be a tactical mastermind by unifying Rome Island under his will and influence. In addition to being the major criminal organization of Rome Island, the Nubian Nation has taken on the additional role and position of being "political leaders" in the community. The City of Haven Police and the City Government of Haven have almost completely removed themselves from the normal day-to-day actions of Rome Island. Only one Police station operates on Rome Island, Police Station 44 better known as Purgatory to the officers that work there. The police officers of this precinct are broken down into two specific, distinct classes, the quick and the dead. The police officers here are more then just living on the edge of law and order; they are living on the brink of their sanity. No one respects their authority, the officers' passion for the job has burned out a long time ago, and if you call for backup after 8:00 pm, you will be out of luck. The Nubian Nation is in complete control of Rome Island, under the total authority of their lord and master, Syrus.

| STR | WILL | AGI | STA | INT | PER | HEA-C |
|-----|------|-----|-----|-----|-----|-------|
| 17 | 14 | 13 | 17 | 14 | 15 | 48 |

| INF | MV | ACC | FV | SUB | CM | HEA-L |
|-----|-----|-----|-----|-----|-----|-------|
| 15 | 17 | 14 | 16 | 15 | 14 | 16 |

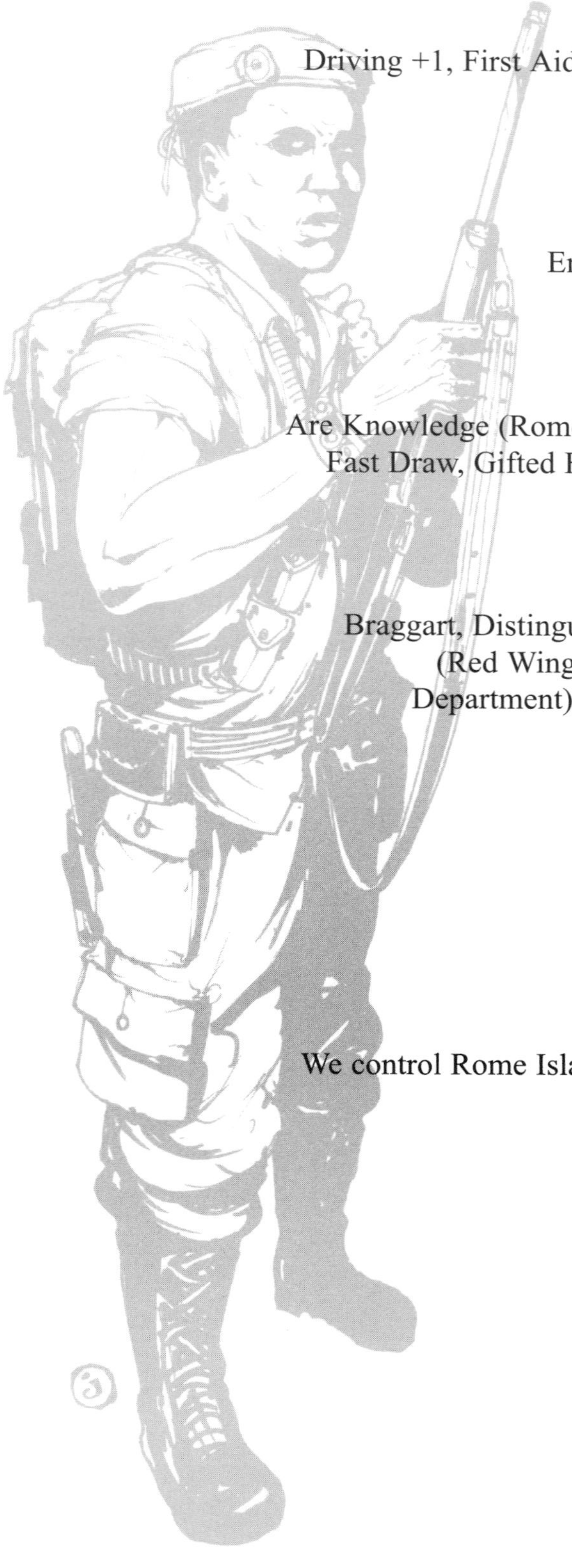

## SKILLS:

Driving +1, First Aid +1, Gambling +1, Military Science +1, Streetwise +2

## LANGUAGES:

English (Native) 16, Spanish 9, Chinese 6

## BENEFITS:

Are Knowledge (Rome Island), Connections (Nubian Nation), Fast Draw, Gifted Fighter, Status (Nubian Nation Member)

## DRAWBACKS:

Braggart, Distinguishable Characteristic (Tattoos), Hatred (Red Wing Tong), Poverty, Pursued (Haven Police Department), Pursuing (Red Wing Tong) Reputation (Organized Crime Organization)

## SPECIAL ABILITIES:

Sixth Sense

## QUOTE:

We control Rome Island. This is our home and we will fight for it to the death.

**nubian nation**

red wing tong

The Red Wing Tong are an imported and "Americanized" version of their "mother" organization, the Crimson Eagle Triad. The Crimson Eagle Triad is one of the most feared and despised criminal organizations on the planet. It has several "sibling offshoots" in several major international cities including New York, London, Paris and now Haven. The Red Wing Tong is one of the most "secure" Criminal organizations in the City of Haven. None of their members have ever betrayed the Red Wing Tong and loyalty is without question. They are under the leadership of Cynthia Yune, the first female to ever run and control a Tong organization. At first, many Tong and Triad members thought this to be a mistake, but Yune has proven her worth as a leader a thousand times over. The Red Wing Tong has made their home in Armistad, but have started to make slight entrances into Golden Heights. Specializing on providing the illegal vices to the citizens of Haven, The Red Wing Tong has placed themselves in a very specialized niche market in the Haven criminal underworld. Many have tried to "break into" the Tongs market, but have meet with resistance on every avenue.

| STR | WILL | AGI | STA | INT | PER | HEA-C |
|-----|------|-----|-----|-----|-----|-------|
| 15 | 15 | 13 | 13 | 18 | 18 | 43 |

| INF | MV | ACC | FV | SUB | CM | HEA-L |
|-----|-----|-----|-----|-----|-----|-------|
| 17 | 14 | 16 | 17 | 18 | 16 | 14 |

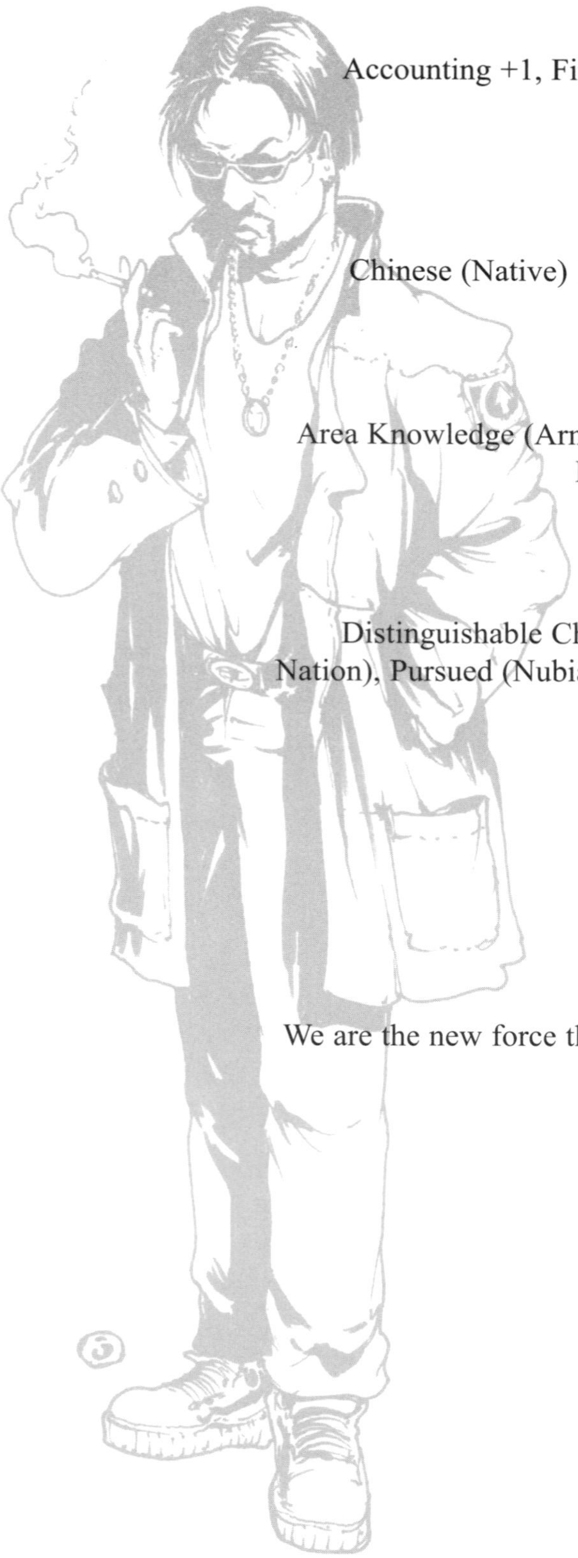

## SKILLS:

Accounting +1, Finance +1, Fine Arts +1, Gambling +1, Philosophy +1, Streetwise +1

## LANGUAGES:

Chinese (Native) 18, English 12, Korean 14, Japanese 8

## BENEFITS:

Area Knowledge (Armistad), Connection (Red Wing Tong), Eidetic Memory, Iron Will, Rapid Fire

## DRAWBACKS:

Distinguishable Characteristic (Tattoos), Hatred (Nubian Nation), Pursued (Nubian Nation, Haven Police Department), Reputation (Ruthless)

## SPECIAL ABILITIES:

Predator

## QUOTE:

We are the new force that has come to Haven and in time we will control it all.

red wing tong

Sangre

Power without knowledge is destructive. Force without reason is chaos. Knowledge is power, but applied knowledge can be outright devastating. The Sangre have learned this lesson a long time ago and realize its implication in the modern world of Haven. While many other organizations believe that brute force and money are the elements of power in the City of Haven, the Sangre understand what is important. Knowledge, Information, and Secrets. These things are the true power of Haven. Without their secrets, certain individuals would be quite vulnerable to attacks by many of their major allies and several of their most trusted "friends". Angel Perelta has done what many did not think was possible: while not as physically powerful as the Carlucci Family, Red Wing Tong or even the Nubian Nation, Sangre compensate for that by informing all interested parts on what is going on, who was involved and what does that mean for those interested. Unlike the other criminal organizations in Haven, the Sangre is ruled more like a family than a criminal organization. The Sangre understand that their power comes from their ability to keep people guessing on where they stand and what they know. The Sangre prefer stratagem and deception to direct confrontation to handle their problems.

| STR | WILL | AGI | STA | INT | PER | HEA-C |
|-----|------|-----|-----|-----|-----|-------|
| 15  | 15   | 17  | 14  | 17  | 17  | 44    |

| INF | MV | ACC | FV | SUB | CM | HEA-L |
|-----|-----|-----|-----|-----|-----|-------|
| 16  | 15  | 17  | 16  | 17  | 17  | 15    |

## SKILLS:

Bureaucratic +1, Driving +1, Forgery +1, Religion +1, Streetwise +1, Thievery +1

## LANGUAGES:

Spanish (Native) 17, Latin 14, English 12 Portuguese 8

## BENEFITS:

Area Knowledge (Freeman Hill), Connections (Nubian Nation), Eagle Eyes, Fast Draw, Sex Appeal, Status (Sangre Member), True Sight

## DRAWBACKS:

Hatred (Templar Knights), Personal Constraint (Family First, Do not Kill women or children), Power Hungry, Pursued (Templar Knights), Reputation (Holder of Secrets)

## QUOTE:

Knowledge is power

# santucci family

Like one side of a coin, the Santucci Family seems to live in the shadow of the Carlucci Family. At one time part of the organized crime Coalition of Haven, but now on their own facing off with many of the new, up-and-coming upstarts of the Underworld, the Santucci seem to have to prove themselves on almost a daily basis. Under the current leadership of Gino Santucci, Jr., the Santucci Family has thrived in a situation that would have normally killed off any other criminal organization. They have been long-time "survivors" in a conflict with the Carlucci Family that has not only cost them in valuable material and goods; it has cost the Santucci Family the ability to grow. With the Santucci Family barely holding on to their control in Haven, it was only a matter of time until that would happen and with that, they would ask for help from outside sources.

| STR | WILL | AGI | STA | INT | PER | HEA-C |
|-----|------|-----|-----|-----|-----|-------|
| 14  | 15   | 16  | 16  | 15  | 15  | 45    |

| INF | MV | ACC | FV | SUB | CM | HEA-L |
|-----|-----|-----|-----|-----|-----|-------|
| 15  | 15 | 16  | 15 | 15  | 16 | 15    |

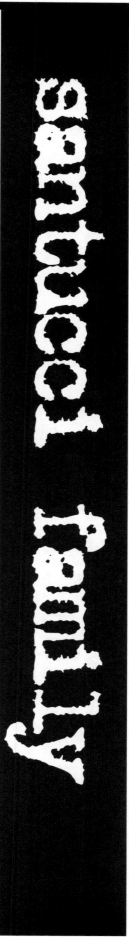

## SKILLS:

Accounting +1, Forgery +1, Gambling +1, Law-Enforcement +1, Streetwise +2

## LANGUAGES:

English (Native) 15, Italian 15, Latin 9

## BENEFITS:

Authority Figure (Santucci Family), Connections (Santucci Family), Fast Draw, Heightened Hearing, Perfect Timing, Rapid Fire, Status (Santucci Family)

## DRAWBACKS:

Braggart, Hatred (Carlucci Family), Power Hungry, Pursued (Carlucci Family), Pursuing (Carlucci Family), Reputation (Organized Crime Organization)

## QUOTE

Soon it will be all ours…

santucci family

# templar knights

It's very easy to keep Haven's citizens at each other's throats, just talk about race relations and how it affects Haven. Haven is a city that is seemingly incapable of making any forward progress in race relations. With so many new hate groups seeming to pop up over night, it was only a matter of time before one person would rule them all, and his name is like what he causes, Fear. With all this power behind Fear, it would be only a matter of time until the larger organized crime families would "sit up and take notice", and invite them into Haven's criminal inner sanctum. Those are Fear's hopes and dreams of the future, but for now, he is content to keep the levels of fear, hatred, and anguish in Haven at a fevered pitch

| STR | WILL | AGI | STA | INT | PER | HEA-C |
|-----|------|-----|-----|-----|-----|-------|
| 17 | 14 | 11 | 13 | 12 | 15 | 44 |

| INF | MV | ACC | FV | SUB | CM | HEA-L |
|-----|-----|-----|-----|-----|-----|-------|
| 15 | 15 | 13 | 15 | 14 | 12 | 15 |

## SKILLS:

Demolitions +1, First Aid +1, Military Science +2, Streetwise +2

## LANGUAGES:

English (Native) 14, German 10

## BENEFITS:

Area Knowledge (Freeman Hill), Fast Draw, Gifted Fighter, Nondescript, Perfect Balance, Status (Neo-Nazi Organizations)

## DRAWBACKS:

Braggart, Distinguishable Characteristic (Nazi Tattoos), Hatred (Nubian Nation, Sangre), Reputation (Neo-Nazi Organization), Pursued (Sangre)

## SPECIAL ABILITIES:

Berserk Rage

## QUOTE:

We are doing what we have to, to save the world from itself.

templar knights

# THE LAST FEW YEARS IN THE CITY OF HAVEN

*"You still think that your ready for this city, well listen up jackass I'm here to tell you what went on back in the good old days. My name is Ulysses Kane; ex-soldier, ex-priest and your little tour guide to the city of Haven. Haven was never the greatest of places to live, but it really went down the toilet within the last five years. I can remember how it went down like it was yesterday."*

*Ulysses Kane*

## FIVE YEARS AGO - THE YEAR OF CHANGE

The year of change began the downfall of the "Good Old Days of Haven" to the pits of hell that we are in now. We knew it could not last forever.

## END OF THE COALITION

Haven was always a city that had crime, but anyone who committed a crime in Haven had to get permission from the Coalition. Yeah, the Coalition ran everything. If you robbed a house, the Coalition had to be notified. If you were embezzling money from a corporation you worked for, then the Coalition better get its cut. The top leaders of the Carlucci, Patrone and Santucci Organized Crime Families set up the Coalition. Each year, the leadership of the Coalition would change from one family to the next. This was enacted so no one Family had control of the leadership for too long, plus anyone who caused trouble in the prior year would normally have to deal with the repercussions of their actions in the next two. The concept of the Coalition was tried and true in the city of Haven and it was thought that it would last forever. Well nothing lasts for forever.

No one knows what really happened or how it went down, but the accepted version is that the Patrone and Santucci factions of the Coalition wanted to take over and obliterate the remaining Carlucci crime family. The plan was that Patrone and Santucci families would then unify themselves one leader, but during the coordinated attack on the Carluccis, the Patrones turned on their partner, the Santucci, in a botched double cross. The three factions barely survived the event and became mortal enemies and the Coalition was shattered forever.

## FIRST CONTACT

With the Coalition in shattered and in pieces, it's void left Haven wide open for the exploration and plundering of its enormous potential by outside sources -- including the remarkably powerful and impressively influential Chinese criminal organization, the Crimson Eagle Triad. With the Crimson Eagle Triad being overcrowded in Asia markets, they thought it best to target Haven as their first American conquest. Several of Crimson Eagle Triad representatives have been seen in the city making inroads for the awaiting Triad members looking to come to America and Haven.

## NEW IMMIGRANTS

At the same time that the breakdown of the Coalition was occurring, Haven's economy began to take-off. With the economy explosion, it created thousands of new jobs available for all the people of Haven. The opening caused a great influx of Asian and Latino immigrants. The rate of Asian and Latino immigration increased 1200 percent during this year alone. The majority of the Hispanic and Latino immigrants filtered into Freeman Hill, while the Asian contingency of immigrants made Armistad their home.

## FACES OF HATE

With such an increase of minority and foreign immigrants from Central and Latin America it was only time before the locals from established European immigrant stock would have a problem with the new Latino immigrants. Several anti-Latino groups begin to crop up. The largest of these groups, the White Aryan Resistance, also known as W.A.R., was the flashpoint for all the anti-Latino and hate groups. These groups began their reign of terror on the new Hispanic and Latino immigrants forcing them to live like hostages in their own homes.

## THE ARRIVAL

On the twenty-sixth day of the month of August, he came. Syrus, the man who would be king of Rome Island. After his arrival on Rome Island, nothing was the same. What would you say to the devil on the first time that he enters Hell? The world of Haven was changing faster than anyone would believe and Syrus was to become one of the most influential players in this New World Order.

## THE LIGHTHOUSE

When the first body showed up on Rome Island by the Lighthouse, it seemed, as if it was some type of unusual gang-related killing. The only thing different about this killing was the victim was crucified on a wooden cross at the Lighthouse's beach and the rancid and putrid smell of sour milk encompassed the body of the deceased. It didn't seem that important at first, then more bodies turned up, all of them crucified and smelling of sour milk. The Haven Police Department took action. After the 36th victim turned up at the Lighthouse, the Haven Police

Department started to stakeout this area for the killer. But it went all wrong, every time that police sent officers to stakeout the Lighthouse, they were found the following morning like the other victims crucified on a wooden cross with the rancid and putrid smell of sour milk surrounding the police officer's body. With all these incidents, the urban legend of Milkbaby was born.

## FOUR YEARS AGO - THE YEAR OF PAIN

After change comes pain. Growing pains. Haven was just discovering what pain really was.

## UNIFICATION

After only a short time on Rome Island, Syrus grew quite influential and powerful. Many individuals tried to covet his power and influence, but they all ended up the same way, dead. Syrus proved to be almost invincible. On one more memorable occurrence, several members of the 42nd Street Boys

caught an unarmed Syrus in an ambush in the Red Hook section of Rome Island. After several minutes in a very heated firefight, all the members the 42nd Street Boys were killed. No one knows how Syrus survived the ambush and killed all the 42nd Street Boys, but one thing was certain. He was not a man to be easily disposed of, or trifled with.

After the ambush, Syrus sought revenge by finding out the identity of his attackers and killing their entire families. He killed their mothers, fathers, brothers, sisters, wives, husbands, sons and daughters. Anyone related to them that lived on Rome Island. He spared no one. It mattered not if the person were a small child to an old and crippled person; all would be crushed under his feet. Syrus' seemingly unnatural ability to survive began to become the stuff of urban myths and legends. Many of the local criminal organizations began to understand what type of influence he would have on Rome Island and many of the organizations wanted to be part of that. So, many of the organizations began to follow Syrus as their new leader after that.

## ASIAN INVASION

With the opening of several car production plants in Armistad, the need for workers was increased by a factor of ten. Many of these new car production jobs went to the newest Asian immigrants in Haven. The Crimson Eagle Triad, realizing the amount of money that would be generated at these plants, decided that it would be best if they help with the employment issue of the workers. The Crimson Eagle Triad formed the Red Wing Tong to conduct its Haven side operations; they imported new workers, managed disputes, but most importantly garnered power. What the Red Wing Tong really wanted was a "powerful influence" over the car manufacture owners to have them hire only the Red Wing Tongs approved employees. This small step was the beginning of the Crimson Eagle Triad and the Red Wing Tongs predominance and immigration into Haven.

## BLOOD ON THE HILL

Freeman Hill went from being a sanctuary for the new immigrants of Haven to something more akin to Nazi Germany. With so many hate groups, including W.A.R., making a home on Freeman Hill, it was only a matter of time before the new immigrants fought back. A group of Latinos from all over Freeman Hill joined to from the Sangre, Spanish for blood. The Sangre took the fight directly to the White Aryan Resistance and other hate groups. If the Sangre saw a member of W.A.R. or any other hate group, the Sangre killed them on sight, violently and publicly. This type of vigilante tactic went over very well in the eyes of the new Latino immigrants to Freeman Hill. The Police investigated the numerous murders of the White Aryan Resistance. The cases were closed for lack of any witnesses to came forward. Payback came looking for the White Aryan Resistance and kicked them right in the nuts.

## THE FALL OF THE PATRONES

After nearly two years of conflict with the Carlucci Family and the Santucci Family, the Patrones were on the horrific and tragic losing end. The Patrone family suffered nearly 85% losses of their forces, armament and money. The current head of the Patrones, Carlos Patrone, made the hardest discussion of his life and disbanded the Patrone Organized Crime Family. Carlos Patrone with his family and the remaining few members of the crime family left the city of Haven. Carlos vowed that one day his family would return to rule over Haven. With the Patrones out of the way, their absence became an invitation that the Crimson Eagles had to accept.

## NEW NEWS

For nearly 50 years, the public of Haven had "assumed" that there was one criminal mastermind running the city, but, it took the reporting skills of the famed Pulitzer Prize winning reporter of Haven Chronicles, Annie Williams, to reveal it all. After years of investigative reporting, she finally discovered the real criminal relationship between the Patrones and the Santucci Family. This report helped truly reveal the power and influence of these two organizations and their dominion on the city of Haven. Even though, a majority of the Patrone and Santucci dealings came to light, oddly enough the Carlucci Family was never implicated in any of the reports.

## THREE YEARS AGO - THE YEAR OF CONFLICT

For there to be any type of change, there will be conflict.

## THE WAR CONTINUES

After nearly three years of death and conflict, the Carlucci / Santucci war had taken heavy losses on both sides of the conflict. The Carlucci Family suffered losses with the death of Nick Perrier, third in command of the Carlucci family, and Manuel Staccio, operational leader of all Arcadian ventures. The Santucci Family suffered major losses with the deaths of Calvin and Nancy DeLunio, husband and wife operational leaders of all Golden Heights ventures, Tony Ventura; fourth in command of the Santucci family, and Reece Gathers, lieutenant in the Santucci crime family. These deaths didn't reduce the amount of conflict between the Carlucci Family and the Santucci Family, it actually increased the violence and vendetta. This conflict between the Carlucci Family and the Santucci Family moved from the back alleys to the streets and the City became an open battleground.

## INFILTRATION

Everything must evolve, change, grow or die. No one understands this rule more than the Red Wing Tong. After years of infiltrating every orifice in Armistad, The Red Wing Tong were looking to expand their power base of control in the underworld. With the never-ending conflicts of the Carlucci Family and the Santucci Family, it made it possible for the Red Wing Tong to slowly and quietly infiltrate themselves into the high stakes and nightlife borough of Arcadia and the ultra elite and impressively influential borough of Golden Heights. Once the Red Wing Tong became ingrained onto these two boroughs, it was made clear that the Red Wing Tong were here to stay.

## BIRTH OF A NATION

With the complete domination of Rome Island finalized, Syrus knew that any great leader needed a great army to follow him and impose his will on the people of Rome Island. Syrus unified the three largest gangs on Rome Island, the Disciples, the Rome Island Demons and the 187 Boys, into his elite military force called the Nubian Nation. The Nubian Nation's main function is to enforce the complete will of Syrus over the people of Rome Island. The Nation also keeps the smaller gangs and criminal organizations in line and makes sure they pay their "tribute" to Syrus and the Nation.

## HATE, LOVE AND WAR

After nearly a year of conflict the battle for the control of Freeman Hill between the Sangre and the W.A.R. come to a head. The Sangre made their final all-out strike against the W.A.R. at their home headquarters in the Citadel section of Freeman Hill. The Sangre killed the headquarters' posted sentries and then set fire to the building Any one who tried to escape was shot down by the Sangre members surrounding the building. This massacre killed the majority of W.A.R.'s members as well as and their leadership in one fell swoop. After this event, just like in the book Animal Farm, the oppressed emulate the activities of their masters. The Sangre begin to assert themselves as the new leader and power in Freeman Hill's underworld, with Angel Peralta in control of everything. The new order of leadership was now in place.

## TWO YEARS AGO - THE YEAR OF FIRE

When any conflict escalates, the heat from the battle causes everything to burn like fire.

## LONG HOT SUMMER

Syrus, always needing to prove that he is always in control and wishing to increase his authority of Rome Island directly planned a head to head confrontation with the City of Haven Police Department. The Nubian Nation made several violent ambushes and sneak attacks on several police department headquarters on Rome Island. After months of these types of attacks on the Haven Police Department, the Police decide to withdrawal roughly 90% of their forces from Rome Island, except for those at Police Station #44, nicknamed "Purgatory". The Mayor of Haven, Arnold Wright, declared that

Rome Island is under Martial Law. Rome Island is under a 7 PM curfew and the Rome Island Police forces are under strict orders to enforce the curfew and martial law at all costs. Truth be told, it is the police who put themselves under curfew.

## ALL FALL DOWN

Haven Memorial Bridge is falling down, falling down, falling down. On the third month of the year of fire, one of the most abhorrent and horrific accidents of all time occurred in Haven. With Haven being one of the major cities on the eastern seaboard it was only time till it fell victim to the deadly act of terrorism. A terrorist group that called itself Helix made a show of force and political statement by bombing the Haven Memorial Bridge during its inaugural opening. At this opening, 73 individuals were killed including Michael and Sarah Carlucci, son and daughter of Dominic Carlucci, leader of the Carlucci Family; and John Carboni and William Santucci, nephew and son of Gino Santucci, leader of the Santucci Family. This event helped to shatter any chance of peace between the Carlucci Family and the Santucci, due to each group blaming the other for the bombing of the bridge and the killings of the family members.

## WHO HAS THE POWER

To prove the extent of their power, the Red Wing Tong attempted to do what only mad men would dream of, the invasion and assimilation of Rome Island. It started off small with one or two new opium dens opening up on Rome Island, then a few prostitution brothels opened up. The Red Wing Tong feeling that Syrus was no real threat decided to steal a page from Syrus' own "play book" by trying to take over the Radcliffe apartment complex. The Red Wing Tong had infiltrated rough fifty percent of the Radcliffe apartment complex, and then Syrus and the Nubian Nation showed the Red Wing Tong why they controlled Rome Island.

Syrus and the Nation went to the home of Raymond Yune, Dragon Head and leader of the Red Wing Tong to leave a message to all of the Red Wing Tong. While there, Syrus and the Nation sexually assaulted and slaughtered Raymond Yune's three sons, two daughters, Yune's mother, and two uncles and three aunts who happened to be living in the mansion at the time. They then burned down his mansion home and several of his businesses. Syrus and the Nation kept Raymond Yune's wife, Cynthia, alive so she could tell the other leaders of the Red Wing Tong that Rome Island was off limits to them and if they were stupid enough to ignore his message he would do the same to their families. The remaining Red Wing Tong leaders decided that the infiltration of Rome Island would not be a profitable venture.

## ALLIES AND ENEMIES

After the long battle with the Red Wing Tong, Syrus made quite an interesting decision on the future of the Nubian Nation. Knowing that an alliance with another underworld criminal organization would strengthen the Nations position in the city of Haven, Syrus went out looking for an ally. After evaluation of the advantages and disadvantages of several organizations, Syrus made what some consider a very unusual decision on the situation. Syrus and the Nubian Nation allied themselves with the Sangre. Even though, the Sangre were nowhere as powerful as the Carlucci Family or the Santucci Family organization, the Sangre had something that neither of these organizations had… loyalty. The reputation of the Sangre member's loyalty was stuff of which legends are made of. No member has ever "turned" on the Sangre. The Sangre's loyalty made truly the best choice of an ally for Syrus and the Nubian Nation. This also helped the Nation establish their presence in Freeman Hill.

## ONE YEAR AGO - THE YEAR OF THE GUN

Give a man a gun and he thinks he's superman, give him two and he thinks he God.

## UNDER NEW MANAGEMENT

With the defeat of the Red Wing Tong at the hands of the Nubian Nation and the murder of their leader, Raymond Yune and his family, the Red Wing Tong was suffering from the 'true' leader of the organization. His wife, Cynthia; after being spared from Syrus' rampage a year earlier, she entertained thoughts of revenge against Syrus and the Nation.

But first she had problems at home that must be dealt with; few in the Red Wing Tong were prepared to offer her respect and only token loyalty. The rules of succession were very clear, these rules were as 'written in stone', no one among the Crimson Eagle Triad or Red Wing Tong could remove Cynthia from power, short of her death.

Since Cynthia was a woman of innovation and unyielding will, she contacted the leaders of the Crimson Eagle Triad with an extremely unusual proposition. She informed them, if she was placed in command of the Red Wing Tong for six months, she would personally increase the profits of the Tong by 500%. If she would be able to do this, the Crimson Eagle Triad would support her in all of her future decision-making and leadership of the Red Wing Tong. If she failed to increase the business profit during this time, she would resign from leadership and pass it on to another. The Crimson Eagle Triad could not pass up an offer like this and agreed to the deal. Cynthia Yune had bought herself enough time to consolidate her position and gain the respect of the other Tong Leaders.

## HATE NEVER SLEEPS

The emotion that is called hate is not easily killed let alone stopped. With the Sangre spreading there influence all over Freeman Hill it was only a matter of time before the terrified Whites still living there would have to fight back against their Hispanic oppressors. Then a man came that would lead the White people of Freeman Hill against the Sangre, they would very aptly call him Fear. Using the old-fashioned guerrilla tactics, Fear and his organization, the Templar Knights, fought back against the Sangre on all possible fronts. Both groups started their conflict on the back alleys and dark places of Freeman Hill, but recently, these of groups have taken their war to the streets and several innocent bystanders have fallen victim to this conflict. Both sides claim that the other side is the reason for the violence and their group is trying to keep the peace.

## ALL OUT WAR

After only five months, Cynthia Yune had increased the Red Wing Tong's profit by nearly 800%. The head members of the Crimson Eagle Triad could hardly believe all this progress was possible in such a short period of time. The Crimson Eagle Triad gave Yune their complete and full support on all future ventures as she had wished and had its blessing, Cynthia Yune began her greatest challenge to date. She openly began to make strikes, both physically and financially, against the Carlucci Family, the Santucci Family, the Nubian Nation, and the Sangre. The Red Wings Tong's spread from their total control of Armistad to Arcadia, Freeman Hill, Haven City and Golden Heights. Yune and the Tong did their best to keep Syrus and the Nation "bottled up" on Rome Island. The Red Wing Tong's conflict turned normally peaceful streets into potential war zones. No one was safe and everyone was out for his or her own personal interests.

## URBAN LEGEND LIVES

During one of the memorable heat waves of Haven's summer a strange occurrence kept happening on the Lighthouse area of Rome Island. Crucified bodies kept turning up on the beaches near and around the lighthouse area. The bodies, like before, all possessed the rank and fetid smell of sour milk that had been left out in the summer too long. After several days of this happening, the Haven Police Department decided to find out once and for all what was going on at the lighthouse. The police sent the S.W.A.T. team to end this thing called Milkbaby. After two nights, the moment that the S.W.A.T. team members were waiting for happened, they saw Milkbaby and all hell broke loose.

The follow morning, the S.W.A.T. team members did not return to the police station. Several police cars were sent out to the Lighthouse to discover what was going on. When they arrived, the police officers said it looked like a war zone. There were bodies and parts of bodies lying around everywhere on the beach. Out of the dozens of S.W.A.T. members that were sent to the Lighthouse only one survived, Officer Steve Balle-Gifford. Officer Balle-Gifford was suffering from shock, various physical traumas and sexual assault. Officer Balle-Gifford kept screaming out about how he had seen the devil and he was coming for us all. After that little fiasco, the Haven Police Department considered the area round the Lighthouse to be off limits to all.

## THE PRESENT - THE YEAR OF FEAR

And now it is the present and everyone is afraid, and the shadow of fear covers all of the City of Haven. What will you do? Who will you trust? Who will you fight? Who will you save? Who do you serve? What will it matter? What will you do to survive? Who is going to be your first victim?

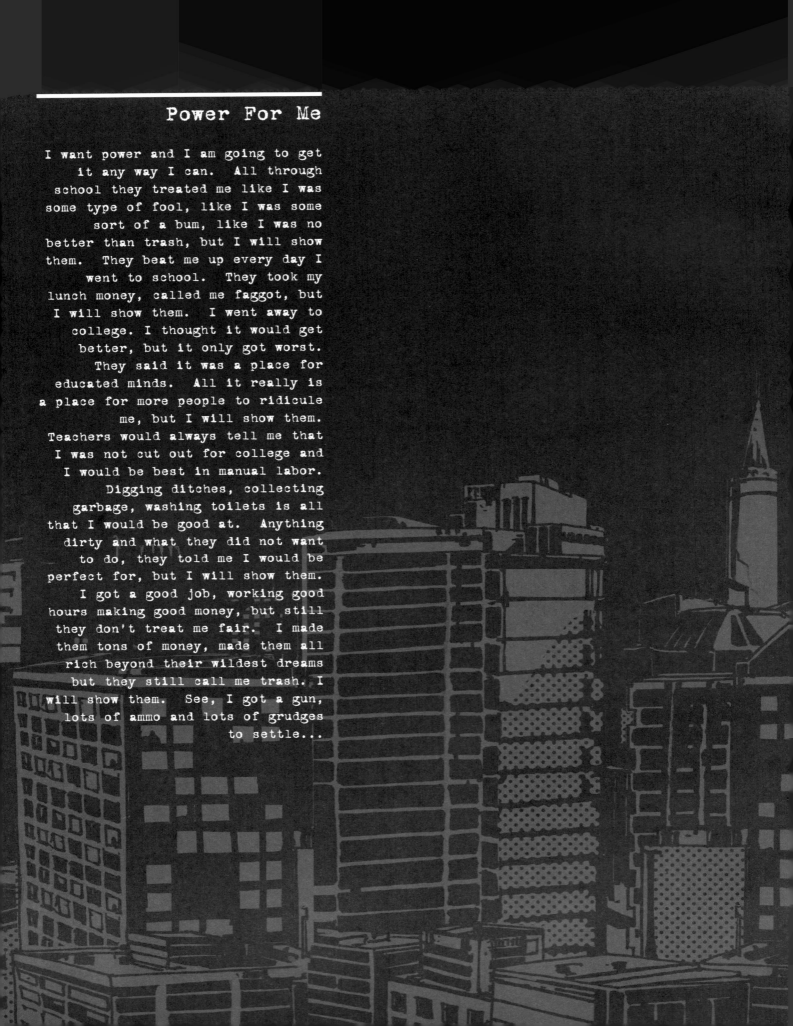

## Power For Me

I want power and I am going to get it any way I can. All through school they treated me like I was some type of fool, like I was some sort of a bum, like I was no better than trash, but I will show them. They beat me up every day I went to school. They took my lunch money, called me faggot, but I will show them. I went away to college. I thought it would get better, but it only got worst. They said it was a place for educated minds. All it really is a place for more people to ridicule me, but I will show them. Teachers would always tell me that I was not cut out for college and I would be best in manual labor. Digging ditches, collecting garbage, washing toilets is all that I would be good at. Anything dirty and what they did not want to do, they told me I would be perfect for, but I will show them. I got a good job, working good hours making good money, but still they don't treat me fair. I made them tons of money, made them all rich beyond their wildest dreams but they still call me trash. I will show them. See, I got a gun, lots of ammo and lots of grudges to settle...

# CHAPTER: 2

## CHARACTER CREATION

*Character builds slowly, but it can be torn down again with incredible swiftness*

*Faith Balwin*

The single most important part of playing any role-playing game and Haven: City of Violence is, no exception to this, is to create a believable character with which to enter this imaginary world. Believability is the key to all good characters, be they heroes or villains, friends, foes, anti-heroes or companions. If the character you create is one who is believable your enjoyment of the game and the enjoyment of your fellow players will be greatly enhanced. That said what makes a believable character? Quite simply the character must be more than just a one-dimensional cardboard cut out. Start with a concept, a core idea or image of what you think your character should be, don't be afraid to change or adapt this mental picture as you progress through character generation. Start by writing a few notes, what does the character look like? How does he dress? Assign a few descriptors to his basic personality, is he quiet and broody or perhaps bold and brash, perhaps he likes practical jokes or Cuban Cigars all these little ideas help to build up the character in your mind and make him more real with every addition.

At this point it's often useful to write a couple of paragraphs about his history and his family, is the character a native of Haven? Where did he grow up? How did his childhood affect him? After all, a character that grew up in the bad side of town is not likely to have a college education for example, unless something in his past radically altered his life. What kind of profession has he taken up and how long has worked it that capacity. Just as importantly you should decide on a few things that might motivate the character. What does he strive for? Why does he want what he strives for and is what he strives for achievable or simply an ideal?

With these core notes in place you can move forward with the process of character generation, the next step is to use the notes and basic sketch of the character so far to shape which attributes you want the character to have and which skills they are good at. What benefits, drawbacks or special abilities they should have. You should note that your character concept may still evolve and change even at this point, as the process of buying all these components of the character suggest ideas or options you had previously not considered.

One final thing should be taken into account when creating a character, role-playing is a social group activity, it is possible and even desirable to create characters that do not always see eye to eye with each other and sometimes fight amongst themselves, but ultimately enjoyment comes from playing as part of a group. It helps if all the players can generate their characters at the same time, this allows for some discussion and co-operation in the group. After all who wants to play a game where all the characters are from rival gangs, who can't get along and just end up killing each other ten minutes into the first gaming session? So discus with the G.O.D. and the other players what kind of characters and game you are going to play within Haven: City of Violence, then have fun.

# CHARACTER CREATION

Choosing a Character Prototype and adding your own touches can easily start your first character. Real leaders, however, make their own destiny and Haven offers an in-depth Character Creation system that lets you build your own personalized character from scratch. G.O.D.s have no excuses for ignorance, thus they should read the Character Creation system to understand how they can create good adversaries and pass on the word to their players the details about character aspects such as Attributes, Skills and Benefits. For those new to a role-playing game pick what looks fun and run with it.

## CHARACTER PROTOTYPES

The following pages are a list of the character prototypes that are commonly seen in Haven. These prototypes can be used to base or compare one's character to the most common person in Haven. A player will determine what type of life their character will follow and activities that they may perform and pursue. All of the listed prototypes are balanced equally so they may be used to run a quick trial game so players can gain a basic understanding of the game. If a long campaign is going to be played by your group, it's going to be best to create your own characters.

| STR | WILL | AGI | STA | INT | PER | HEA-C |
|-----|------|-----|-----|-----|-----|-------|
| 16 | 11 | 14 | 15 | 14 | 14 | 42 |

| INF | MV | ACC | FV | SUB | CM | HEA-L |
|-----|-----|-----|-----|-----|-----|-------|
| 13 | 16 | 14 | 15 | 14 | 14 | 14 |

## body guard

### SKILLS
Law Enforcement +1, Military Science +1, Streetwise +1

### LANGUAGES
Native Language, Any additional two languages

### BENEFITS
Area Knowledge, Connections (Haven Police Dept.), Direction Sense, Eidetic Memory, Gifted Fighter

### DRAWBACKS
Distinguishable Characteristic (Scars), Hatred (Assassins), Pursuing (Assassins), Reputation (Body Guard), Secret

### SPECIAL ABILITIES
Anti-Hero, Sixth Sense,

### STARTING EQUIPMENT
Work Clothes

### BACKGROUND
This is the type of character who specializes in the field of protection of all different types of people and things. These types of characters will normally be hired to keep another person or item out of harm's way and these people are normally well known for their work in underworld circles. Sometimes out of admiration and sometimes out of rivalry, it's a hazard of the occupation and a measure of their success. Several of the more infamous bodyguards include Hawk from the Robert B. Parker, Spenser novels and Spenser for Hire television show.

### QUOTE
"You betta come wit me if you want to live!"

| STR | WILL | AGI | STA | INT | PER | HEA-C |
|-----|------|-----|-----|-----|-----|-------|
| 14 | 14 | 13 | 15 | 14 | 14 | 43 |

| INF | MV | ACC | FV | SUB | CM | HEA-L |
|-----|-----|-----|-----|-----|-----|-------|
| 14 | 15 | 14 | 14 | 14 | 14 | 14 |

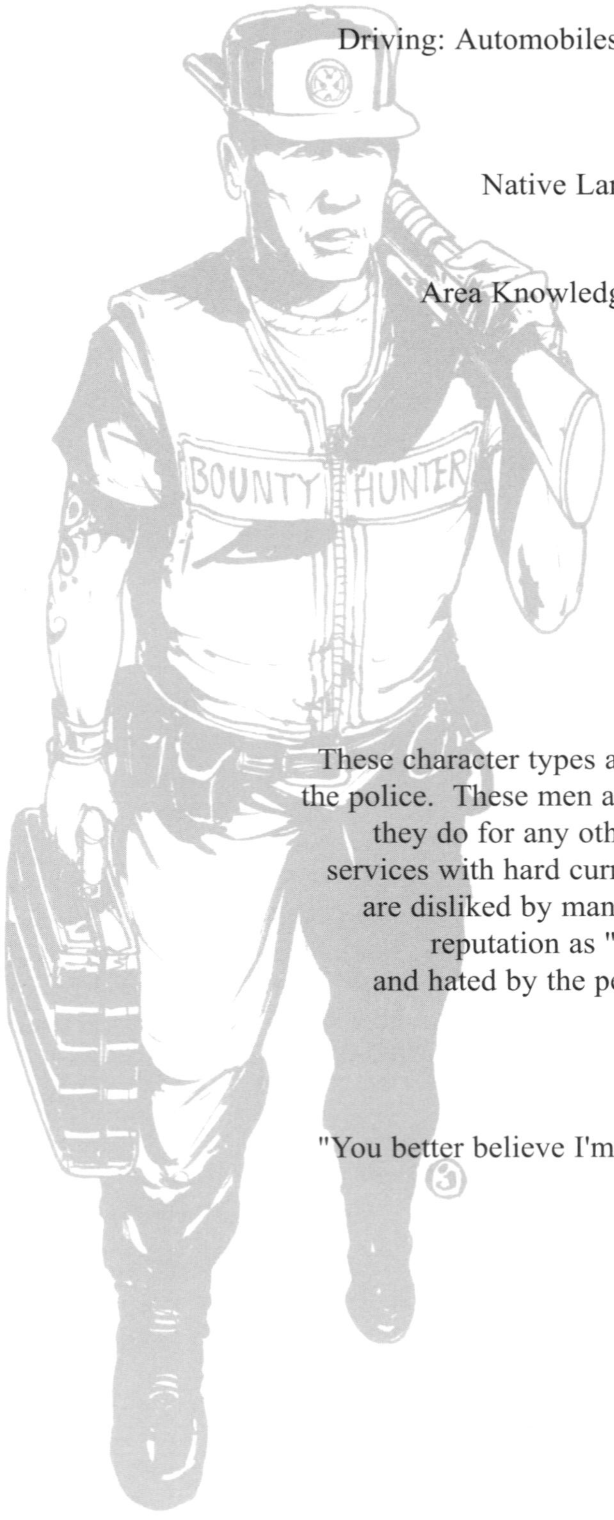

# bounty hunter

## SKILLS

Driving: Automobiles +1, Law Enforcement +1, Streetwise +3, Tracking +3

## LANGUAGES

Native Language, Any additional two languages

## BENEFITS

Area Knowledge, Connections (Haven Police Dept.), Marksman

## DRAWBACKS

Reputation (Bounty Hunter), Secret

## SPECIAL ABILITIES

Predator, Trick Shot

## STARTING EQUIPMENT

Work Clothes

## BACKGROUND

These character types are considered to be a lower version of the police. These men and women do not perform the job that they do for any other reason other than payment for their services with hard currency. The majority of bounty hunters are disliked by many law enforcement groups due to their reputation as "unskilled people doing the police job" and hated by the people they collect a bounty on, usually criminal types.

## QUOTE

"You better believe I'm going to get my man. He is worth 25 grand, dead or alive - damn it."

| STR | WILL | AGI | STA | INT | PER | HEA-C |
|---|---|---|---|---|---|---|
| 13 | 11 | 12 | 13 | 14 | 15 | 37 |
| INF | MV | ACC | FV | SUB | CM | HEA-L |
| 13 | 13 | 14 | 14 | 15 | 13 | 12 |

## SKILLS
Military Science +2, Streetwise +3, Thievery +3

## LANGUAGES
Native Language, Any additional two languages

## BENEFITS
Area Knowledge, Connections, True Sight

## DRAWBACKS
None

## SPECIAL ABILITIES
Dodge, Predator

## STARTING EQUIPMENT
Work Clothes

## BACKGROUND
These character types are considered to be the lowest of the low. They don't work for any other reason than money. They will do anything from just old-fashioned protection work, to extortion, to the extremes of murder and assassination. For these types of characters it is all about the money, you pay the man and you get the job done. That is how they live and that is how they survive.

## QUOTE
"Hey, it's only a job. You punch a time clock; I punch a face. I think you're pissed just because I get paid more. ... Well that and a couple of your teeth are on the floor."

| STR | WILL | AGI | STA | INT | PER | HEA-C |
|-----|------|-----|-----|-----|-----|-------|
| 14  | 13   | 12  | 14  | 14  | 16  | 41    |

| INF | MV | ACC | FV | SUB | CM | HEA-L |
|-----|-----|-----|-----|-----|-----|-------|
| 15  | 14  | 14  | 14  | 15  | 13  | 14    |

## SKILLS

Law +1, Law Enforcement +2, Streetwise +2

## LANGUAGES

Native Language, Any additional two languages

## BENEFITS

Area Knowledge, Connections (Haven Police Dept.), Eagle Eyes, Fast Draw, Status (Police Officer),

## DRAWBACKS

Pursuing (Criminals), Pursued (Criminals)

## SPECIAL ABILITIES

Cop's Eyes

## STARTING EQUIPMENT

Police Uniform, 9mm Glock 19 with (3) magazines of FMJ ammunition, Night Stick, Handcuffs, Mace

## BACKGROUND

These types of characters work on a very low scale of crime prevention, in specific places from small towns to large cities. Several famous police officers include John McClane from the Die Hard movies and Clint Eastwood's character Harry Callahan from the Dirty Harry movies. These types of characters only seem to care about law and order, right and wrong and anything else would deter them from this job.

## QUOTE

"BLAM! BLAM! BLAM! Freeze Police! If you don't stop I'll shoot you in the other leg!"

# police officer

# politician

| STR | WILL | AGI | STA | INT | PER | HEA-C |
|-----|------|-----|-----|-----|-----|-------|
| 9 | 14 | 10 | 12 | 14 | 13 | 35 |

| INF | MV | ACC | FV | SUB | CM | HEA-L |
|-----|-----|-----|-----|-----|-----|-------|
| 14 | 11 | 12 | 12 | 14 | 12 | 12 |

## SKILLS

Actor +1, Bureaucratic +2, Finance +1, Law +1, Political Science +3

## LANGUAGES

Native Language, Any additional two languages

## BENEFITS

Area Knowledge (Haven City, Arcadia), Connections (City Hall, Haven Police Department. Local Citizens), Status (Politician)

## DRAWBACKS

Reputation (Politician)

## SPECIAL ABILITIES

Cop Eyes, Future Days

## STARTING EQUIPMENT

Business Suit

## BACKGROUND

Whatever you have heard about politicians is totally true. This type of person is the greatest legal con man that the world has ever created. The characters will prefer to talk themselves out of a situation rather than shoot it out with someone.

## QUOTE

"I'm off to kiss some butt and shake some babies."

| STR | WILL | AGI | STA | INT | PER | HEA-C |
|-----|------|-----|-----|-----|-----|-------|
| 13  | 15   | 13  | 13  | 14  | 14  | 41    |

| INF | MV | ACC | FV | SUB | CM | HEA-L |
|-----|----|-----|----|-----|----|-------|
| 15  | 13 | 14  | 14 | 14  | 14 | 14    |

## SKILLS

Interrogation +2, Law Enforcement +2, Streetwise +2

## LANGUAGES

Native Language, Any additional two languages

## BENEFITS

Area Knowledge, Connections (Haven Police Dept.),
Iron Will

## DRAWBACKS

Reputation (Private Investigator)

## SPECIAL ABILITIES

Cop Eyes, Sixth Sense

## STARTING EQUIPMENT

Work Clothes

## BACKGROUND

This type of character is one who has started down the road of
law enforcement but taken a turn in life. Now these persons
work directly for the people who at one time they may have
"served and protected." Several famous private investigators
include Spenser from the Robert B. Parker Spenser novels and
Spenser for Hire television show and Jake Gittes from the
movies, Chinatown and the Two Jakes.

## QUOTE

"Don't kill the messenger. Remember you asked me to find
out if your husband was cheating."

**private investigator**

# CHARACTER CREATION SYSTEM

Congratulations, you decided to have us stop spoon-feeding your lazy ass. Like making your own street machine, this system will let you fine tune your character concept into a mean son of a bitch who will take on the streets with his own bare hands. Making your own savior or satan of the city takes five steps. On your first try, take things slow. You will find out that as you go, that you will discover that there are advantages you may need to retrofit into your character.

- Step 1: Start with a Pool of 100 Character Points (CPs).
- Step 2: Create Primary Abilities and Secondary Abilities.
- Step 3: Choose Skills, Languages, Benefits, Drawbacks and Special Abilities.
- Step 4: Choose Equipment with the starting $1,000.
- Step 5: Finalize the characters background concept and notes into a History.

## STEP 1

All players begin the creation of their character with 100 Character Points (CPs). Character Points are used to purchase the character's Primary Abilities, Skills, Benefits and Special Abilities. Often it is useful to track these numbers on a piece of scrap paper during character creation.

## STEP 2

All the player character's Primary Attributes begin at "0". The intensity of each of these can be increased by spending CPs on them. The more points spent the better the Attribute and the greater the chance of succeeding at tests of ability. Primary Attributes are all bought at a rate of 1 point for each CP spent on them. Secondary Attributes are all derived from the Primary Attributes and are thus not bought directly.

| INTENSITY | DEFINITION |
|-----------|------------|
| 1 to 3 | Low |
| 4 to 8 | Below Average |
| 9 to 15 | Average |
| 16 to 20 | Above Average |
| 21+ | Superior |

# PRIMARY AND SECONDARY ABILITIES

There are six Primary Abilities that decide how well the character can perform particular acts. These are: STRENGTH (STR), WILL (WILL), AGILITY (AGI), STAMINA (STA), INTELLIGENCE (INT) and PERCEPTION (PER). The majority of Primary Abilities are normally fixed items, though they may be increased over time.

The Secondary Abilities include the character's current level of health, how fast they can run and how much money they own. The Secondary Abilities consist of INFLUENCE (INFL), MOVEMENT VALUE (MV), ACCURACY (ACC), FIGHTING VALUE (FV), SUBTERFUGE (SUB), COUNTER MEASURES (CM) and HEALTH (HEA). Unlike the Primary Abilities, Secondary Abilities may change drastically during an adventure.

# PRIMARY ABILITIES
## STRENGTH (STR)

- The measure of physical power.
- The greater the intensity of this attribute the stronger the character and the more weight they can lift.
- Used to determine the Secondary Abilities: Movement Value, Fighting Value and Concussive and Lethal Health.

## WILL (WILL)

- The measure of mental strength and ability to control one's actions.
- Decides how much resistance that character can provide against mental domination, hypnosis or mind control.

- Used to determine the Secondary Abilities: Influence and Concussive and Lethal Health.

# AGILITY (AGI)

- The measure of personal agility, reflexes and nimbleness.
- Used to decide the Secondary Abilities: Accuracy and Counter Measures.

# STAMINA (STA)

- The measure of the personal endurance and physical resistance.
- This is also used to determine actions that may take a long time to accomplish a task.
- Used to determine the Secondary Abilities: Movement Value and Concussive and Lethal Health.

# INTELLIGENCE (INT)

- The total measure of one's reason, wisdom and intuition.
- This ability is used to determine the success in building and repairing items.
- Used to determine the Secondary Abilities: Fighting Value and Subterfuge.

# PERCEPTION (PER)

- The ability to comprehend and distinguish the difference in various items and actions.
- Used to determine the Secondary Abilities: Influence and Accuracy.

# SECONDARY ABILITIES
## INFLUENCE (INFL)

- The measure of the character's natural appeal and charisma.
- Can be used to acquire information from friends, get equipment from associates and general favors.
- Influence is the combination of the character's Perception and Will, divided by two, with all fractions rounded up.

# MOVEMENT VALUE (MV)

- Total distance a character can move within a six-second period (1 combat round).

- Movement Value is the combination of the character's Strength and Stamina, divided by two, with all fractions rounded up.

# ACCURACY (ACC)

- This will determine your ability to use firearms and throw objects. This will be covered in the combat section.
- Accuracy is the combination of the character's Agility and Perception, divided by two, with all fractions rounded up

# FIGHTING VALUE (FV)

- The measurement of the character's hand-to-hand ability and total fighting skill.
- Characters that possess a higher intensity level are better fighters and can make multiple attacks.
- Fighting Value is the combination of the character's Strength and Intelligence, divided by two, with all fractions rounded up

# SUBTERFUGE (SUB)

- The ability to deceive others by obvious traditional methods or unusual and unconventional ways.
- Subterfuge is the combination of the character's Intelligence and Perception, divided by two, with all fractions rounded up.

# COUNTER MEASURES (CM)

- The ability to manipulate mechanical devices, including deactivating security systems, concealed traps or snares and concealed items.
- Counter Measures is the combination of the character's Agility and Intelligence, divided by two, with all fractions rounded up.

# CONCUSSIVE AND LETHAL HEALTH (HEA)

- This ability is used to measure the amount of physical damage a character can deal with before losing consciousness.
- A character's HEA is divided into specific types: Concussive and Lethal. Concussive HEA is the ability to resist blunt or physical trauma of various types. Concussive attacks include any type of attack with punches, kicks, even clubs or

falls. Lethal HEA is the ability to resist immediate and fatal injury. Lethal attacks includes being shot with a firearm or arrow, stabbed or cut with a knife or sword, burned by fire or even electrocuted.

- The character's Concussive HEA is made up of the combination of Strength, Will and Stamina.
- The character's Lethal HEA is made up of the combination of Strength, Will and Stamina, divided by three, with all fractions rounded up.
- HEA points are lost during the adventuring due to combat, life threatening situations and various accidents.
- For every 15 points of Concussive HEA damage a character may suffer, they will also lose 1 point for their Lethal HEA.
- If the character's Concussive HEA is reduced to zero, the character is unconscious. If the character's Concussive HEA is reduced to half of their normal Concussive HEA in negatives, the character dies. If the character's Lethal HEA is reduced to zero, the character dies.

## STEP 3

The character's unique abilities are defined as follows:

## SKILLS:

Skills are very common aptitudes and under normal conditions, everyone will have them. Skills are normally learned or acquired through training. Everyone will have a degree of "common sense" that will get him or her through the basic situations in life. Skills are that particular edge that can "help" when specifically needed. They can vary from basic everyday items including general trivia to the cutting edge of scientific understanding, such as of molecular biology. Skills can be used to modify any Primary or Secondary ability, expect for Concussive and Lethal HEA.

The number of skills that a character receives is determined by their INT. The character will receive as many skills as their INT divided by three, rounded up. If a character has an INT of 15, they can initially start off with five skills, while if another character

starts off with an INT of 10 they will initially start off with four skills. All skills when initially chosen cost no CPs and they give the character a +1 to any ability when using that skill. So if a character has INT of 14 and took medicine as one of their initial skills they would increase their INT to 15 when dealing in the field of medicine. Characters can choose to purchase their skill to give them a higher intensity when dealing with a specific topic. Characters can raise their skill bonus to a maximum of +5. The chart lists the cost, level of skill and increase to the particular ability being used.

*Example: If a character wanted to hold a Masters degree in history, it would increase any ability when dealing with History by +3 and cost 2 CPs. While if a character wanted a to be a Ph.D. in Ecology and an Expert in Animal Training, it would cost the character 3 CPs for the Ph.D. and 1 CP for the expert rating in Animal Training for a total of 4 CPs.*

## SKILL DESCRIPTIONS
### ACCOUNTING

The character with this skill has some training or experience in financial bookkeeping. A character with this skill will be able to adjust the financial records of an organization or someone's personal finances for example.

| Activity | Modifier |
|----------|----------|
| Small Business | Average (-5) |
| Corporate Office | Hard (-9) |
| IRS High Level Audit | Amazing (-19) |

### ACROBATICS

The character that possesses this skill has trained their body to be extremely supple and nimble giving them the ability to move with tumbling or gymnastic maneuvers. Any time the character uses any abilities to perform gymnastic actions they will receive a specific ability adjustment to that ability.

| CP COST | LEVEL OF SKILL | MODIFIER |
|---------|----------------|----------|
| None | High School Degree or General Training | +1 |
| -1 | Bachelors Degree or Expert Training | +2 |
| -2 | Masters Degree or Master Training | +3 |
| -3 | Ph.D. or Grand Master Training | +4 |

# LIST OF SKILLS

Accounting
Acrobatics
Actor
Aeronautical Engineering
Agriculture
Animal Training
Archeology
Artist
Astronomy
Biology
Botany
Bureaucratic
Chemistry
Civil Engineering
Computers
Demolitions
Disguise
Driving
Ecology
Electrical Engineering

Electronics
Escape Artist
Espionage
Finance
Fine Arts
First Aid
Forensic Medicine
Forgery
Gambling
Genetics
Geography
Geology
Journalism
History
Industrial Engineering
Interrogation
Law
Law Enforcement
Mechanical Engineering
Medicine

Metallurgy
Military Science
Mimicry
Occult
Philosophy
Photography
Physics
Piloting
Political Science
Psychology
Religion
Social Science
Streetwise
Thievery
Tracking
Trivia
Ventriloquist
Weaponsmith

| Activity | Modifier |
|----------|----------|
| Walking a balance beam | Easy (-2) |
| Juggling Balls | Average (-5) |
| Juggling knives | Hard (-9) |
| Walking a tightrope | Extreme (-14) |
| Walking a tightrope on a windy day | Amazing (-19) |

| Activity | Modifier |
|----------|----------|
| Local High School Performance | Easy (-2) |
| College Level Performance | Average (-5) |
| Golden Globe Winning Performance | Extreme (-14) |
| Oscar Winning Performance | Amazing (-19) |

## ACTOR

This character possesses the ability to perform, be it on stage, in front of a blue screen, or before a TV camera. Often this skill can be intensely useful for adopting the mannerisms and poise of others.

## AERONAUTICAL ENGINEERING

The field of engineering is extremely wide and varied, but a character with this skill has a good understanding of the technologies and theories behind modern aircraft. Naturally, this skill can be used to build, repair of diagnose potential problems in this field.

| Activity | Modifier |
| --- | --- |
| Replace a Basic Part | Easy (-2) |
| Repair a Basic Part | Average (-5) |
| Scratch Build a Basic Part | Hard (-9) |
| Scratch Build a Specific Part | Extreme (-14) |
| Major Part Repair | Amazing (-19) |

# AGRICULTURE

The character has studied horticulture, plant and animal physiology and reproduction as it relates to modern farming practices.

| Activity | Modifier |
| --- | --- |
| Working on a Small Farm | Average (-5) |
| Working on a Large Farm | Extreme (-14) |

# ANIMAL TRAINING

The character that possesses this skill has been taught to train various types of animals. The character with this skill can instruct various animals to perform stunts or tricks and is aware of how to correctly handle his charges.

| Activity | Modifier |
| --- | --- |
| Voice Command Training | Easy (-2) |
| Whistle Command Training | Hard (-9) |
| Look Command Training | Amazing (-19) |

# ARCHEOLOGY

The character has studied in the area of archeology. Though many archeologists have their own particular favorite period or field; they may be considered to have a good general knowledge of many myths, legends and customs of the ancient world.

| Activity | Modifier |
| --- | --- |
| Native American Arrowheads | Average (-5) |
| Statues from the Forbidden City | Extreme (-14) |
| Pyramids of King Tut | Amazing (-19) |
| Finding artifacts from Atlantis | Nearly Impossible (-25) |

# ARTIST

Art and artistic expression has many forms including poetry, painting, sculpture and creative writing. The artist skill can be seen as a general indication of the creative artistic spirit behind the work despite the artists favored form.

| Activity | Modifier |
| --- | --- |
| Original Piece of Music | Easy (-2) |
| Greco-Roman Columns and Statues | Average (-5) |
| Creating a New Music Style (Jazz, Blues) | Extreme (-14) |
| Creating a Masterpiece | Nearly Impossible (-25) |

# ASTRONOMY

Characters with this skill possess a basic understanding of the celestial bodies in the universe, planetary movement and alignments with their satellites, in addition to the current day theories of cosmology.

| Activity | Modifier |
| --- | --- |
| Discovering a Nebula | Average (-5) |
| Discovering a Planet | Hard (-9) |
| Discovering a New Star | Extreme (-14) |
| Discovering a New Galaxy | Amazing (-19) |
| Discovering a Black Hole | Nearly Impossible (-25) |

# BIOLOGY

Biology is an extremely broad science, encompassing as it does many aspects of the other sciences as they relate to the biological and natural world. For the purposes of easy distinction the biology skill here is assumed to relate specifically to animal biology, while plant biology is covered by the Botany skill.

| Activity | Modifier |
|---|---|
| Discovering a new virus | Average (-5) |
| Discovering a new organism | Hard (-9) |
| Curing a New Virus | Extreme (-14) |
| Creating a Man-made Virus | Amazing (-19) |

## BOTANY

The character has a background with the study of plants or any other multi-celled organism that does carry out photosynthesis to survive.

| Activity | Modifier |
|---|---|
| Discovering new Plant life | Average (-5) |
| Cross Breeding plants | Hard (-9) |

## BUREAUCRATIC

The character with this skill has been trained to deal with bureaucracy in all of its various forms from speaking to the "right person" to "cut through red tape".

| Activity | Modifier |
|---|---|
| Circumvent Secretary | Easy (-2) |
| Circumvent Low Level Bureaucrat | Average (-5) |
| Circumvent Mid-Level Bureaucrat | Hard (-9) |
| Convince other to not follow established policy | Extreme (-14) |
| Circumvent High Level Bureaucrat | Amazing (-19) |
| Convince other to break policy by doing an illegal act | Nearly Impossible (-25) |

## CHEMISTRY

The character with this skill will receive a specific ability adjustment to any ability the deals with the area of chemistry, including identification of chemicals by sight, taste, smell or touch, creating new chemical compounds and other similar items.

| Activity | Modifier |
|---|---|
| Identifying Chemicals with proper equipment | Average (-5) |
| Identifying Chemicals with sight or smell | Hard (-9) |
| Discovering a new element | Amazing (-19) |

## CIVIL ENGINEERING

The character with this skill will receive a specific ability adjustment to any ability that deals with the area of Engineering, including the building and construction of various items, discovery of any object and its particular uses and other related items.

| Activity | Modifier |
|---|---|
| Replace a Basic Part | Easy (-2) |
| Repair a Basic Part | Average (-5) |
| Scratch Build a Basic Part | Hard (-9) |
| Scratch Build a Specific Part | Extreme (-14) |
| Major Part Repair | Amazing (-19) |

## COMPUTERS

The character with this skill will receive a specific ability adjustment to any ability that deals with the area of computers, including programming of computers, creation and development of artificial intelligence and other related items.

| Activity | Modifier |
|---|---|
| Creating a Program | Easy (-2) |
| Modifying an existing Program | Average (-5) |
| Bypassing an Average Security System | Hard (-9) |
| Bypassing an Advanced Security System | Extreme (-14) |

## DEMOLITION

The character with this skill has been trained to deal with demolitions. The character has knowledge of bomb making and explosive technology, which type of explosive agent they may use and how to place it for maximum effect.

| Activity | Modifier |
|---|---|
| Setting an explosive | Easy (-2) |
| Building explosives with a kit | Average (-5) |
| Building explosives from scratch | Hard (-9) |
| Disarming explosives built with a kit | Extreme (-14) |
| Disarming explosives built from scratch | Amazing (-19) |

## DISGUISE

The character is proficient with a number of techniques that are useful when trying to create a disguise, from basic make-up artistry to latex masks and full body molding. This skill has a place on the film set and also in undercover operations.

| Activity | Modifier |
|---|---|
| Alter Minor Details (Eyes or Hair) | Easy (-2) |
| Alter Basic Details (Height and Weight) | Hard (-9) |
| Alter Distinct Details (Age or Skin Color) | Extreme (-14) |
| Alter Major Details (Sex) | Amazing (-19) |

## DRIVING

The character has spent time developing his ability to drive or ride a number of motor vehicles, from motorbikes to eighteen wheeled land rigs to motorized watercraft.

| Activity | Modifier |
|---|---|
| Avoid Obstacle | Easy (-2) |
| Aggressive Driving Style | Hard (-9) |
| Complex Driving Styles and Techniques | Amazing (-19) |

## ECOLOGY

The character has studied the direct and indirect relationship of animals and plants in an ecological system and how these forms of life interact with each other.

| Activity | Modifier |
|---|---|
| Identifying Flora and Fauna | Average (-5) |
| Causes of Global Warming | Hard (-9) |
| Cure for Global Warming | Extreme (-14) |
| Gaia Environment | Amazing (-19) |

## ELECTRONICS

Characters with this skill have been exposed to the concept and designs of electronics. The character with this skill will receive a specific ability adjustment to any ability that deals with the area of electronics, consisting of the creation and repair of various types of electronic devices and other related items.

| Activity | Modifier |
|---|---|
| Replace Part | Easy (-2) |
| Repair Part | Average (-5) |
| Scratch Build Part Creation | Hard (-9) |
| Major Part Repair | Amazing (-19) |

# ESCAPE ARTIST

The character with this skill is a time-practiced expert both in theory and practice of escaping from locks, bonds and other such restraining devices.

| Activity | Modifier |
| --- | --- |
| Escape Rope Restraints | Average (-5) |
| Escape Handcuffs | Hard (-9) |
| Escape Handcuffs and Leg Restraints | Extreme (-14) |
| Escape Straightjacket | Nearly Impossible (-25) |

# ESPIONAGE

A character who has trained in espionage is proficient with various forms of surveillance and the equipment commonly used in such tasks, including bugging, laser microphones and phone tapping.

| Activity | Modifier |
| --- | --- |
| Examine & Surveillance | Easy (-2) |
| Analyze Photography and Video | Hard (-9) |
| Conceal or Find Bugs | Extreme (-14) |

# FINANCE

The character with this skill has a background in the corporate world, economics and finance.

| Activity | Modifier |
| --- | --- |
| Mom and Pop Shop | Average (-5) |
| Small Corporation | Hard (-9) |
| Mid-sized Corporation | Extreme (-14) |
| Large Corporation | Amazing (-19) |

# FINE ARTS

A character with this skill has been train in the recognition and identification of works of painted art, expensive ceramics and precious gemstones and jewels.

| Activity | Modifier |
| --- | --- |
| Tiffany Diamond | Average (-5) |
| Picasso | Hard (-9) |
| Ming Vase | Extreme (-14) |
| Mona Lisa | Amazing (-19) |
| Hope Diamond | Nearly Impossible (-25) |

# FIRST AID

The character has had basic first aid training and may even be certified in CPR and other basic emergency procedures. In general, first aid covers the ability to stabilize victims' wounds long enough for the arrival of paramedic assistance, including techniques for emergency resuscitation and for stemming blood flow from gunshot wounds.

| Activity | Modifier |
| --- | --- |
| Small Cuts | Easy (-2) |
| Jammed Fingers | Average (-5) |
| Dislocated Shoulder | Hard (-9) |
| Broken Arm | Extreme (-14) |

# FORENSIC MEDICINE

The character has been trained in various techniques of forensic examination, including crime scene evidence gathering and forensic pathology to determine the cause of injury or death to a victim. A reasonable degree of legal understanding in terms of law and legal investigative procedures are included in this skill.

| Activity | Modifier |
| --- | --- |
| Death by Natural Causes | Easy (-2) |
| Death by Firearm | Average (-5) |
| Death by Poison | Hard (-9) |
| Multiple shooting with multiple Firearms | Extreme (-14) |
| Faking a Death | Amazing (-19) |

## FORGERY

An extremely variable skill, which permits the character to duplicate handwriting, issue fake documentation, or recreate an artistic masterpiece (though the appropriate Fine Arts skill is also required for the latter).

| Activity | Modifier |
| --- | --- |
| Forging a non-specific handwriting | Easy (-2) |
| Forging a non-specific document | Average (-5) |
| Forging a specific handwriting | Hard (-9) |
| Forging a specific document | Extreme (-14) |
| Forging an item with anti-forgery system (Hologram, Watermark) | Amazing (-19) |

## GAMBLING

The gambling skill permits the character to play a variety of skill based gambling games (usually card based), to understand the rules and procedures of play and to not give away his hand in the process. Gambling based on random chance is not covered by skill, its just potluck!

| Activity | Modifier |
| --- | --- |
| Straight | Easy (-2) |
| Flush | Average (-5) |
| Full house | Hard (-9) |
| Four of a kind | Extreme (-14) |
| Straight Flush | Amazing (-19) |
| Royal Straight Flush | Nearly Impossible (-25) |

## GENETICS

The character with this skill will receive a specific ability adjustment to any ability that deals with the area of genetics, consisting of creating and discovering new life forms, development of humans and animals, cures to genetic defects and other related items.

| Activity | Modifier |
| --- | --- |
| Blood Typing | Easy (-2) |
| Genetic Engineered Foods | Hard (-9) |
| Cloning | Amazing (-19) |
| Genetic Engineering | Nearly Impossible (-25) |

## GEOGRAPHY

The character is at least competent in reading a map and using a compass; he is also able to draw maps with reasonable accuracy and has a basic understanding of geographic features that effect local ecologies.

| Activity | Modifier |
| --- | --- |
| United States | Average (-5) |
| North Dakota | Hard (-9) |
| Togo | Extreme (-14) |
| Curaçao | Amazing (-19) |

## GEOLOGY

This includes geological stability of landmasses, the mineral composition of a particular area, identification of rocks and minerals and other related items.

| Activity | Modifier |
| --- | --- |
| Reasoning for Earthquakes | Average (-5) |
| Age of the Earth | Hard (-9) |
| Creating Synthetic Diamonds | Extreme (-14) |
| Creating a Natural Diamond | Nearly Impossible (-25) |

## JOURNALISM

With the skill of journalism, the character has been involved and can perform in the field of writing, reporting and research. The character is usually able to layout a story in an interesting format and gets his point across with written words.

| Activity | Modifier |
|---|---|
| Writing for a High School Paper | Easy (-2) |
| Writing for a Local Newspaper | Average (-5) |
| Writing for a Major Newspaper or Magazine | Hard (-9) |
| Writing a Best Seller | Extreme (-14) |
| Writing a Pulitzer Prize | Amazing (-19) |

## HISTORY

The character with this skill has knowledge of general history to the historical effect that a particular event played to another.

| Activity | Modifier |
|---|---|
| Discovery of America | Average (-5) |
| The Crusades | Hard (-9) |
| Ancient Mayan Civilizations | Extreme (-14) |
| Fall of the Roman Empire | Amazing (-19) |

## INDUSTRIAL ENGINEERING

A character with this skill can apply scientific principles toward the design, construction and operation of efficient and economical structures, equipment and systems. This skill also includes the commercial production and sale of goods and services. The character knows what is being shipped into an industrial area, he can predict what is being built or set up in that area and vice versa.

| Activity | Modifier |
|---|---|
| Sales of Goods | Easy (-2) |
| Predict what is being built with materials on hand | Extreme (-14) |
| Predict what is being built with no materials on hand | Amazing (-19) |

## INTERROGATION

The character is a master of the interview technique; he can use subtle psychological manipulations to break down a suspect's will to resist, when attempting to obtain information. This skill also includes the use of more direct means of getting a suspect to talk, from intimidation to torture.

| Activity | Modifier |
|---|---|
| A young Child | Easy (-2) |
| Your Mother | Average (-5) |
| Your Boy or Girlfriend | Hard (-9) |
| Professional Interrogators | Extreme (-14) |
| Professional Interrogators with Chemicals | Amazing (-19) |

## LAW

This skill indicates that the character has at the very least attended law school and has a good grasp of legal language and terminology. He may or may not actually be qualified as a professional lawyer.

| Activity | Modifier |
|---|---|
| Grand Jury Arraignment | Average (-5) |
| Murder Court Case | Hard (-9) |
| Death Row Appeal | Extreme (-14) |
| Arguing a Supreme Court Case | Amazing (-19) |

## LAW-ENFORCEMENT

The character has been trained in law enforcement procedures, including the correct manner in which to caution and handcuff suspects, how to investigate a crime scene and how to present information when called to testify in a courtroom.

| Activity | Modifier |
|----------|----------|
| Profiling | Average (-5) |
| Serving a Warrant to the Carluccis | Hard (-9) |
| Undercover work in the Red Wing Tong | Extreme (-14) |
| Narcotic Trafficking | Amazing (-19) |
| Undercover work in the Nubian Nation | Nearly Impossible (-25) |

## MECHANICAL ENGINEERING

Characters with this skill know how to apply scientific principles toward the creation and application of mechanical power and the production, design and use of the most complex machines and tools.

| Activity | Modifier |
|----------|----------|
| Replace a Basic Part | Easy (-2) |
| Repair a Basic Part | Average (-5) |
| Scratch Build a Basic Part | Hard (-9) |
| Scratch Build a Specific Part | Extreme (-14) |
| Major Part Repair | Amazing (-19) |

## MEDICINE

The character with this skill is trained in various facets of medicine, from human anatomy and physiology to toxicology, pathology and for very skilled individuals - surgery. To possess this skill, the character must have attended medical school and is most likely a practicing clinician.

| Activity | Modifier |
|----------|----------|
| High Blood Pressure | Average (-5) |
| Heart Attack | Hard (-9) |
| Stoke | Extreme (-14) |
| Quadruple Heart Bypass | Amazing (-19) |

## METALLURGY

Characters know the science or procedures of extracting metals from their ores, of purifying metals and of creating useful objects from metals. A character can identify metal in an object and ore being brought from a mine on sight. The character with this skill will receive a specific ability adjustment to any ability dealing with the area of metallurgy.

| Activity | Modifier |
|----------|----------|
| Identifying Metals | Average (-5) |
| Smelting Ore | Extreme (-14) |
| Creating Alloys | Amazing (-19) |

## MILITARY SCIENCE

The character with this skill has either served in the military or had some experience dealing with the military. The character is familiar with military procedures and may have some degree of knowledge concerning policy, strategy and tactics used by military forces.

| Activity | Modifier |
|----------|----------|
| Boot Camp | Average (-5) |
| US Marine Corp. Recon | Hard (-9) |
| US Army Rangers | Extreme (-14) |
| US Navy S.E.A.L.s | Amazing (-19) |

## MIMICRY

The character has a talented voice that can be used to mimic another's voice, vocal pattern and mannerisms or can even combine the skill with ventriloquism.

| Activity | Modifier |
|----------|----------|
| Average Person | Average (-5) |
| The President of the United States | Hard (-9) |
| Eddie Murphy | Extreme (-14) |
| Jerry Lewis | Amazing (-19) |

## OCCULT

The character that possesses this skill has acquired knowledge of the occult, magical histories and magical and mystical backgrounds.

| Activity | Modifier |
|---|---|
| Tarot or Palm Reading | Easy (-2) |
| Government Conspiracies | Hard (-9) |
| Big Foot or Sasquatch Sighting | Extreme (-14) |
| Loch Ness Monster Sighting | Amazing (-19) |
| Bermuda Triangle Disappearance | Nearly Impossible (-25) |

## PHILOSOPHY

The character with this skill will receive a specific ability adjustment to any ability that deals with the area philosophy.   This includes the ability to discuss and research any areas of philosophy, the historical background of the "fathers" of philosophy and other such topics.

| Activity | Modifier |
|---|---|
| Contemplating an concept of idea | Easy (-2) |
| Ancient Philosophy & Classical Thought | Average (-5) |
| Medieval Thought & Philosophy | Hard (-9) |
| Metaphysics | Extreme (-14) |

## PHOTOGRAPHY

The character is practiced in the area of photography; he is familiar with cameras in general and with many photographic styles and techniques.  The character is also able to use a dark room to develop prints and may be sufficiently skilled to analyze existing pictures to ascertain whether or not they are genuine of photo-composites.

| Activity | Modifier |
|---|---|
| Familiar with the inner working of a Camera | Average (-5) |
| Can develop own photographs | Hard (-9) |
| Can tell if photograph has been faked on sight | Amazing (-19) |

## PHYSICS

The character that possesses this skill is well versed in the field of physics, consisting of high school basic physics to sub-atomic theory.  The character with this skill will receive a specific ability adjustment to any ability that deals with the area of physics that includes motion, flight and other related items.

| Activity | Modifier |
|---|---|
| Newton' Law of Gravity | Easy (-2) |
| Newton's Third Law | Average (-5) |
| Creating a new law of physics | Extreme (-14) |
| Discovering new high energy particle | Amazing (-19) |
| Negating gravity | Nearly Impossible (-25) |

## PILOTING

The character with this skill has trained as a professional pilot and will receive a specific ability adjustment to any ability that deals with the area of piloting aircraft.  This skill permits the character to fly anything from a small display plane up to a Jumbo jet.

| Activity | Modifier |
|---|---|
| Avoid Obstacle | Easy (-2) |
| Aggressive Piloting Style | Hard (-9) |
| Complex Piloting Styles and Techniques | Amazing (-19) |

## POLITICAL SCIENCE

The character with this skill has been train in the areas of political science, including international history, geopolitics and political theory.  The character with this skill will receive a specific ability adjustment to any ability that deals with the area of political science and political theory.

| Activity | Modifier |
|---|---|
| Creating a trade agreement | Average (-5) |
| Getting two warring parties to meet at the peace table | Hard (-9) |
| Abolishing Apartheid in South Africa | Extreme (-14) |
| Peace Treaty between Arabs and Jews | Nearly Impossible (-25) |

## PSYCHOLOGY

The character that possesses this skill has been trained in the art of psychology and psychotherapy. When using this skill, the character will receive a specific ability adjustment to any ability that deals with the area of psychiatry, psychology, mental manipulation, hypnosis and other related items.

| Activity | Modifier |
|---|---|
| Anxiety Attack | Average (-5) |
| Nervous Breakdown | Hard (-9) |
| Dealing with Multiple Personalities | Amazing (-19) |

## RELIGION

The character that possesses this skill knows the expressions of humanity's belief in and reverence for a superhuman power recognized as the creator and governor of the universe. The character with this skill will receive a specific ability adjustment to any ability that deals with the area of religion, religious beliefs and other such matters.

| Activity | Modifier |
|---|---|
| Performing generic religious service | Easy (-2) |
| Performing specific religious service | Hard (-9) |
| Performing exotic religious service | Amazing (-19) |

## SOCIAL SCIENCE

A character with this skill can comprehend the study of social behavior, institutions and development of human society in general. The character with this skill will receive a specific ability adjustment to any ability that deal with the area of social sciences.

| Activity | Modifier |
|---|---|
| Building a General Organization | Average (-5) |
| Building a Specific Organization | Hard (-9) |
| Revitalizing a Poor Neighborhood | Extreme (-14) |
| Solving the Plight of the Poor | Nearly Impossible (-25) |

## STREETWISE

A character with this skill has a great amount of experience with "life on the street". Many times this type of skill is best used when dealing with situations that include blending in with in a local crowd of people with out drawing attention to yourself, dealing with black market or underworld items, people and other related items. When using this skill the character will receive a specific ability adjustment to any ability when dealing in these situations

| Activity | Modifier |
|---|---|
| Blend in at Haven City | Easy (-2) |
| Blend in at Arcadia | Average (-5) |
| Blend in at Freeman Hill | Hard (-9) |
| Blend in at Armistad | Extreme (-14) |
| Blend in at Golden Heights | Amazing (-19) |
| Blend in at Rome Island | Nearly Impossible (-25) |

## THIEVERY

The character with this skill has been trained as an expert thief. The character is able to deal with a number of professional problems from lock picking, pick pocketing and various other related items. Many "upstanding" individuals often shun this skill but it can become a very impressive lifesaver when necessary.

| Activity | Modifier |
|---|---|
| Picking a Simple Lock | Easy (-2) |
| Picking an Average Lock | Average (-5) |
| Hotwiring an Automobile | Hard (-9) |
| Picking an Above Average Lock | Extreme (-14) |
| Picking a Superior Lock | Amazing (-19) |

## TRACKING

The character that possesses this skill is a specialist in the area of tracking animals and people. The ability to track prey may be used on any type of environment, with the possible exception of a city street. The character with this skill will receive a specific ability adjustment to the intensity level of all abilities dealing with tracking a quarry.

| Activity | Modifier |
|---|---|
| Easy trail to follow | Easy (-2) |
| Average Trail to follow | Hard (-9) |
| Very few clues or tracks to follow | Amazing (-19) |

## TRIVIA

The character that possesses this skill is a specialist in one specific area. The area of trivia could be anything from television history to gemstones to African religions. The character with this skill will receive a specific ability adjustment to the intensity level of all abilities dealing with trivia.

| Activity | Modifier |
|---|---|
| What is Batman's Real Name? | Easy (-2) |
| What are the name of the Seven Dwarves from Snow White? | Hard (-9) |
| For Whom the Bell does Toll? | Extreme (-14) |
| What is the answer to the Riddle of Life? | Nearly Impossible (-25) |

## VENTRILOQUIST

The character with this skill is trained in the art of "throwing" ones voice, making it seem that a person's voice is coming from another location. The character with this skill is able to throw their voice. When using this skill the character will receive a specific ability adjustment to the intensity level of all abilities dealing with the field of ventriloquism.

| Activity | Modifier |
|---|---|
| With a Mannequin | Average (-5) |
| While Smoking | Hard (-9) |
| While Drinking Water | Amazing (-19) |

## WEAPONSMITH

The character with this skill is trained in the art of creating and manufacturing any type of weapon of offensive device from a knife or sword to firearms. When using this skill the character will receive a specific ability adjustment to the intensity level of all abilities dealing with the field of weapon creation, development and research.

| Activity | Modifier |
|---|---|
| Repair Weapon | Average (-5) |
| Scratch Build a Weapon | Hard (-9) |
| Scratch Build an Exotic Weapon | Extreme (-14) |

## LANGUAGES:

All characters in the Haven: COV are able to speak, read, write and understand at least one language. This initial language will be, of course, the character's native tongue. Characters with higher levels of Intelligence may have learned more languages than just their native language. Consult the table below to find out how many languages your character can speak.

A player character has a language rating for their native language that is equal to 10 plus a D10 dice roll. Any languages additional to a character's native language have a starting rating of 5 plus a D10 dice roll. A character with a rating of 12 or higher is considered to be completely fluent in the language.

A character with a 16 or higher rating is considered to be able to speak with such proficiency that these people could pass as someone who has lived extensively in a particular place or was even born there. A character's additional languages can be equal to the character's native language, but they can never be higher than the character's native language. If the additional language rating is higher than the native language rating then those rating numbers will be switched for each other. The following is a list of languages.

| Intelligence (INT) | Languages Spoken |
|---|---|
| 1 - 7 | 1 (Native) |
| 8 - 12 | 2 (Native + 1) |
| 13 - 15 | 3 (Native + 2) |
| 16 - 18 | 4 (Native + 3) |
| 19 - 20 | 5 (Native + 4) |
| 21+ | 6 (Native + 5) |

# LANGUAGES

Afrikaans
Albanian
Arabic
Aramaic
Armenian
Bengali
Bulgarian
Chinese
Czech
Danish
Dutch
English
English - United Kingdom
English - Australian
Finnish

Flemish
French
German
Greek
Hindi
Hebrew
Hungarian
Icelandic
Indonesian
Italian
Japanese
Korean
Latin
Maltese
Norwegian

Persian
Polish
Portuguese
Rumanian
Russian
Serbo-Croatian
Slovak
Spanish
Swedish
Thai
Turkish
Ukrainian
Vietnamese
Yiddish

# BENEFITS:

Benefits are some unique abilities or advantages that give a character a particular edge in their existence. The benefit could be anything from the ability to have others follow a player character with their Leadership Benefit to being able to use both hands with equal proficiency with the Ambidextrous Benefit. The character may have as many benefits that they wish, as long as they can pay for them with their CPs. Some particular benefits, including Connections, may be chosen multiple times. The following is a list of the Benefits that can be chosen multiple times:

- Area Knowledge
- Connections
- Immunity
- Prodigy
- Status

# DEFINITIONS OF BENEFITS

## AMBIDEXTROUS

*You got two hands, right? Then use 'em!*

The character with this ability is able to use both their hands and perform actions without any difficulty. Characters with this benefit do not suffer negatives to their ACC when firing two firearms in combat.

*Cost: -4*

# BENEFITS

Ambidextrous
Area Knowledge
Authority Figure
Connections
Direction Sense
Eagle Eyes
Eidetic Memory
Fast Draw
Gifted Fighter

Heightened Hearing
Immunity
Iron Will
Lucky
Marksman
Natural Athlete
Natural Linguist
Night Vision
Nondescript

Perfect Balance
Perfect Timing
Rapid Fire
Sex Appeal
Soothing Voice
Status
True Sight
Wealthy

## AREA KNOWLEDGE

*Hell, I grew up in this neighborhood.*

The character with this benefit has a very intimate knowledge of a certain location. The character may have grown up in the location or has spent an extreme amount of time at this location, interacting with various people. Along with this benefit, it is very logical to also choose the benefit Connections, stating that this character has made various "friends" during their time in this location.
*Cost: -2*

## AUTHORITY FIGURE

*Whenever he walked into the room, his workers were instructed to not turn their heads, to not glance aside at him or offer him a good morning. If he stood by them as they did their work, they were to act as though nothing was there. This was the way he ran his offices: with the absolute respect that complete silence and invisibility would award him*

The character with this benefit is looked up to and admired by other characters, whether the person with this benefit is a police officer, mercenary or an assassin. When the character with this benefit inter-acts with others, depending on the character, that character will receive a +3 to all their INFL rolls.
*Cost: -2*

## CONNECTIONS

*He can score anything at anytime. Everyone in Haven, from Mayor Wright to Gino Santucci to Archbishop Charles Dutton owes him something.*

*Need a brand new Porsche 911 in two hours with the pink slip? Need a full dinner Buffet for 200 people? Need a Stinger Rocket Launcher? He can find it for you.*

This asset provides a "contact" for a character. These consist of a person or group, from which he can often get information, funding, or comfort. The connection can consist of persons from previous interactions, teachers, or someone that might have helped the person in the past. This connection is considered an ally to the character and is trusted in any way within normal means. The character cannot abuse this relationship, to the point where it might place the contact in personal danger. The Game Operation Director, G.O.D. for short, will decide the type of relation possessed and the lengths and limits to this relationship.
*Cost: -3*

## DIRECTION SENSE

*What do you mean turn left? We need to go north, right? Then go straight!*

The character possesses an almost supernatural sense of direction and can always tell in which direction they are facing even when blindfolded or disoriented. The character with this benefit cannot use it to help find out where they are if they are lost but they will be aware in what direction they are facing at any given time.
*Cost: -1*

## EAGLE EYES

*I see you!!!!!*

A character with this benefit has been born with natural abilities that make them able to see better than the majority of people. The character with this benefit will receive an additional +3 to their PER roll when looking or searching.

*Cost: -2*

## EIDETIC MEMORY

*I can still see my notes, imprinted and burned into my brain. It's still there for me to see. Everything is still there for me to see.*

The character possesses an eidetic or "photographic" memory. The character's mind is able to record any and every thing that the character is exposed to and to can recall it with no trouble at all. The events that the character is exposed to can be items that were either studied or seen.

*Cost: -2*

## FAST DRAW

*Everything seemed to slow down in the bar, casting a silence that sank deep into the walls. Before anyone else could make a move, there was a flash and the smell of gunpowder and his body was on the floor.*

The character with this benefit is able to ready their weapon, whether it is a pistol, sword, or any other weapon of this type, almost instantaneously. The character with this benefit can ignore their holster modifier when drawing any type of weapon.

*Cost: -4*

## GIFTED FIGHTER

*Most people think similar thoughts when they go up against him. "How bad could a round with the champ be?"*

A character with this benefit has been born with natural instincts and abilities that make him a fighter with which to be reckoned. The character with this benefit will receive an additional action when engaged in hand-to-hand combat.

*Cost: -3*

## HEIGHTENED HEARING

*I can hear a pin drop in the middle of a thunderstorm.*

A character with this benefit has been born with natural abilities that make them able to hear better than most. The character with this benefit will receive an additional +3 to their PER roll when listening.

*Cost: -2*

## IMMUNITY

*Poison doesn't work on me. Next time try a gun.*

For some unknown reason, the character possesses natural immunity to common and even to extreme, exotic poisons, diseases, or both. The following chart will determine how many points taking the benefit will cost. If a character takes an immunity that has other intensities under it they will receive immunity to the lower intensities as well with no additional cost. Characters can choose to purchase either immunity to poisons or immunity to diseases separately.

*Example: Marcus decides to take the immunity to exotic poisons and rare disease. Since there are two other lower intensities for poison, rare and general, he will receive that immunity at no extra cost. But, since Marcus purchased the lowest intensity for disease he will be only immune to those and nothing higher.*

| POINTS | TYPE OF IMMUNITY |
|---|---|
| -2 | General Poisons (Arsenic) or Diseases (Basic Flu) |
| -4 | Rare Poisons (Cobra Venom) or Diseases (Scarlet Fever) |
| -6 | Exotic Poisons (Portuguese Man-O-War Venom) or Disease (Eboli) |

**Cost: Variable**

## IRON WILL

*I gave him five doses of truth serum and he still wouldn't break.*

This benefit gives the character an incredibly strong will that makes them even more resistance to brain washing or interrogation. The character receives an additional +3 to their WILL against these types of mental assaults and manipulations such as brain washing and post-hypnotic suggestion.

*Cost: -2*

# LUCKY

*For the sixth time in a row, he rolled sevens.*

The character is unusually lucky. This will give the character the ability to accomplish almost incredible feats with uncanny ease and ability. For gaming purposes, this means the character can re-roll up to three rolls, per adventure, that they may have failed.

*Cost: -10*

# MARKSMAN

*Line them up in the crosshairs and squeeze the trigger.*

With this benefit, the character is an expertly trained sharpshooter and marksman. The character with this benefit will gain a +2 to their ACC with any type of firearm at medium or long range.

*Cost: -1*

# NATURAL ATHLETE

*You want me to perform a forward roll into a leaping one-half twisting forward jump into a one-armed handstand? Piece of cake!*

A character with this benefit has been born with natural instincts and abilities that make them the dream of any sports team and coaches. The character with this benefit will receive an additional +2 to their AGI score when engaged in any athletic endeavors, including catching or dodging objects, and throwing items. This benefit cannot be used when shooting.

*Cost: -1*

# NATURAL LINGUIST

*If I can hear it, I can speak it.*

The character is able to translate and speak languages that they have heard. The benefit is on

a totally subconscious level of the character and cannot be controlled. The first time a character speaks with or hears a language that they have not been exposed to before, the character must make an INT roll. If the character succeeds with the roll, they will acquire and speak this language equal to the character's native language at Hard (-9) modifier. If the character fails, they may not speak this language and may not try again until they come across someone else who speaks that particular language.
*Cost: -3*

## NIGHT VISION

*I got eyes just like a cat.*

A character with this benefit is able to see in complete darkness as well as a bright summer day. The character with this benefit suffers no negatives to their abilities when in dark situations or environments.
*Cost: -3*

## NONDESCRIPT

*What did she look like? Yeah, I remember. Well, she had red....wait....no....blond...no, wait .... brunette ..... wait....or was it a he?*

The character with this benefit is hard to remember as are very specific items or information about the person. The character, when described, will be talked about with generalization. This will be related to the character's height, weight, age, hair color and sometimes to an extreme if the person was male or female or black or white.
*Cost: -6*

## PERFECT BALANCE

*Watch mom! No hands!*

The character was born with an innate sense of balance so much so that this character can walk a tightrope automatically and a rope with slack in it with an AGI roll. The character can also survive falls up to three stories if they land on their feet, with an AGI roll.
*Cost: -3*

## PERFECT TIMING

*Time passes slowly for those who wait.*

The character is able to detect the passage of time down to the exact second with innate skill and ability. The character can use this benefit at anytime with no resistance to it.

*Cost: -1*

# RAPID FIRE

*He was killed due to lead poisoning, the 9mm type.*

The character with this benefit is able to shoot particular firearms faster than normally possible. A character with this benefit is able to fire an additional shot per round to any weapon that has a rate of 1 shot per round.

*Cost: -6*

# SEX APPEAL

*It must be a crime to look this good!*

Members of the opposite sex find a character that acquires this benefit amazingly attractive. This makes others more susceptible to his or her charms. Any time the character interacts with a member of the opposite sex, he or she will receive a +3 to all their INFL rolls.

*Cost: -2*

# SOOTHING VOICE

*Just calm down son. Think about what you're doing. Look at the gun and make sure you want to do this. Listen to me.*

The character with this benefit has been blessed with the "angelic voice of God himself." This character is said to be able to calm the wildest animal with a simple whisper from their voice. Any time that the character is speaking, they can add +3 to their INFL rolls.

*Cost: -2*

# STATUS

*Everyone at the club knew who he was. To not know him was to be nothing. To know him was to get at least a hundred in tips from his table, every night.*

The character with this benefit is considered to hold some type of important status in the regular world or even in the criminal underworld. The character may be a captain of industry, an actor or performer, or even the leader of a nation or country. Any time the character interacts with a person that recognizes their status the character will receive a +4 to all their INFL rolls.

*Cost: -2*

# TRUE SIGHT

*Something tells me you're lying.*

The character with this benefit, by some unknown reason or ability can detect if someone is being untruthful or deceptive to them in any ways. Examples of this benefit include a character being able to see a person's real face even if they had a mask or make-up covering it or detecting if the character is being lied to.

*Cost: -2*

# WEALTHY

*Show me the money!!!!!!!!!*

A character that chooses this benefit has some form of additional financial resources. This can take the form of a family fortune, inheritance, or from an unknown source. For gaming purposes, this means the character starts the game with $2,000.

*Cost: -3*

# DRAWBACKS:

Drawbacks are some special disadvantages that give a character a particular defect on their existence. The drawback could be anything from the constant battle between two foes that causes a Feud to a character that wishes everyone to know who they are with Public Identity. Each drawback will give character points back to a player, in contrast to benefits. The character may initially gain up to a maximum of 12 Character Points from drawbacks, anymore than that amount of drawbacks will make the characters generally unplayable. Characters can gain drawbacks during an adventure, but they will not gain additional Character Points for those acquired. Some particular drawbacks, including Psychological Disorder, may be chosen multiple times. The following is a list of the Drawbacks that can be chosen multiple times:

# DRAWBACKS

| | | |
|---|---|---|
| Absentminded | Functionally Illiterate | Pursued/Pursuing |
| Amnesia | Hatred | Reputation |
| Blind as a Bat | Loner | Rivalry |
| Braggart | Personal Constraint | Secret |
| Coward | Phobia | Traumatic Flashback |
| Dependency | Physical Disability | Ugly as Sin |
| Distinguishable | Poverty | Uncoordinated |
| Characteristic | Power Hungry | Unlucky |
| Foolhardy | Psychological Disorder | |

- Dependency
- Distinguishable Characteristic
- Hatred
- Personal Constraint
- Phobia
- Physical Disability
- Psychological Disorder
- Pursued
- Pursuing
- Reputation
- Rivalry
- Secret
- Traumatic Flashback

# DEFINITIONS OF DRAWBACKS

## ABSENTMINDED

*Did I remember to…?*

The character is extremely forgetful and has a major problem remembering even the most basic of items. The character will misplace items, forget clues in an investigation or even the names of people they will meet. Any time a character needs to recall any fact they must make an INT roll; if they need to remember an important fact they receive an Average (-5) modifier to INT rolls.
*Cost: +2*

## AMNESIA

*His name eluded him for so long. But still, his real name and his real past eluded him*

The character with this drawback is totally unable to remember anything about their past. The character with this drawback can have other benefits and drawbacks that the character does not know about, including being pursued by an unknown enemy, or that they are wealthy.
*Cost: +2*

## BLIND AS A BAT

*I can't see a thing. I have lost my glasses again.*

A character with this drawback has been born with natural disabilities that make them unable to see as well as the majority of people. The character with this drawback will suffer an additional Average (-5) modifier to their ACC and PER roll when looking, searching or shooting.
*Cost: +3*

## BRAGGART

*Yeah, I know Syrus! Taught the boy everything he ever learned! Who do you think set him up where he is on Rome Island, huh?*

A character with this drawback has an "incredibly high opinion of him- or herself" and is not afraid to let everyone else know about it. The character will constantly boast about their past deeds, exaggerating their talents and powers to an almost godlike status. They may never actually do anything, but they will talk a great deal and try to convince everyone that they will. A Braggart may never have skills or abilities to back up the statements they make and this may cost them in battle.
*Cost: +1*

## COWARD

*Things were going so well. No one in the bank gave him trouble and it took two shots to drop the guard. Now only if the driver had stuck around....*

The character that possesses this drawback is completely against the idea of risking their life for any reason. "They will be the person who always sounds like they will be right by your side if something does happen", they will be right by your side, but in reality they will be the first ones to leave if the situation turns bad. Characters that are cowards will leave a dangerous situation the minute they feel that their existence could be threatened. When playing with this character in a group, this character can develop into an utterly bad liability.
*Cost: +1*

## DEPENDENCY

*Just one more hit, just one more hit, just one more hit....*

The character is either physically or psychologically dependent upon a certain item. The dependency may range from an alcoholic beverage to illegal drugs to a weapon they like to use. The character must constantly be in contact with the item to which they are dependent. One example is characters that are dependent on illegal drugs to make them function normally; if they do not take them they will begin to go through withdrawal. If the character spends more than two hours without their dependency, they will suffer an Average (-5) modifier to all their primary abilities with no change in their secondary abilities. The character will go to extreme lengths to acquire the source of their dependency and will not let anything get in their way, including friends and family. Their abilities will return to normal when the character reacquires the "item".
*Cost: +4*

## DISTINGUISHABLE CHARACTERISTIC

*This tattoo is one of a kind. No one has anything like this.*

The character has some type of physical trait that will make the character more easily noticeable than the average person. An example of this would be

unusual eye color, such as gray eyes, a tattooed face, someone that wears an eye patch and various others.
*Cost: +1*

## FOOLHARDY

*Lets see. ten guys all armed with MP-5's and all I got is a .22 with five bullets. Sounds like a good plan.*

Characters possessing this drawback are monstrously overconfident of their skills and abilities, which will prove dangerous to themselves and others. The character only wishes to do the most dangerous and exciting stunt so everyone can see. The notion of battling with a thousand soldiers at once is not too much of an exaggeration for persons that possess this drawback. In any situation that could be considered dangerous, the foolhardy character is the first one to spin into action against the enemy.
*Cost: +1*

## FUNCTIONALLY ILLITERATE

*Just because I can't read does not mean I'm an idiot*

Characters that possess this drawback are able to communicate orally with others with no difficulty but the character cannot read at all. The character is able to communicate with characters as if they did not possess this drawback, but anytime the character is forced to read a book, plans or even the simplest map they are incapable of reading it.
*Cost: +1*

## HATRED

*Jesus hates you and so do I.*

Characters that possess this drawback have an incredibly long-lasting vendetta with another person, which has caused a large number of battles to be fought. Anytime the character meets up with their Hatred opponent they will attack on sight. This is with no regard to themselves, other party members, the mission, or the opponent. The character will always choose this opponent above all else in the game play, including the mission itself.
*Cost: +3*

## LONER

*People stepped away from him as he shuffled down the sidewalk. The gray sky cast down its indifference to the city. The concrete jungle is a cold and deaf world.*

The character with this drawback has a difficult time being a member of a group of any type. They will normally alienate themselves from all types of collective units and work alone in just about every aspect. The character with this drawback will never join any type of team membership or group for more than a limited time at best.

*Cost: +1*

## PERSONAL CONSTRAINT

*There are some lines that I will not cross...*

This drawback is any type of restriction that the character has placed upon themselves, some may even call it a "code of honor," though sometimes it may have nothing to do with morals. This type of drawback, should not be too specific, including your character cannot attack people wearing the color red on a Saturday during a lunar eclipse.

*Cost: +1*

## PHOBIA

*I'm not afraid ... really.*

The character that possesses this drawback has an irrational, obsessive and intense fear focused on a specific circumstance, idea, or item. Exposure to the phobia may cause characters to suffer a variety of symptoms, including dizziness, palpitations, nausea and immobilization. Different types of phobias include claustrophobia; fear of being enclosed in a small space, including an elevator; agoraphobia, fear of being in or crossing through a wide open space; or acrophobia, a fear of heights. In gaming terms, when the character is exposed to a situation where the phobia is present, the character must roll against their WILL to overcome the phobia. If the character passes the roll, then the Phobia does not affect the character. If the character fails the roll, the phobia will overcome them so much that they will become mentally disjointed mound of flesh. The effects of the drawback Phobia will last 1D10 rounds. Depending on the level of the condition of the Phobia, the character will receive minuses to their roll. Use the following chart as the modifiers:

- The character is close to the source of their Phobia. An example is someone who has agoraphobia, fear of being in or crossing through a wide?open space, they would have this penalty to pass through a desert. WILL penalty: Easy (-2) modifier

- The character must perform some action that involves the source of their Phobia. An example of this could be someone who has claustrophobia being forced to fight enemies underground. WILL penalty: Average (-5) modifier

- The character is forced into direct contact with the object of their fear. An example of this could be a character with acrophobia, being forced to rescue someone who is suspended high in the air. WILL penalty: Hard (-9) modifier

*Cost: +3*

## PHYSICAL DISABILITY

*Your back is broken. You will never walk again.*

The character with this drawback suffers some type of physical disability or affliction. Blindness, deafness, missing limbs, or even some chronic illnesses are some possibilities. When the character chooses this drawback, the player must make life difficult for the character, but it must not be so extreme that the character is completely hopeless. Often, the characters with Physical Disability will normally lead to a character acquiring the Distinguishable Characteristic drawback. An example of this would be someone who is blind and would have no optical nerves to see. The following chart will determine how many points taking the physical disability will attain.

| POINTS | TYPE OF PHYSICAL DISABILITY |
|---|---|
| +6 | Blind (ACC is reduced to 0) |
| +3 | Chronic Illness (STA is reduced to Hard (-9) modifier) |
| +4 | Deaf |
| +2 | Missing One Arm (Average (-5) modifier to STR) |
| +1 | Missing One Eye (Easy (-2) modifier to PER and ACC) |
| +1 | Missing One Hand |
| +2 | Missing One Leg (MV is halved) |
| +3 | Mute |
| +4 | Paraplegic (MV is reduced to 3) |

**Cost: Variable**

## POVERTY

*I wish someone would show me the money.*

A character that chooses this drawback has some form of financial difficulty. This can take the form of being in debt from gambling, born into poverty, or other various ways. For gaming purposes, this means the character starts the game with only $500 dollars.
**Cost: +2**

## POWER HUNGRY

*I want it all.*

The character with this drawback is constantly looking for ways to increase their personal power no matter if it is physically or monetarily. The characters with this drawback will be constantly looking for ways to increase their abilities and will even place themselves, enemies, or even friends in danger to acquire more power. No risk is too much for this character to acquire power.
**Cost: +3**

## PSYCHOLOGICAL DISORDER

*I'm not crazy. You're the one who is crazy.*

The character for some unknown reason suffers from a type of mental or emotional disorder, whether it is from just basic kleptomania to the extremes of multiple personalities and insanity. Although Phobia is a psychological fear, the Psychological Disorder forces the character to take on a more severe side of abnormality. As with other certain drawbacks, this one should not be so overpowering that the character is unable to function normally in any situation ever. It should be something that could "pop up" at any time (G.O.D.'s decision) but does not have to.
**Cost: +4**

## PURSUED/PURSUING

*I've got a name, I've got a number and I'm coming after you.*

The character that chooses this drawback is pursuing or being pursued by a particular person or organization. This may stem from a longtime conflict

between the two parties or just something that has happened recently to change the two parties' positions on each other. Whatever the case is, the character is being pursued or pursuing, with a good chance of them running into their predator or prey. Anytime the character may encounter this target they will always choose this opponent above all else. This will, in some extreme instances, include the specific mission itself.
*Cost: +1*

## REPUTATION

*Tonight, an officer shot and killed a prisoner while he was being transported from his cell. This is the sixth such prisoner to have died under his supervision.*

The character that possesses this drawback has a noted history where they have performed particular actions that have gained themselves prominence in the general standings of others. For gaming purposes, this means the character will perform the action that they are so noted for anytime the opportunity will reveal itself. The G.O.D. will determine at what time this would be opportune. The Reputation could be anything from being a heinous killer, being remarkably unemotional and even occasionally another drawback listed.
*Cost: +3*

## RIVALRY

*I'm better than you are.*

The character that possesses this drawback has developed a rivalry with another person, whether the rivalry is professional, friendly, or even to some extremes hostile. The rivalry drawback can be formed, between two persons that are the best of friends or two that are the worst of enemies. In any situation that a character is a rival to another, the characters will always try to out do each other in every way. The character will also place themselves in dangerous situations to out show the other person.
*Cost: +1*

## SECRET

*He won't say it outright, but you can see his secrets in his pupils.*

The character with this drawback has some type of secret; if uncovered or discovered that would be a great embarrassment or danger to the character. The secret consists of anything from an abused childhood, a criminal past, or even if a person was the father, mother, son, or daughter of a particularly important person.
*Cost: +1*

## TRAUMATIC FLASHBACK
*Don't make me relive the death of my parents again.*

Characters possessing this drawback have had some event in their lives traumatically imprinted on their mind triggered by some type of stimuli. The flashback is so overpowering that anytime this character is exposed to the stimuli they must make a WILL roll. If they fail the roll, they collapse just remembering that tragic event for 1D10 rounds. The stimuli may be as general as children crying to a particular brand of alcohol. Nevertheless, do not make the stimuli too general, so that the character is having these flashbacks every second or so vague that the sound of a dog barking at a full moon in the middle of a rainstorm in November will set it off.
*Cost: +3*

## UGLY AS SIN
*Damn! Is that your face or did your neck throw up?!?*

You so ugly you have to sneak up on a glass of water. You have been beaten way too many times with the ugly stick. This drawback makes a character appear amazingly unattractive to members of the opposite sex. Any time the character interacts with a member of the opposite sex, he or she will receive an Average (-5) modifier to all INFL rolls.
*Cost: +2*

## UNCOORDINATED
*I tripped on a rock and broke both of my legs.*

A character with this drawback has been born with those natural instincts and abilities that make them "a complete klutz" when doing anything that may require manual dexterity. This drawback makes them the nightmares of sports coaches, everywhere. The character with this drawback will receive a Easy (-2) modifier to their AGI score when engaged in any athletic endeavors, including throwing or dodging objects, except shooting or marksmanship.
*Cost: +1*

## UNLUCKY
*If you did not have bad luck, then you would not have any luck at all.*

The character is more than just unusually unlucky. This person is the god of unlucky. This character could trip over a rock then injure his arm, fall into a patch of poison ivy, then while trying to get out, trip and break his leg. This will give the character the ability to almost fail even the most mundane actions. For gaming purposes, this means the character must re-roll any successful first roll that they may have had during an adventure.
*Cost: +8*

## SPECIAL ABILITIES:

Special Abilities are specific abilities that are unique to each individual character. These abilities are completely separate from a character's Benefits and Drawbacks. These abilities have an almost magical quality about them, from the implied power of a police officer to the supernatural quality of a bodyguard able to sense danger. The following is a list of these special abilities.

# SPECIAL ABILITIES

| | | |
|---|---|---|
| Anti-Hero | Death Trance | Predator |
| Berserk Rage | Detect Flaw | Sixth Sense |
| Chi | Dodge | Tough as Nails |
| Cop Eyes | Future Days | Trick Shot |

# DEFINITIONS OF SPECIAL ABILITIES

## ANTI-HERO

*Good. Bad. Who the hell gives a damn?*

The character that possesses this endowment has an uncommon ability to act like both the "hero" and the "villain" in the game. Anti-Heroes are able to commit various crimes including robbery, assaults and even to the extreme, murder, while still being able to prevent destructive crimes, conspiracies and misdemeanor crimes. Characters with this special ability, gain an additional 50 experience points per gaming session.

*Cost: -7*

## BERSERK RAGE

*Don't make me angry. You wouldn't like me when I'm angry.*

The character with this ability will reach the berserk rage of a wild beast in combat. Before starting combat, the character must make a WILL roll at a Hard (-9) modifier. If the character passes the roll, they may attack normally. If they fail, the character will attack their target with little to no regard for themselves. The character gains +3 to their STR and ACC while receiving an Average (-5) modifier to their PER and the character will not make any defensive tactics or retreat from battle. If the character defeats their target, they will move to the next closest enemy target. The character will continue to perform this action until there are no more enemy targets for them to combat. When there are no targets left, make a WILL roll, if the character passes the roll, then the character returns to normal. If the character fails the roll, they will begin to attack their teammates as if they were their foes.

*Cost: -7*

## CHI

*Focus and take the pebble from my hand.*

A character with this ability is able to focus their internal energies and increase one of their primary or secondary abilities. A character with this special ability gains +5 to any primary ability for a maximum of 1 round, up to D4 times a day.

*Cost: -4*

## COP EYES

*The eyes are the mirrors to the soul...*

A character with this ability "seems to look like the law." Everything about this person seems to say, "Hello, I am a officer of the law." None of that may be true; the person could be everything from Satan to a mob enforcer, but the general public on first sight gets the feeling that this person "wears a badge." This ability is chosen often by law enforcement characters to help with their natural influence. The following is a list of powers this ability holds for characters.

- Law enforcement badges are extremely influential in the general public and normal populace. Characters with this ability add points to their INFL when they show their badge. When showing or using their badge, police officers add +2 to their INFL.
- Characters with this ability can also make arrests on persons. Even though the common citizen can make a "citizen's arrest," a law enforcement character's arrest carries more influence with the general populace. More people are willing to help and become involved when dealing with a person with this ability.

*Cost: -4*

## DEATH TRANCE

*They loaded the body in the back of the sedan. They thought he was dead. They got quite a surprise when they learned he wasn't.*

The character with this power is able enter into a death-like state. In this state, the character will be considered to be "dead" to average medical scans and general investigation. In this state the character can stop the damaging effects certain particular environments including intense cold. The character can enter in this death-like state for as many hours equal to their WILL. Characters that enter into a Death Trance are not aware of their surrounds or events that are taking place, but may choose to recover from the Death Trance at any time they feel necessary.

*Cost: -4*

## DETECT FLAW

*Everything has a weakness and I am going to find it.*

The character that possesses this benefit is able to detect flaws and stress points in objects. With this knowledge he can attack these items in these specific places that will cause all items to be easily broken or destroyed. With this ability characters can halve the modifiers when they are trying to force any type of lock.

**Cost: -3**

## DODGE

*He just knew he should be dead, that the metal should have torn a hole in his head and not just brushed past his hair.*

A character with this ability is able to dodge objects in flight from simple items such as thrown stones and knives to the extreme of actual firearm rounds. A character is able to dodge up to D6 times a day any thrown object or firearm. The character must declare to the G.O.D. that they are dodging before the attack is played out, even though the attack may miss normally.

**Cost: -10**

## FUTURE DAYS

The future is now.

The character with this power possesses the ability to see the future in quick flashes of information. This power is only as effective as the information given. Due to the unusual and specific nature of time, it can never be truly determined due to the large number or variety of possible alternate futures. The future is also mutable and constantly changing. If a character with this power sees an assassination of the President in the near future, they can attempt to warn the target of the assassination or capture the assassin before the assassination.

A character with this ability will make a WILL roll every time they go to sleep. If they fail their roll, the character doesn't receive a vision that night. If the character passes their roll, then they will receive a quick burst of information including a three-second flash of a picture. If the character passes their roll by

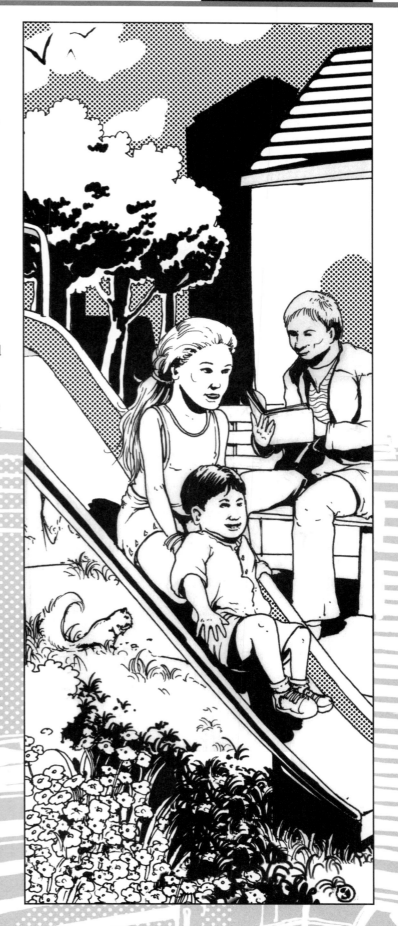

four or more, then they will receive ten seconds of information of things to come.

*Cost: -9*

## PREDATOR

*I am the hunter and you are the prey.*

Characters that possess this unique ability to "track" can follow a quarry by using learned abilities, logical guess and other unknown abilities. The character is able to place themselves in the mind of whoever they are after and guess the next location where they will be. All characters wanting to discover the next location their "prey" might be at must make a WILL roll. If the character fails the roll, they cannot think where the person would be and can try again in an hour. If the character succeeds in the roll, the G.O.D. will inform the character of the next future location of the "prey" for up to three hours.

*Cost: -5*

## SIXTH SENSE

*Watch out. Something does not feel right.*

Certain persons have a natural instinctual sense of danger. Many say it is as if they have "eyes in the back of their head and they can see into the future". This sixth sense will warn the character of any impending danger that might affect the character. In these situations, the G.O.D. will notify the character that there is danger, but not the specific nature of the danger.

*Cost: -7*

## TOUGH AS NAILS

*What will it take to stop you?*

A character with this benefit is considered to have almost an inhuman ability to resist being knocked out or put down. Unlike when normal characters reach 0 Lethal HEA they are considered dead, characters with this ability are able to keep on fighting until their Lethal HEA reaches half their total Lethal HEA in negatives. If a character has a 20 Lethal HEA and possesses Tough as Nails, they could keep attacking in combat until the Lethal HEA reached -10 HEA and at that point they would be dead. If combat ends and the character's Lethal HEA is below 0 but not half their total Lethal HEA in negatives, the character is considered to have a Lethal HEA of 1, just

enough life to be considered barely alive in game standards.

*Cost: -8*

## TRICK SHOT

*Off the steel wall, off the backyard grill and off the frying pan in Carmen's right hand...*

The character possesses expert skill in the area of trick shooting. The character's body can record and mimic exactly any trick shot they may happen to see. In gaming terms, this means the character can ignore any location modifier when trying to perform a called shot.

*Cost: -10*

## STEP 4

Now you know a lot about what the character can do and what he can't, you should have some idea of the sort of image he likes to portray, any specialized kit that he carries or keeps stashed in the trunk of the car and what kind of piece he keeps close to his heart or under his pillow at night. The actual equipment lists can be found in the next section of this book and you have $1,000 to buy whatever equipment that may be required to keep you alive from this point out. If there is something your character needs that isn't on the list then check with the G.O.D., to see whether or not you can have it and how much it'll set you back.

## STEP 5

Time to tie everything together, look back over the character so far, the attributes, skills, special abilities and his idea concept. What you have so far is a framework, now its time to put flesh over the bones. Different people like to do this different ways some start with the character as is and work backwards through the characters life so far, others start at the beginning and work forward. Some prefer to detail several major points in the characters life path and then link them together. Regardless, the true test of a character is can you, the player, hold a convincing conversation in character about the characters experiences.

# Full Metal Taste

The gun in my mouth tasted bitter
and cold when moments before I had
it all. All I had to do was to
leave. I had the money I stolen
from them. I had the weaponry and
firearms they were going to sell.
I had both sides thinking that the
other one double-crossed them for
the money. I had the ticket to
fly out of here to Japan. I had
it all, but I had to come back. I
had to get greedy. I wanted to
humiliate them like they did to me.
They took it all away from me.
They moved me from a very powerful
position in the organization to
nothing better than a lap dog.
They didn't care. They embarrassed
me in private and in public to
"friends of ours". I helped make
them powerful. I did everything
for them and in the end the just
shit all over me. It was business, nothing personal they said.
When you take 30 millions dollars
of money and products from people
you better fucking believe it's
personal. Besides fucking somebody's wife, there is nothing more
personal than taking somebody's
money. You'd think after all the
money I made for them that they
would not worry about a little bit
of money that I took for myself.
Call it a severance package for all
my good work and years of loyalty.
I didn't think that it is so much
to ask for. So here it is. I
don't have the money and I had got
a gun in my mouth. It tasted
bitter and it was cold.

# CHAPTER : 3

## ABILITIES

*Ability is nothing without opportunity.*

*Napoleon Bonaparte*

At this point in the book, you should have your own character created. Now let's talk about how the character is used in the game. In the role-playing situation, you are cast as a main character. You, the player, are controlling the actions and reactions of your character. Your character is limited in what he or she can do as a result of the character's limited abilities. Any time you check against these abilities to see if you complete an action, you are making an ability roll.

# THE ABILITY ROLLS

An ability roll determines the success of any action. You make an ability roll in the following fashion:

* Determine the Ability or Skill you are checking.
* Find out the modifier to the Ability or Skill.
* Roll dice to determine the success or failure of the action.

## TYPES OF ABILITY ROLLS

The following are the different types of ability rolls that can be called for during the course of the game.

Primary Ability rolls are those that rely on one of the six primary abilities: STRENGTH (STR), WILL (WILL), AGILITY (AGI), STAMINA (STA), INTELLIGENCE (INT), and PERCEPTION (PER). Skills or the existing situation may alter these rolls. Secondary Ability rolls are those that rely on one of the six Secondary Abilities: INFLUENCE (INFL), MOVEMENT VALUE (MV), ACCURACY (ACC), FIGHTING VALUE (FV), SUBTERFUGE (SUB), and COUNTER MEASURES (CM). Skills or the existing situation may alter these rolls, like Primary Abilities. Skill rolls are those that rely on the character's skills, where the skill modifies a specific ability for an ability roll.

## POSSIBLE AND NEARLY IMPOSSIBLE ROLLS

The majority of the time when a character tries a particular action, there is a good chance that the character will be able to perform the action, sometimes automatically, sometimes with great difficulty and on a few occasions the action will be considered impossible. The difficulty of the action is dependant on the situation and the intensity of the character's relevant skills. No matter the situation there is always a slim margin of success or failure, a roll of a 1 on a D20 is always a success, while a 20 is always a failure.

**Automatic Actions:** Certain actions can be performed without any difficulty to the character. Walking, speaking, thinking, and other examples of a similar nature will not need a roll to determine their success. In general anything that the average Joe in the street can be expected to do characters should not have to test for.

**Possible Actions:** Certain actions can just be performed without needing some type of roll. Several of these types of actions include attacking another character, trying to influence others, and trying to discover and research new technological devices. The G.O.D. will determine the complexity of any possible actions.

**Nearly Impossible Actions:** Certain actions can be performed with a great amount of difficulty to the character. This may include trying to lift past a strength limit or holding your breath for hours or any feat that may seem superhuman or extremely unlikely to occur.

The following is a listing of how difficult any type of actions may be and its particular modifier. A character need only roll equal to or less than the number to succeed at the task.

| Difficulty | Modifier |
|---|---|
| Automatic | 0 |
| Easy | -2 |
| Average | -5 |
| Hard | -9 |
| Extreme | -14 |
| Amazing | -19 |
| Nearly Impossible | -25 |

**Automatic:** No thought needed. Breathing and heart beating fall under this category.

**Easy:** Most every day items or events. Leaping over a small puddle in the middle of the walkway would fall under this rating.

**Average:** This category contains items or events that normally challenge a person, solving a math problem in one's head or catching a ball.

**Hard:** Just like the name says this is hard. This will consist of the more difficult tasks in life. Walking a tightrope or programming a computer would fall under this ranking.

**Extreme:** This complexity level takes it to the limit. Catching a throwing knife from out of the air would fall under this category.

**Amazing:** After someone performs an event at this level you have to stand up and clap. Dodging an arrow in mid-flight would fall under this category.

**Near Impossible:** The one in a million shot. Catching an arrow that has been fired from a compound bow in mid flight would fall under this category

**Example:** *Marcus is walking when three kids armed with rocks come out of nowhere and being to throw them at him. Marcus, being in a good mood and decides to teach them all a little lesson. Marcus waits as the first kid throws and decides he wants to catch the rock. Marcus' AGI is 15 and the G.O.D. determines to catch a rock is an Average (-5) modifier, which mean he needs to roll a 10 or less on a D20. Marcus rolls a 3 and catches the rock and waits till the second boy throws.*

*Marcus decides that he is going to throw his rock at the second boy's rock as it is in the air to deflect it.*

*The G.O.D. determines to deflect the rock is a Hard (-9) modifier, which Marcus needs a 6 or less to succeed. Marcus rolls a 5 and the second attacker's rock is deflected.*

*The last boy throws his rock and Marcus decides to get cute. Marcus plans to catch the rock and then ricochet it off all three of the boy's heads. Marcus' AGI is 15 and the G.O.D. determines to catch a rock is an Average (-5) modifier, which mean he needs to roll a 10 or less on a D20, which he rolls a 9. Then he suffers an Amazing (-19) modifier to his AGI to make it only possible if Marcus rolls a 1. Marcus rolls a 1 and hits all three boys. The boys scatter off feeling bitter.*

## ABILITY MODIFIER CHALLENGES

The following are tables of the common activity modifiers based off of the particular primary ability. These tables are best used to help determine how difficult a specific action will be in comparison to others.

| STR Activity | Modifier |
|---|---|
| Press up to 50 lbs. | Automatic (-0) |
| Press up to 100 lbs. | Easy (-2) |
| Press up to 200 lbs. | Average (-5) |
| Press up to 300 lbs. | Hard (-9) |
| Press up to 400 lbs. | Extreme (-14) |
| Press up to 500 lbs. | Amazing (-19) |
| Press up to 600+ lbs. | Nearly Impossible (-25) |

| WILL Activity | Modifier |
|---|---|
| Casual Suggestion | Automatic (-0) |
| Persuasion | Easy (-2) |
| Intimidation | Average (-5) |
| Hypnosis | Hard (-9) |
| Brainwashing | Extreme (-14) |
| Expert Brainwashing | Amazing (-19) |
| Manchurian Candidate | Nearly Impossible (-25) |

| AGI Activity | Modifier |
|---|---|
| Flipping a coin | Automatic (-0) |
| Walking a balance beam | Easy (-2) |
| Juggling Balls | Average (-5) |
| Juggling knives | Hard (-9) |
| Catching a thrown knife | Extreme (-14) |
| Dodge arrow in flight | Amazing (-19) |
| Catch arrow in flight | Nearly Impossible (-25) |

| STA Activity | Modifier |
|---|---|
| Walking | Automatic (-0) |
| Light Jogging | Easy (-2) |
| Jogging | Average (-5) |
| Marathon | Hard (-9) |
| Biathlon Marathon | Extreme (-14) |
| Iron Man Marathon | Amazing (-19) |
| Pentathlon | Nearly Impossible (-25) |

| INT Activity | Modifier |
|---|---|
| IQ of 1 to 30 | Automatic (-0) |
| IQ of 31 to 60 | Easy (-2) |
| IQ of 61 to 90 | Average (-5) |
| IQ of 91 to 120 | Hard (-9) |
| IQ of 121 to 150 | Extreme (-14) |
| IQ of 151 to 180 | Amazing (-19) |
| IQ of 181 or higher | Nearly Impossible (-25) |

| PER Activity | Modifier |
|---|---|
| Bump on a log | Automatic (-0) |
| Detailed work | Easy (-2) |
| Darkness | Average (-5) |
| Three Card Monty | Hard (-9) |
| Camouflage | Extreme (-14) |
| Expertly hidden | Amazing (-19) |
| Needle in a haystack | Nearly Impossible (-25) |

# TIME

*Tempus fugit*

*Ovid*

Time is the one factor that no one can truly control. Time in Haven: COV is only important in very specific instances. These may include a bomb counting down to explode or finding a particular object quickly.

# PHASES, ROUNDS, AND TURNS

In the Haven: COV RPG system, time is based on the conceptual grouping of six seconds of real time, into what is called a round. A round is enough time for two combatants to attack each other or have a quick conversation or greeting or walk up a flight of stairs. A phase is one second of real time. So, six phases are equal to one round. A turn is a ten-minute grouping of time or 120 rounds. Based on the following information, a one-minute period has 12 rounds in it; a ten-minute period has 120 rounds or 1 turn; an hour has 720 rounds or 6 turns in it. The majority of the time characters will not have to record the passage of time. The following chart shows the real time equivalence to the game time counter parts.

- 1 Phase = 1 Second
- 1 Round = 6 Seconds or Phases
- 1 Turn = 10 minutes

# MOVEMENT VALUE

Movement is simply defined as the ability to travel from one point to another. It seems extremely easy but in reality it takes many forms. The movement value is the combination of the character's STR and STA, divided by two, with all fractions rounded up. This number will determine the Movement Value (also called their MV or Move). This number will determine the distance or speed that the character can travel in one round. All movement of the character can take place before, after, or during any type of combat. The following chart lists the movement value rate and athletic feats that are normally possible within their movement value.

| Movement Value | 1 to 6 | 7 to 13 | 14 to 20 | 21+ |
|---|---|---|---|---|
| Bicycling | 9 mph | 25 mph | 40 mph | 53 mph |
| Body Throw (160 lbs) | 2 feet | 7 feet | 12 feet | 17 feet |
| Crawling | 6 feet | 12 feet | 18 feet | 24 feet |
| Deep Drive with SCUBA | 78 feet | 222 feet | 342 feet | 456 feet |
| Deep Drive without SCUBA | 48 feet | 144 feet | 222 feet | 294 feet |
| Grenade Toss (1 lb.) | 24 feet | 70 feet | 105 feet | 143 feet |
| High Dive into Water | 30 feet | 84 feet | 126 feet | 168 feet |
| Holding Breath | 23 sec | 64 sec | 98 sec | 131 sec |
| Motorcycle jump | 32 feet | 90 feet | 135 feet | 185 feet |
| Rollerblading | 4 mph | 11 mph | 18 mph | 25 mph |
| Rope Climb | 1.5 feet | 3 feet | 4.5 feet | 6 feet |
| Rowing | 2 mph | 5.5 mph | 8 mph | 11 mph |
| Running | 72 feet | 90 feet | 108 feet | 126 feet |
| Running and Dodging | 42 feet | 48 feet | 54 feet | 60 feet |
| Running High Jump | 1.5 feet | 4 feet | 6 feet | 8 feet |
| Running Long Jump | 5 feet | 14.5 feet | 23 feet | 30 feet |
| Skateboarding | 7 mph | 22 mph | 36 mph | 50 mph |
| Standing Broad Jump | 3.5 feet | 6 feet | 8.5 feet | 11 feet |
| Standing Vertical Jump | .5 feet | 1.5 feet | 2.25 feet | 3 feet |
| Swimming | 12 feet | 18 feet | 24 feet | 30 feet |
| Swimming w/ Fins | 18 feet | 24 feet | 30 feet | 36 feet |
| Treading Water | 13 hours | 37 hours | 56 hours | 76 hours |
| Wading | 6 feet | 12 feet | 18 feet | 24 feet |
| Walking | 24 feet | 30 feet | 36 feet | 42 feet |

When using this system, a character can normally move up to one-sixth of their full movement value, per phase of the round. The following example is a break down of that.

**Example:** *Blade Wilson his running down the street after being shot at, looking to find a spot to return fire to the assailant. Blade's movement value is 15.*

- The first phase, Blade runs 18'.
- The second phase, Blade runs 18'.
- The third phase, Blade runs 18'.
- The fourth phase, Blade runs 18'.
- The fifth phase, Blade runs 18'.
- The sixth phase, Blade stops, turns around, and returns fire to the assailant.

*Blade ran for a total of 90' in that turn. If Blade had chosen to run and shoot instead of shooting during his last phase of the round, he would have traveled the normal 108' instead of 90' and take modifiers to his ACC to hit.*

Characters can only attain their maximum MV speeds and distances for as many rounds as their STA amount when they are unencumbered. Characters can maintain up to 25% of their maximum speed for as many hours as their STA amount when they are unencumbered. Characters can maintain up to 50% of their maximum speed for as many minutes as their STA amount when they are unencumbered. For every round past their STA limits, characters will loses 5 Concussive HEA points until they stop, reduce their speed or fall Unconscious (see Unconsciousness).

## MOVEMENT WHILE CARRYING WEIGHT

Under normal conditions, characters can lift and carry a maximum of 15 times their STR amount, characters can drag a maximum of 25 times their STR amount and characters can push a maximum of

10 times their STR amount. Characters may move and carry up to 33% of their maximum weight, for as many turns as equal to their STA. Characters may move and carry up to 66% of their maximum weight, for as many minutes as equal to their STA. Characters may move and carry up to 100% of their maximum weight, for as many rounds as equal to their STA.

While carrying up to 25% of their maximum weight, a character may move at 75% of their MV. While carrying up to 50% of their maximum weight, a character may move at 50% of their MV. While carrying up to 75% of their maximum weight, a character may move at 25% of their MV. While carrying up to 100% of their maximum weight, a character may move at 10% of their MV. While dragging up to 33% of their maximum weight, a character may move at 75% of their MV. While dragging up to 66% of their maximum weight, a character may move at 50% of their MV. While dragging up to 100% of their maximum weight, a character may move at 25% of their MV. While pushing up to 33% of their maximum weight, a character may move at 50% of their MV. While pushing up to 66% of their maximum weight, a character may move at 25% of their MV. While pushing up to 100% of their maximum weight, a character may move at 10% of their MV.

## UPWARD AND DOWNWARD MOVEMENT

Upward movement consists of movement by walking up stairs and riding elevators. Vertical movement is measured in distance by floors. For gaming purposes, one floor is equal to 10' in height. The character's MV determines the amount of floors that can be transversed in one round. Characters with an MV of 1 to 10 can travel at a rate of one floor per round. Characters with a MV of 11 to 20 can travel at a rate of two floors per round. Characters with an MV of 21 or greater are able to travel at a rate of three floors per round.

One of the most common types of vertical movement is the elevator. Elevators normally travel at various speeds due to the specific nature of elevators. Older elevators travel at the rate of four floors per round while the majority of modern elevators will travel at a rate of eight floors per round. Service elevators are built to move large objects and not for speed and they only move five floors per round while express elevators move at a rate of 12 floors per round.

Downward movement works in the complete inverse of upward movement. Characters with a MV of 1 to 10 can travel at the rate of one floor per round. Characters with a MV of 11 to 20 can travel at the rate of two floors per round. Characters with a MV of 21 or greater are able to travel at the rate of three floors per round.

## FALLING AND FALLING DAMAGE

One of the most common types of downward movement is falling. When you are falling, it is not the fall that kills you; it's the sudden stop at the end of the trip. Characters can fall up to 10' and take no damage from the fall. A fall from a distance 11' to 20' makes a player roll a D20 and on a roll of 4 or less, his character takes a D10 Concussive HEA points damage. A fall from 21' to 30' will cause 2D10 Concussive HEA points damage. A fall from 31' to 40' will cause 3D10 Concussive HEA points damage and so on. Anytime a character receives damage from a fall, they will be automatically stunned. Stunned characters will not be able to act in any fashion for as many rounds as the points of damage they may have acquired due to the falling damage.

## FIRE AND ICE

The following sections deal with particular environmental issues and endangering situations, and how the G.O.D. should handle them.

## EFFECTS OF FIRE

As with most items in life, fire can come in various intensities according to the size and combustible material that may be available. Fire affects people and the surroundings in two very distinctive forms,

| Event | Concussive HEA | Lethal HEA |
|---|---|---|
| Blast Furnace | 3D10 | 3D20 |
| Burning Explosive Chemicals | 2D6 | 2D12 |
| Burning House | D8 | D20 |
| Burning Non-Explosive Chemicals | D4 | D10 |
| Burning Room | D4 | D8 |
| Burning Warehouse | 2D8 | 2D20 |
| Campfire | - | D4 |
| Pack of Matches | - | D4-3 |

one being from the heat the other being from the fire itself.

Heat damage in Haven: City of Violence is considered to be Concussive HEA damage, while actual fire damage is considered to be Lethal HEA damage. If a target is engulfed by fire they will take Lethal HEA damage from the flames, people inside of a burning room, however, will take Concussive HEA damage from the heat as long as they are not on fire. The range of the heat's Concussive HEA damage is equal to that of the fire's Lethal HEA damage in feet. For example, a house is on fire and the fire does 19 points of Lethal HEA damage, then those with in 19 feet of the fire will suffer from heat Concussive HEA damage. The chart is a list of events and their intensities.

Fire will spread at a movement rate of one area of 20 feet by 20 feet every D4 rounds, whether it is horizontal or vertical. Depriving it of air, cooling its heat, or depriving it of fuel can reduce a fire's strength. Normal fire extinguishers are capable of putting out a fire in an area of 20 feet by 20 feet in six rounds. Normal Fire Hoses are capable of putting out a fire in an area of 20 feet by 20 feet in two rounds and a range of 60 feet. Other amounts of water will affect the fire accordingly to the amount of water used. A fire deprived of fuel burns itself out in D6 rounds. Effects of fire on a material vary according to the material in question. If the flames are not able to burn the material, the fire will not damage the material, though it will carry the heat through its substance. Therefore, a steel rod with one end in a fire can burn someone grabbing the other end, causing Lethal HEA equal to the fire's heat Concussive HEA damage.

# EFFECTS OF ICE

Ice has an AV of 7 in thickness of up to 6 inches. For every 6 inches of ice, the AV increases by +2. While ice is quite resistant against physical attack, against heat and fire, ice has an AV of 1, no matter the thickness.

# SURPRISE

Everyone likes a surprise, unless they are kissing the business end of a shotgun. The ability to surprise another character is directly determined by the character's PER score. When a character is trying to surprise another, the intended victim and attacker will need to make a PER roll with a Hard (-9) modifier. If the attacker rolls equal to or less than the number, they have not managed to surprise their intended target, but may act as normal. If on the other hand, the attacker rolls higher than the victim's roll then, the attacker gains all the advantages of surprise. The victim of the surprise suffers a Hard (-9) modifier to all their rolls for that round. On the following round, the victim is no longer surprised and may act as normal.

# SEARCHING

The most common way of attaining information about a person or place is to search for it. The police and law enforcement agencies and sometimes bodyguards or bounty hunters, are the people who most commonly rely on this type of information gathering. The ability for a character to search another person is determined by the character searching's CM minus the searched for item's SUB. If the searching character passes the roll, then they have located something when they were searching. If a character fails the roll, then the searched person has hidden the item well enough that it could not be found. To completely search a person takes two rounds. To search a 20' X 20' space or acutely search a 10' X 10' space will take ten rounds. Areas larger than that will take more time respectively. For each additional person added to a search, the search time is reduced by half. Smaller objects are harder to find than large ones causing them to have modifiers, G.O.D.'s decision, to the searcher's CM.

# SECURITY SYSTEMS

Any intelligent person realizes the need for a security system to prevent the bad guys from getting in. The need for security systems in the Haven: COV becomes prevalent when characters plan to break into various locations. When planning to break into an area, a character must compare their CM skill versus the modifier of the security device. Normal door or pad locks have an Easy (-2) modifier. Electrical tape or electrical eye systems have an Average (-5) modifier. Combination locks, pressure pads and wall safes have a Hard (-9) modifier. Bank vaults, fine wall safes or thermal imaging systems have an Extreme (-14) modifier. Motion detection systems and thumb print scans have an Amazing (-19) modifier. Retina Scans and Voice Print Scans have a Nearly Impossible (-25) modifier. If one or more types of locks are used as a security deterrent, then the modifiers are calculated together for their effective modifier.

# HANDCUFFING

The easiest way to control a person who is being a problem and does not want to be restrained is to slap the 'old steel bracelets' or ankle shackles on them, sometimes both are necessary. Handcuffs, straight jackets or any type of wrist restraint will reduce a character's AGI by an Average (-5) modifier. If ankle cuffs or leg restraints are used, the AGI is reduced by a Hard (-9) modifier and their MV is reduced by Extreme (-14) modifier. If both of these

types of restraints are used on a person the reduction to AGI and MV are cumulative. To escape these types of items, a character must make a CM roll with an Average (-5) modifier to escape rope restraints; a Hard (-9) modifier to escape handcuffs; an Extreme (-14) modifier to escape handcuffs and leg restraints; and Nearly Impossible (-25) modifier to escape a straightjacket. Characters with the skill, Escape Artist, will gain modifiers to their CM to escape.

# FORCING A LOCK

There are times when a character will use their brute strength to open a locked door or other locked object. When this is done, the character will use their STR as their ability number minus whatever other modifiers there are to affect the roll. Apartment Doors and windows have an Easy (-2) modifier, House Doors have an Average (-5) modifier, Fire Doors a Hard (-9) modifier, and Steel Doors an Amazing (-19) modifier.

If a character uses a ram bar to help with forcing a lock on a closed door, the character will add +4 to their STR. When brute strength may fail, characters may choose to shoot a lock off with their firearm. The character will use the firearm and ammunition's AP as its strength to shoot off the lock minus any modifiers.

# LOCK PICK SETS

There are two types of lock pick tools used in the Haven: COV RPG, mechanical or electronic. Mechanical lock picks employ a tension bar and pick while electronic lock picks amplify tumbler sounds and analyzes them into the code combinations for opening locks. Mechanical lock picks are only useful against key-operated locking devices. Electronic lock picks can only operate on combination, or tumbler locks.

Mechanical lock picks increase the character's CM score by +4 when attempting to open a key-operated lock. Electronic lock picks increase the character's

CM by +6 when attempting to open a combination lock. These devices are normally equipped with a memory device that makes it able to record the combination once it has been discovered.

# EXPERIENCE POINTS

*What does not destroy me makes me stronger.*

*Friedrich Wilhelm Nietzsche*

Experience Points, or XP as there are better known as, are considered to be the ruler by which all characters are judged and measured. The more experience a character has, the more competent they will become. In Haven: COV, characters that gain experience points are able to convert experience points to help raise their Primary Abilities, which in turn increase their Secondary Abilities, or Skills, Benefits, and Special Abilities. The maximum amount of experience points that a player character can gain per gaming session is 300 XPs. The chart is a listing of the type of experience that can be gained during a gaming session.

# INCREASING ABILITIES AND ABILITIES OVER 20

Everyone dreams of being the best at what they want to do. Besides, doves don't fly for the death of amateurs. This is also true in Haven: COV. Any character can increase their Primary Abilities, which in turn increase the Secondary Abilities, by trading in their experience points. For every 200 XPs, a character can increase a Primary Ability by one point. Experience Points can be saved between games so that even if you don't gain enough in one session of play, over several games you could save enough to be useful.

## ROLEPLAYING (100 XP MAXIMUM PER SESSION)

| Event | XPs |
| --- | --- |
| Acted out of character | -30 |
| Increased the drama of the game | 20 - 50 |
| Made the G.O.D.'s evening enjoyable | 5 - 20 |
| Player showed enthusiasm | 20 - 40 |
| Player showed little interest | -20 |
| Player showed up for the game | 10 |
| Player stayed in character | 10 - 30 |

## ADVENTURING (200 XP MAXIMUM PER SESSION)

| Event | XPs |
| --- | --- |
| Character discovered a major plot or clue | 25 |
| Character discovered a minor plot or clue | 10 |
| Character failed to discover a plot or clue | -25 |
| Character used skills or abilities in a unique fashion | 5 - 20 |
| Defeated a major villain or his agenda | 30 - 75 |
| Defeated a minor villain or his agenda | 10 - 30 |
| Failed at the adventure | -50 |
| Performed an action that proved vital to the session | 10 - 30 |
| Strategically outmaneuvered the opposition | 5 - 20 |
| Worked as a team to overcome obstacles | 20 - 40 |
| Worked individually to overcome obstacles | 5 - 15 |

*Example:* "Gunner" McNeil has completed several adventures and has acquired 843 experience points. Gunner chooses to increase his AGI by 3 and his PER by 1, which come to a total of 800 experience points. Gunner can retain the remaining 43 experience points for later use.

Due to the nature of this gaming system, there is truly no limit on how high a character can advance their Primary or Secondary Abilities. If a character has an ability that is higher than 20, the ability number is still used as the intensity of that ability. No matter what the percentage of the ability, the character will always have at least a 5%, 1 out of 20 on a D20, chance of success.

An example of this would be if a character had calculated their chance of success as less than zero. No matter what the score was, the character will still succeed on a roll of 1 out of 20. The inverse to the previous state is also true. A character will never have greater than a 95% chance to succeed. An example of this would be if a character had a calculated chance to succeed over 20 on a D20. No matter what the score is they will still fail on a roll of 20 out of 20.

## SKILL ADVANCEMENT AND ADDITION

All characters have the ability to increases their skill's intensity number or learn a new skill by educating themselves on a particular topic. To increase an existing skill, characters will have to trade in their experience points for this knowledge. A character can increase a skill's ability intensity by +1, to a maximum of +5, for each 150 Experience points they spend. If a character wishes to acquire a new skill, the character must pay 200 experience points for each new skill. The character with the new skill will start off with a +1 to the particular ability when dealing with this skill.

## LANGUAGE ADVANCEMENT AND ADDITION

All characters have the ability to learn new languages or increase their ability of currently learned ones.

The increases or additions to languages are normally brought about learning it from a school or from a person who knows the specific language. To increase an existing language, characters will have to trade in their experience points to acquire this knowledge. A character can increase language ability intensity by +1, to a maximum of 20, for each 75 Experience points they spend. If a character wishes to acquire a new language, the character must pay 200 experience points for each new language. The character with the new language will start off with a rating of 8 in that particular language.

## ACQUIRING NEW BENEFITS AND SPECIAL ABILITIES

All characters have the ability to acquire new benefits and special abilities by purchasing them with experience points. The reasoning behind acquiring this new benefit or special ability must be acceptable to the G.O.D. For a character to acquire a new benefit or special ability, they must purchase this benefit or special ability at one hundred times the original cost in experience points.

*Example:* Morgan wants to acquire the benefit Night Vision, which costs 3 points, and the special ability Dodge, which is 9 points. The price of Night Vision costs 300 experience points. The price of Dodge is 900 points. The total cost is 1,200 experience points for both advancements. It may be a long time before Morgan gets these new abilities.

## ACQUIRING NEW DRAWBACKS

Acquiring a drawback for a player is extremely easy to attain but the reasoning for them must be acceptable to the G.O.D. If a character loses an arm due to some unfortunate mishap, they will acquire the drawback, Physical Disability: One Arm. The character will not gain any additional experience points for acquiring this drawback as when they did when first creating the character.

## OVERCOMING DRAWBACKS

Often a character can overcome their previous background and rise above that to elevate themselves to new heights. This could be anything from a secret that has been revealed to the world to a cure for a fatal disease. Whatever it is, it is possible to improve one's self. A character can nullify the drawback by finding some way to have the drawback reasonably invalidated. The G.O.D. must approve of the reasoning for this change, and may direct you on how to resolve this during a gaming scenario or campaign. Once these conditions have been approved of by the G.O.D., the character must pay back two hundred times the original cost in experience points.

*Example: Morgan has the drawback Traumatic Flashback, due to an event that happened in his past. After a few months of seeing a psychiatrist, Morgan overcomes his Traumatic Flashback and no longer suffers from it. The G.O.D. agrees with this solution to the drawback, Morgan pays his 600 experience points and it is erased from Morgan's character sheet.*

# EQUIPMENT

Everyone needs goods and equipment. Without equipment, even the simplest task would seem almost impossible. In the Haven: COV setting, characters are capable of purchasing various types of equipment and firearms that should be needed for their character's use. It is also important to note that a character should posses the money to purchase an item. Of course receiving the item in a timely fashion to make it useful is a totally different matter. While in some cases and instances it may not be possible to acquire all items or equipment through legal channels, characters can also choose a more interesting and somewhat primitive and often illegal way of acquiring certain goods and services. The following tables list the most common items found in this gaming system. Any items not found can be created or produced by the G.O.D., at his or her discretion.

| General Clothes | Cost |
| --- | --- |
| Attaché case | $15 |
| Backpack | $20 |
| Belt | $8 |
| Boots | $45 |
| Cane | $10 |
| Casual outfit | $75 |
| Formal outfit | $250 |
| Gloves | $15 |
| Goggles | $5 |
| Hat | $20 |
| Jacket, casual | $20 |
| Jacket, leather | $150 |
| Jumpsuit | $50 |
| Money belt | $15 |
| Overcoat | $65 |
| Purse | $10 |
| Scarf | $5 |
| Shoes, athletic | $60 |
| Shoes, formal | $50 |
| Suit, causal | $100 |
| Suit, formal | $125 |
| Suitcase | $50 |
| Sweater | $25 |
| Umbrella | $5 |
| Work clothes | $50 |

| Specialty Items | Cost |
| --- | --- |
| Binoculars | $75 |
| Bulletproof shield and helmet | $225 |
| Bulletproof vest | $350 |
| Camera, 35mm | $250 |
| Chain, 10' | $5 |
| Counterfeit money | 10% of value |
| Crampons/climbing irons | $20 |
| Flashlight | $10 |
| Handcuffs | $15 |
| Lock pick set | $200 |
| Lock pick set, electronic | $800 |
| Makeup kit | $55 |
| Metal Cutting Torch | $275 |
| Photographic film | $5 |
| Piano wire. 10' | $2 |
| Rope. 10' | $3 |
| Rubber gloves | $3 |
| Steel cable, 10' | $7 |
| Telescope, tripod mount | $150 |

| Weapons | Cost | | |
|---|---|---|---|
| Billy club | $15 | Gas mask | $25 |
| Bow | $75 | Grenade | $30 |
| Bow, Compound | $200 | Hypodermic needle and syringe | $3 |
| Brass knuckles | $5 | Knife | $10 |
| Crossbow | $180 | Light intensifier goggles | $240 |
| Dart | $1 | Magazines. Empty | $3 |
| Dart gun | $100 | Plastic explosive, per oz. | $60 |
| Dynamite. 1 stick | $15 | Stiletto | $35 |
| Firearms Holster | $5 | Switchblade | $30 |

# AMMUNITION TYPES

When using any type of firearm the most important ingredient in the weapons success is the type of ammunition, whether it is armor piercing explosive rounds or whisper rounds or shotgun slugs. The following is a listing of information on the common types of ammunition in this gaming system.

## ARMOR PIERCING (AP) ROUNDS

This illegal ammunition is a hardened steel or tungsten core surrounded by a slim, long, flat-tipped metal jacket and hardened steel core. These types of rounds are created and designed to penetrate lightly armored items or vehicles. With this design, the ammunition will pass through living targets with little damage. In gaming terms, these types of rounds add +D6 points to a firearm's AP. This type of round is useable in any type of firearm. Armor Piercing rounds do 1 point of additional Lethal HEA damage.

## ARMOR PIERCING EXPLOSIVE TIPPED (APE) ROUNDS

This type of round is a combination of an armor piercing and explosive tipped round. This round is created with a hardened steel or tungsten core surrounded by a slim, long, flat-tipped metal jacket and the center core of this bullet is filled with an explosive material that will explode on contact with the target. In gaming terms, these types of rounds add +D6 points to a firearm's AP. This type of round is usable in any type of firearm, but is illegal to have in one's possession and is very expensive to acquire. Armor Piercing Explosive Tipped rounds do an additional D4+1 points of Lethal HEA damage.

## ARMOR PIERCING INCENDIARY (API) ROUNDS

This illegal ammunition is a combination of an armor piercing and incendiary round. This round is created with a hardened steel or tungsten core surrounded by a slim, long, flat-tipped metal jacket and the center core of this bullet is filled with an incendiary material that will ignite on contact with the target. In gaming terms, these types of rounds add +D6 points to a firearm's AP. This type of round is usable in any type of firearm. Armor Piercing Incendiary rounds do an additional 3 points of Lethal HEA damage.

## DUPLEX (D) ROUNDS

This is a unique type of round; it contains two projectiles within it. When firing a duplex round, the character subtracts an Easy (-2) modifier from the first projectile's ACC and then subtracts an Extreme (-14) modifier from the second projectile's ACC. Due to the nature of this round, if there is another person within 5' of the intended target and the second projectile has missed, there is a 1 in a D4 chance that the second projectile with hit the other target. Duplex rounds do an additional 2 points of Lethal HEA damage.

## EXPLOSIVE TIPPED (E) ROUNDS

This type of bullet has the tip of the round hollowed out and filled with an explosive material that will explode on contact with the target. This type of ammunition, unlike the armor piercing explosive or armor piercing incendiary round, can be stopped by a minor barrier or even to an extreme a pane of glass.

This type of round is useable in any type of firearm, but is illegal to have in one's possession and very expensive to acquire. Explosive rounds do an additional D4 points of Lethal HEA damage.

## EXPLOSIVE TIPPED INCENDIARY (EI) ROUNDS

This type of round is a combination of incendiary and explosive tipped round. This type of bullet has a center core that is filled with explosive and incendiary materials that will explode and ignite on contact with the target. A minor barrier or even a pane of glass can stop this type of ammunition, unlike the armor piercing explosive or armor piercing incendiary round. This type of round is usable in any type of firearm, but is illegal to have in one's possession and very expensive to acquire. Explosive Tipped Incendiary rounds do an additional D4+2 points of Lethal HEA damage.

## FLECHETTE (F) ROUNDS

Flechette rounds fire a cloud of fine airfoil flechettes at the target. Flechettes are usually made of a dense polymer, with excellent armor-piercing characteristics against lightly armored items. This type of ammunition round cannot penetrate hard armor surfaces such as body armor or bulletproof vests. In gaming terms, these types of rounds add +1 points to a firearm's AP. Flechette rounds do an additional 1 points of Lethal HEA damage.

## FULL METAL JACKET (FMJ) ROUNDS

This type of bullet is the most common type of ammunition in existence. It is a full-jacketed sleeve round with a standard lead core.

## GLAZER (G) ROUNDS

This is a generic name for a type of ammunition that is called a "safety round." This type of round works identical to a shotgun pellet shell. The round is filled with several tiny ball bearings that when hit cause traumatic damage to the target. This type of round, due to their construction, has no effect on bulletproof devices including bulletproof vests and glass. Glazer rounds do an additional 2 points of Lethal HEA damage.

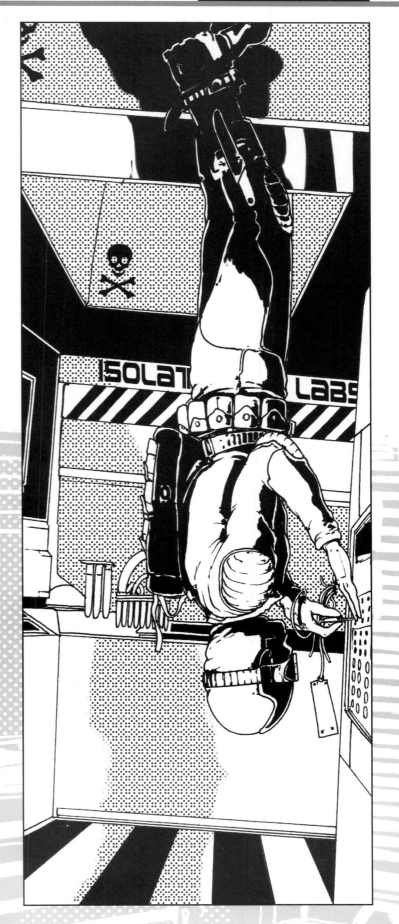

## HOLLOW POINT (HP) ROUNDS

This bullet contains a soft hollow nose. This ammunition is made so that it may "tumble" in flight causing greater damage to the target. Hollow Point rounds do an additional 2 points of Lethal HEA damage.

## INCENDIARY (I) ROUNDS

This type of bullet has a center core that is filled with an incendiary material that will ignite on contact with the target. Unlike the armor piercing incendiary round, a minor barrier or even a pane of glass can stop this type of ammunition. This type of round is usable in any type of firearm, but is illegal to have in one's possession and very expensive to acquire. These types of rounds cannot be purchased as normal ammunition would be, and must be acquired by illegal means. Incendiary rounds do an additional 2 points of Lethal HEA damage.

## TRACER (T) ROUNDS

These types of rounds are coated with a light-producing chemical including magnesium or phosphorus. When fired, the round ignites setting off a glow that allows the shooter to see where their round is going. This type of round gives those that fire it an additional +2 to their ACC to any following shots from the tracer round. This type of ammunition is used often by snipers and professional assassins to help with their shooting ability. Tracer rounds do an additional 1 point of Lethal HEA damage.

## WADCUTTER (WC) ROUNDS

These rounds are almost identical in nature to the Full Metal Jacket round, but these rounds are primarily used for target shooting. Wadcutter rounds do an additional 1 point of Lethal HEA damage.

## WHISPER (WP) ROUNDS

This type of ammunition is also known as low velocity ammunition, this type of ammunition travels just below the speed of sound. In normal terms, this means the bullet does not make a sonic boom when fired, unlike the majority of other ammunition.

# SHOTGUN SHELLS
## BIRDSHOT SHELLS

This type of shell is filled with extremely small round projectiles, similar to a BB. These projectiles are so small that they do not contain much of their initial energy when fired. With this type of shell, minor cover, including walls, can stop it. Birdshot shells do an additional 5 points of Lethal HEA damage.

## BUCKSHOT SHELLS

This type of shell is similar to the Birdshot, but the interior of this shell is filled with large ball bearing type projectiles. This shell, unlike the Birdshot, does retain its initial energy when fired, making it deadly ammunition. Minor cover does not stop this type of shell, unlike the Birdshot. Buckshot shells do an additional 8 points of Lethal HEA damage.

## SLUG

This type of ammunition is quite different from the majority of shotgun shells. Instead of having some type of shot in the shell, it has been replaced with a large piece of solid metal. This type of ammunition is quite similar to a Full Metal Jacketed round. This type of ammunition will easily penetrate most common types of cover. Slugs do an additional 10 points of Lethal HEA damage.

## PENETRATER

This type of slug is equivalent to an armor piercing round. These types of shells are created and designed to penetrate lightly armored items or vehicles. With this type of design, this type of shell will pass through living targets with little damage. This type of shell is usable in any type of firearm but is illegal to have in one's possession. This type of shell cannot be purchased as normal ammunition would be, and must be acquired by illegal means. Penetrater shells do 3 points of additional Lethal HEA damage.

# FIREARM MODIFICATION

Very often, characters will like to customize their firearms to make it more personal to themselves. This may include everything from adding a scope,

laser sight, a recoil compensator, and flash suppressor. All of these modifications will improve the weapon's performance in one way or another. All of these modifications can be used in conjunction with each other. The following listed items are the most common of all customizable items for firearms.

## BARREL EXTENSION

This device extends the length of a firearm's barrel helping to increase this weapon's accuracy at the cost of making the weapon harder to conceal. When a barrel extension is placed on a weapon the shooter receives a +1 to ACC and -3 to the weapon's SUB.
*Cost: Additional 20% of firearm's cost*

## FLASH SUPPRESSOR

A flash suppressor is to the firearm's powder flash as a silencer is to the noise of the firearm shot. A flash suppressor is used primarily when in combat in dark or night conditions. When looking for a weapon that uses a flash suppressor, all characters suffer an Extreme (-14) modifier to PER versus their sight.
*Cost: Additional 20% of firearm's cost*

## LASER SIGHT

This device is one of the most-used of the newly created devices for firearms. This device works by emitting a laser light beam from itself on to the item it is targeting, locating where the shot will go. When this device is used, the shooter receives a +3 to their ACC when firing in either light or dark conditions at point blank, short, and medium ranges.
*Cost: $100*

## RECOIL COMPENSATOR

These devices were created to help with the character's ability to handle a weapon's recoil when firing a semi-automatic or automatic weapon including an assault rifle or submachine gun. The recoil compensator will add +1 to a character's ACC after the 1st shot fired in that round. For example, Morgan is armed with a 9mm Beretta 92R with a recoil compensator. The Beretta is able to fire up to 3 shots per round. For every shot after the 1st, Morgan will receive a +1 to his ACC to those shots. Even though this device is found the majority of time in assault

rifles or submachine guns, it can be used in pistols and shotguns.
*Cost: Additional 10% of firearm's cost*

## SCOPE

A scope, or telescopic sight as it is also known, is a device that helps magnify a target making it possible to see them more clearly at great distances. Scopes come in various powers from 4X power, 6X power, 8X power, and 12X power. The scope helps improve the character's ability to hit their target at medium and long range only. A 4X scope increases a shooter's ACC by +2; 6X scope increases a shooter's ACC by +3; 8X scope increases a shooter's ACC by +4; and 12X scope increases a shooter's ACC by +6. Scopes can be placed on any type of firearms, but a 4X scope is the only scope that can be placed on a pistol.
*Cost: 4X - $125, 6X - $175, 8X - $225, 12X - $275*

## SILENCER

A silencer is a device that helps reduce the sound of the firearm going off to a point where the sound is similar in value to a muffled cough. When listening for a weapon that uses a silencer, all characters suffer an Extreme (-14) modifier to PER versus their hearing. The cost of making the weapon nearly silent is it makes the weapon harder to conceal. All silencer-used weapons suffer an Easy (-2) modifier to the weapon's SUB.
*Cost: $150*

## STARLIGHT SCOPE

This type of scope works by amplifying the surrounding ambient light making it possible for the shooter to see in the dark. When using this device, the shooter will negate the modifiers when firing in dark or night conditions.
*Cost: $300*

## SUPPRESSORS

A suppressor is a larger version of a silencer, which is used for fully automatic firearms including the AK-74 and the Uzi. When listening for a weapon that uses a suppressor, all characters suffer an Extreme (-14) modifier to PER versus their hearing.

The cost of making the weapon nearly silent, it makes the weapon harder to conceal. All suppressor used weapons suffer an Average (-5) modifier to the weapon's SUB.
*Cost: $125*

## AMMUNITION COST (PER 50 ROUNDS)

| Type | .21 to .30* | .31 to .40** | .41 to .50 |
| --- | --- | --- | --- |
| AP | $120 | $140 | $150 |
| APE | $350 | $400 | $450 |
| API | $150 | $165 | $200 |
| D | $4 | $5 | $5 |
| E | $250 | $300 | $350 |
| EI | $300 | $350 | $400 |
| F | $4 | $4 | $5 |
| FMJ | $2 | $2 | $2 |
| GS | $15 | $20 | $25 |
| HP | $3 | $3 | $4 |
| I | $80 | $85 | $90 |
| T | $15 | $25 | $25 |
| WC | $1 | $1 | $1 |
| WP | $2 | $2 | $2 |

\*-5.56mm and 7.62mm
\*\*-9mm and 10mm

## SHOTGUN AMMUNITION COST (PER 20 ROUNDS)

| Shotguns | 12 Gua. |
| --- | --- |
| Birdshot | $10 |
| Buckshot | $12 |
| Sabot | $15 |
| Slug | $20 |
| Penetrator | $50 |

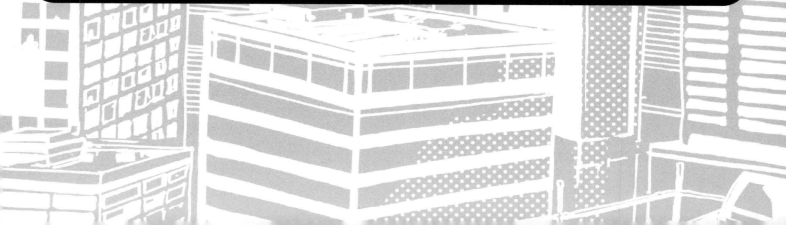

# Disposal

Disposal

Christ, I can tell you one thing
about getting rid of bodies.
Probably not what you expect.  You
probably think I'm gonna tell you
the best way to chop a guy up,
best way to get rid of his legs,
best place to put his remains so
no one ever, ever finds him.  You
probably think I'm gonna tell you
what its like smelling a guy that's
swollen like a purple balloon with
three bullets in his face.  What
it's like being covered with
rotten, stinking blood, so old its
black.  You probably think that's
what body disposal is all about.
It is, but it's about a whole lot
more.  Let me tell you what it is.

All they do is get rid of the
other guy's breathing and mind.
We're the ones who got to get rid
of everything else.  We're the ones
who've gotta get rid of 180 pounds
of flesh right now.  We're the
ones who've got those street assassins by the balls.  They come
running to you, nearly crying,
they've got to get rid of these
two bodies in the trunk, some guy
under the sheets in a hotel downtown, a few arms and torsos inside
a duffel bag.  That's when you've
got them against the wall.  That's
when they'll pay you anything,
anything, man, just to make sure
you make that body disappear
forever.

# CHAPTER: 4

## COMBAT & CONFLICT

*Friends may come and go, but enemies accumulate*

*T. Jones*

Often human beings cannot solve their differences by "normal" non-violent means and the situation devolves into physical combat. The following section describes how combat is resolved in Haven: City of Violence. This section has been broken down to cover the many different aspects of personal combat governed by the game system.

# SHOOTING INITIATIVE

The first action when resolving a firearm combat situation is to figure who gets to make that all important first attack, is know as Initiative in Haven. Initiative is determined by the character's AGI, sometimes with modifiers. The character with the highest AGI, after all the modifiers have been calculated, gets to act first. The person with the second highest AGI then gets to act and so on from highest to lowest. If two or more individuals have the same initiative, then they will attack at the same time. If the two or more persons are engaged in combat and one of the persons is killed and has the same initiative, the newly deceased person will still be able to perform their action. This is due to the actions and events occurring at the same instant in time. So it is possible for a "dead" man to kill his killer!

In each round of combat the character will determine initiative to find out who will proceed first in that round of combat. The holster type modifier is only used in the first round that the character draws their weapon out of their holster. If the weapon is already drawn, the character does not suffer any holster negatives to their AGI. Weapon types also modify the shooter's initiative. The following chart lists the type of modifiers for holsters and weapon types.

| Holster Type | Modifier |
|---|---|
| Hip | Easy (-2) |
| Shoulder or Waistband | Average (-5) |
| Neckband | Hard (-9) |
| Ankle | Extreme (-14) |

| Firearm | Modifier |
|---|---|
| Pistols | Easy (-2) |
| Assault Rifles, Sawed-off Shotguns, Sub Machine Guns | Average (-5) |
| Rifle and Shotgun | Hard (-9) |

*Example: Blade Wilson and "Gunner" McNeil meet up on a busy street. Both Blade and Gunner are armed with pistols. Blade's AGI is 17 and he is drawing his pistol, Easy (-2) modifier, from a waistband holster, Average (-5) modifier. Gunner's initial AGI is 15 and he is drawing his pistol, Easy (-2) modifier, from his shoulder holster, Average (-5) modifier. In the end Blade's final AGI for initiative is 10, while in comparison, Gunner's is 8, hence Blade is able to shoot first . . . bang.*

# SHOOTING DETERMINATION

When a character uses any type of firearm or projectile weapon, they have a chance to hit their target. Once the player has determined their character's Accuracy (ACC), they must roll a D20 to resolve whether or not they are able to hit their target. The character's ability to hit their target is calculated from the character's initial ACC, modified by various factors of the environment, the shooter's movement and their target's movement, etc. If the player's roll is higher than the character's ACC, they have missed their target. If the roll is lower than or equal to their character's ACC, then a successful hit has been scored in a particular target location.

A character can use and fire one firearm in each hand, at the firearm's rate of fire. The specific type of firearm in each hand does not matter. The character can have a .380 Sig Saur P230 in one hand and a 9mm Uzi in another. The character can still shoot once per round with the Sig Saur P230 and up to five times per round with the Uzi. Though, the character can fire each weapon, they will receive specific modifiers to their ACC when firing two weapons simultaneously. Even though the character is using two weapons concurrently, the player must make a separate roll for each shot that is fired from each firearm.

No matter what the character's ACC is, as long as the target of the shot is within range of the weapon, the shooter will always have at least a 1 out of D20 chance of hitting the target. A character will never have greater than a 20 on a D20 chance to hit the target. On a rolled score of 20 on a D20, the result is a miss, misfire, or jam. Roll a D4 to determine the results. If the character rolls a 1 on a D4, then the shot is a normal miss. If the character rolls a 2 or 3 on a D4, then the shot is a misfire. If the character rolls a 4 on a D4, then the shot is a jam. Any target that is out of the range, lies beyond 2501 feet, or has an X in the range column, does not utilize the 1 out of D20 hit rule. The following charts are lists of modifiers and factors that can influence the ACC of the character.

A shooter will suffer an Easy (-2) modifier to their ACC when they are shooting at a target behind soft cover like a small tree or small pile of rubble, firing more than one shot per round cumulative, shooting with the wrong hand or is wounded, in gun hand or arm. A shooter will suffer an Average (-5) modifier to their ACC when they are shooting at a target behind hard cover or firing two weapons. A shooter will suffer a Hard (-9) modifier to their ACC when they are shooting at night or in complete darkness.

## FIREARMS WEAPONS CHART

**PB:** Point blank range is from 0' - 5'
**S:** Short range is from 6' - 40'
**M:** Medium range is from 41' - 500'
**L:** Long range is from 501' - 2500'
**Rate:** The maximum number of shots that can be fired in a round

| Shooting Determination | Modifier |
|---|---|
| Target behind Soft Cover (Small Tree of Small Rubble) | Easy (-2) |
| Firing more than one shot per round cumulative | Easy (-2) |
| Shooting with the wrong hand or is wounded, in gun hand or arm | Easy (-2) |
| Target behind Soft Cover | Easy (-2) |
| Target behind Hard Cover | Average (-5) |
| Firing two weapons | Average (-5) |
| Shooting at night or in complete darkness | Hard (-9) |

| Assault Rifles | PB | S | M | L | Rate | Ammo | Cost | AP | SUB |
|---|---|---|---|---|---|---|---|---|---|
| 5.56mm Colt M16A1 | +1 | 0 | -11 | -25 | 7 | 30 | 1000 | D10+5 | NC |
| 5.56mm Colt M16A2 | +2 | 0 | -10 | -21 | 5 | 30 | 1200 | D10+5 | NC |
| 5.56mm Steyr AUG | +2 | 0 | -13 | -24 | 7 | 32 | 1400 | D10+5 | NC |
| 7.62mm AK-47 | +1 | 0 | -12 | -19 | 6 | 30 | 1100 | D10+7 | NC |
| 7.62mm Galil Arm | +2 | 0 | -9 | -20 | 7 | 35 | 1350 | D10+7 | NC |
| 7.62mm Springfield Armory M1A | +2 | 0 | -14 | -27 | 7 | 20 | 1000 | D10+7 | NC |

| Rifles | PB | S | M | L | Rate | Ammo | Cost | AP | SUB |
|---|---|---|---|---|---|---|---|---|---|
| .50 Barrett M82A1 | +5 | +2 | 0 | -16 | 1 | 11 | 2900 | D10+9 | NC |
| 5.56mm SIG SG-3000 | +2 | +1 | -1 | -11 | 1 | 5 | 1200 | D10+5 | NC |
| 7.62mm Druganov SVD | +4 | 0 | -2 | -9 | 2 | 10 | 1750 | D10+7 | NC |
| 7.62mm Heckler & Koch G3SG/1 | +3 | 0 | -5 | -15 | 2 | 20 | 1650 | D10+7 | NC |
| 7.62mm Heckler & Koch PSG-1 | +3 | 0 | -2 | -13 | 1 | 5 | 1100 | D10+7 | NC |

**Ammo:** The maximum number of shots fired before reloading
**Cost:** The cost of the firearm in dollars

**AP:** The weapon's Armor Penetration value
**SUB:** The change in the character's SUB when hiding the firearm.  NC means that the weapon can not be concealed

| Pistol-Automatic | PB | S | M | L | Rate | Ammo | Cost | AP | SUB |
|---|---|---|---|---|---|---|---|---|---|
| .22 American Derringer | +2 | -14 | X | X | 1 | 1 | 300 | D10-5 | +2 |
| .357 Magnum Desert Eagle | +2 | -1 | -17 | X | 1 | 9 | 1450 | D10+2 | -5 |
| .380 Sig Sauer P230 | 0 | -4 | -15 | X | 1 | 7 | 500 | D10-1 | 0 |
| .40 S&W Glock 22 | 0 | -1 | -15 | X | 1 | 17 | 650 | D10 | -3 |
| .40 S&W Heckler & Koch USP | 0 | -2 | -12 | X | 1 | 10 | 650 | D10 | -3 |
| .44 Magnum Desert Eagle | 0 | -2 | -18 | X | 1 | 8 | 1350 | D10+2 | -5 |
| .45 Colt 1991A1 | 0 | -4 | -18 | X | 1 | 8 | 550 | D10+1 | -4 |
| .45 Smith & Wesson Model 4500 | 0 | -5 | -20 | X | 1 | 8 | 500 | D10+1 | -4 |
| .50 AE Desert Eagle | +1 | -3 | -19 | X | 1 | 7 | 1250 | D10+4 | -6 |
| 9mm Beretta 92F | 0 | 0 | -15 | X | 1 | 16 | 750 | D10 | -2 |
| 9mm FN Browning "Fast Action" | +1 | -2 | -18 | X | 1 | 14 | 850 | D10 | -2 |
| 9mm Ruger P89 | 0 | -4 | -17 | X | 1 | 10 | 800 | D10 | -2 |
| 9mm Sig Sauer P228 | 0 | -3 | -17 | X | 1 | 13 | 800 | D10 | 0 |

| Pistol-Revolver | PB | S | M | L | Rate | Ammo | Cost | AP | SUB |
|---|---|---|---|---|---|---|---|---|---|
| .357 Magnum Colt Python | +3 | -2 | -18 | X | 1 | 6 | 700 | D10 | -2 |
| .38 Smith & Wesson Model 64 | 0 | -3 | -17 | X | 1 | 6 | 675 | D10 | -2 |
| .41 Smith & Wesson Model 57 | +3 | -1 | -15 | X | 1 | 6 | 675 | D10+1 | -5 |
| .44 Magnum Colt Anaconda | +4 | -3 | -13 | X | 1 | 6 | 750 | D10+2 | -5 |
| .44 Magnum Ruger Blackhawk | +3 | -3 | -12 | X | 1 | 6 | 775 | D10+2 | -5 |
| .44 Magnum Smith & Wesson Model 29 | +3 | -2 | -12 | X | 1 | 6 | 750 | D10+2 | -5 |
| 9mm Ruger SP-101 | +1 | -4 | -15 | X | 1 | 5 | 600 | D10 | -2 |

| Sub-Machine Gun | PB | S | M | L | Rate | Ammo | Cost | AP | SUB |
|---|---|---|---|---|---|---|---|---|---|
| .45 Ingram M10 | +4 | -1 | -12 | -21 | 4 | 30 | 900 | D10+3 | -5 |
| 9mm Heckler & Koch MP5K | +5 | -4 | -8 | -26 | 7 | 30 | 2000 | D10+3 | -5 |
| 9mm Mini-Uzi | +2 | +1 | -10 | -21 | 4 | 30 | 1200 | D10+3 | -5 |
| 9mm Tec-9 | +1 | -3 | -15 | -24 | 4 | 32 | 700 | D10+3 | -5 |
| 9mm Uzi | +4 | -2 | -9 | -24 | 5 | 40 | 1300 | D10+3 | -10 |

| Shotgun | PB | S | M | L | Rate | Ammo | Cost | AP | SUB |
|---------|----|----|----|----|------|------|------|----|----|
| 12 gau. Benelli 121 M1 | +3 | -6 | -19 | X | 1 | 7 | 900 | D10+5 | -10 |
| 12 gau. Mossberg 500ATP | +5 | -4 | -22 | X | 1 | 8 | 1000 | D10+5 | -10 |

*-Saw off version only works at Point Blank or Short range

## CALLED SHOTS

There are times when it is necessary to hit a certain location on the target. Naturally, the smaller the target area the harder it will be to hit. A called shot must be declared before the character calculates their ACC to hit. Shooting at an arm or a leg is an Average (-5) modifier; foot or hand is a Hard (-9) modifier; and a headshot is an Extreme (-14) modifier.

## SHOOTING MORE THAN ONE TARGET

Often when characters are able to fire more than one shot per round they may choose to shoot at more than one target. When choosing to fire at more than one target, or "spray an area', as it is better known, the character will miss one shot for every additional person they fired upon. So if a character was able to shoot 5 times in a round they could reasonably hit up to 3 targets.

The first shot would be aimed at the first target, the second shot would miss, the third shot would be at the second target, the fourth shot would miss, the fifth, and the final shot would be at the target. This combination of hit and automatic misses can be put in desired order.

## EMPTYING A MAGAZINE

Very often, it is necessary for a character to fire more shots than they are normally capable of doing. This is most common in action-adventure movies where the hero fires off all the rounds in their pistol in a six-second interval. In Haven: COV system, a character can fire off all the rounds or shots in their firearm, but they suffer extreme penalties in the accuracy of their shots. Characters wishing to empty a magazine must observe the following rules:

- Acharacter wishing to empty a magazine must be using a pistol to fire with. It is impossible for all other firearms to empty their magazines in this fashion.
- A character must follow all the normal rules of shooting when using this technique including when shooting more than one target.
- The character shooting receives a Hard (-9) modifier to each of their shooting rolls in addition to any other shooting modifiers. Characters with the benefit Rapid Fire only suffer an Average (-5) modifier to each of their shooting rolls in addition to any other shooting modifiers
- The character must fire all the shots in the magazine that round, so that in the subsequent round they must reload their weapon.
- When shooting in this fashion, all scopes and sights are considered totally ineffective. The character when firing in this fashion does not acquire their additions to their base ACC rating.

## MISFIRES AND JAMS

In very rare instances, a character may suffer a setback in combat; if they roll a 20 on a D20, which causes either a misfire or a jam (see Shooting Determination). Roll on a D4, on a result of a 1 or 2 the firearm has suffered a missed; 3 the firearm has suffered a misfire; on a roll of 4, the firearm has suffered a jam. A misfire is when the firearm improperly chambers a round. When using an automatic pistol, such as the Beretta 92F or the Desert Eagle, the weapon jams and the magazine feed will be stopped. This will take one round to to be fixed. The shot from the firearm is considered to be a missed shot. A character must manually operate the firearm's slide for the next round to chamber the following bullet. On all other automatic, semi-automatic, and non-automatic firearms when there is a misfire the shot is ruled as a missed shot.

A jammed shot occurs when a shot is lodged incorrectly inside the firearm. This event can happen to any type of firearm. When a weapon is jammed the character cannot fire from the weapon until the jam is cleared. If firing from a weapon that fires more than one shot per round, any shots fired before the jam act as normal. Clearing a jam from the firearm's barrel will take the round that the weapon was jammed and two additional rounds.

## MISSED SHOTS

One of the most common instances in firearm combat is someone missing their target. This is not a problem when the two opponents who are shooting are in a completely open field, where there is no chance of anyone else getting hurt. On a busy street corner, however, this is a big problem. Any time a player misses their target, there is a chance that the shot will hit another person unintentionally. If a shot has missed its target and there are other persons within 5' of the intended target, the player must roll a D20. If the result is 4 or higher, the shot misses anyone near them. If the result is 1, 2, or 3, the shot has hit an unintended target and must reference the injury chart as normal (see injury chart).

## CAN'T MISS SHOTS

In some cases, a person may be at a distance where they could not miss a shot. The distance for these shots cannot be more than a foot away from the target. When shooting at this range, a character needs only to make any roll amount on a D20 roll, except a 20. Characters at this range can also choose at what body location they are shooting with no modifiers to the roll. Also, all damage at this range is double the normal shooting damage.

## SHOOTING INTO HAND-TO-HAND COMBAT

This is very dangerous act, but happens more often than you think. Characters who shoot into hand-to-hand combat will suffer a Hard (-9) modifier to their ACC, in addition to any other shooting modifiers. If

a character makes a successful ACC roll they will hit their target. If a character fails their ACC roll they will hit the other hand-to-hand opponent. If the character misses their ACC by more than 6 points, they have missed both of the targets.

## INJURY

If a target is hit by an opponent's shot, the player must roll a D10 for the location of the shot, the amount of damage that is taken. If the attacker hits a location on the target that is covered by some type of hard solid protection, including a steel wall, the attack will miss even if the character had scored a successful hit. The following chart will notify the characters of their damage, body location to the attack. All damage in firearm combat is considered to be Lethal with the damage removed from Lethal HEA.

| D10 | Body Location | Damage |
|-----|---------------|--------|
| 1 | Right Leg | D8 |
| 2 | Left Leg | D8 |
| 3 - 4 | Abdomen | D10 |
| 5 - 7 | Chest | D12 |
| 8 | Right Arm/Hand | D6 |
| 9 | Left Arm/Hand | D6 |
| 10 | Head/Neck | D12+D8 |

## FIREARM AMMUNITION AND CALIBER DAMAGE MODIFIERS

Certain types of ammunition and weapon caliber do more damage to a target than normal. It is only logical that an armor-piercing explosive round would do more damage than a normal full metal jacketed round. Following with this premise, assault rifles and rifles do more damage than pistols, due to being physically larger than the pistol bullets.

All assault rifles and rifles will add an addition +3 Lethal HEA points damage to their respective Firearm Caliber Damage Modifiers in addition to ammunition type. All magnum or action express firearms, such as a .50 AE Desert Eagle, will add an additional +2 Lethal HEA points damage to their

| Firearm Ammunition And Caliber Damage | Damage Modifier |
|---|---|
| All assault rifles and rifles | +3 Lethal HEA damage |
| All magnum or action express firearms | +2 Lethal HEA damage |

respective Firearm Caliber Damage Modifiers in addition to ammunition type.

***Example:** Jack has been shot in the chest with a .50 AE Desert Eagle with hollow point rounds. The damage done is two points of damage due to the type of ammunition and another two points of damage due to the weapon magnum caliber. This is a total of four points of damage in addition to the normal damage of the firearm.*

## BLEEDING

After a being wounded by bullets and knifes, there is a nasty little event that will always happen to a character - the character will start bleeding. Sometimes, they bleed just a few drops and sometimes they will bleed buckets full of blood. Either way, this does

have a very direct way of hampering the character. After being wounded by firearm's fire or an edged object, a character will lose points to their Lethal HEA if they do not seek aid or bandage themselves correctly. For every 10 minutes, or one turn, that a character does not bandage themselves they will lose 1 Lethal HEA point from each of their wounds. If the character has been shot or stabbed five times, then they have five wounds and will lose 5 Lethal HEA points every turn if they do not bandage themselves. If the character's Lethal HEA reaches 0 in this fashion, they have bled to death.

Characters can try to locate bandages to stop the bleeding or they can create "makeshift" bandages. If a character uses normal bandages, the wound's bleeding will stop within five minutes, half of a turn. If a character uses "makeshift" bandages they will

| Lethal HEA | 1 | 2 | 3 | 4 | 5 | 6 | 7 | 8 | 9 | 10 |
|---|---|---|---|---|---|---|---|---|---|---|
| 0 or less | 20 | 40 | 60 | 80 | 100 | 120 | 140 | 160 | 180 | 200 |
| 1 - 2 | 10 | 20 | 30 | 40 | 50 | 60 | 70 | 80 | 90 | 100 |
| 3 - 5 | 9 | 18 | 27 | 36 | 45 | 54 | 63 | 72 | 81 | 90 |
| 6 - 8 | 8 | 16 | 24 | 32 | 40 | 48 | 56 | 64 | 72 | 80 |
| 9 - 13 | 7 | 14 | 21 | 28 | 35 | 42 | 49 | 56 | 63 | 70 |
| 14 - 16 | 6 | 12 | 18 | 24 | 30 | 36 | 42 | 48 | 54 | 60 |
| 17 - 19 | 5 | 10 | 15 | 20 | 25 | 30 | 35 | 40 | 45 | 50 |
| 20 - 22 | 4 | 8 | 12 | 16 | 20 | 24 | 28 | 32 | 36 | 40 |
| 23 - 25 | 3 | 6 | 9 | 12 | 15 | 18 | 21 | 24 | 27 | 30 |
| 26 - 28 | 2 | 4 | 6 | 8 | 10 | 12 | 14 | 16 | 18 | 20 |
| 29 or greater | 1 | 2 | 3 | 4 | 5 | 6 | 7 | 8 | 9 | 10 |

not stop the bleeding, but slow it down. Characters using "makeshift" bandages will lose 1 Lethal HEA point every 20 minutes, instead of 10 minuets as with normal bleeding. Characters with medical or first aid skills can stop the bleeding in one minute, and "makeshift" bandages will lose 1 Lethal HEA point every 40 minutes.

# UNCONSCIOUSNESS

The above chart is used to determine the amount of time that a character will be unconscious due to tear gas or anesthetic gas, for example. A player will roll a D10 and compare that result with the top row, and then cross-index that result against their current Lethal Health of the character to determine the amount of time, in minutes that the character will be unconscious.

# KILLING CHARACTERS

If a character reaches zero Lethal HEA, they are dead. If a character is unconscious, they can be killed by anyone in one round. The attacking character may only need to state that they are killing the unconscious character and by the following round, the unconscious character is dead.

# HEALING

A character will normally gain one-eighth of their STA intensity in Lethal HEA per week following the last damage done, rounded up. If any additional damage is done to the character while the character is healing they must start from that last point of damage. If the character is under the care of a doctor or standard medical care, the healing rate is increased to one-quarter of the character's STA per week.

*Example: Ace's starting STA was 20 and Lethal HEA was 18, but he had been in several conflicts with the wrong people and has had his Lethal HEA reduced to 10. Ace has decided to take some time off from being foolish and rest. For each week that Ace stays at home, he will gain 3 points to his Lethal HEA per week, for a total of three weeks to gain back his normal total Lethal HEA of 18. If Ace had chosen to spend this time in a hospital he would gain 5 points to his Lethal HEA per week, for a total of 2 weeks to gain back his normal total Lethal HEA.*

# FIREARM HIT

There are rare occasions when a character's firearm can be hit by another person's shot. When this occurs, roll a D4. On the roll of a 1, the projectile has been lodged in weapon but it does not affect the firearm's use. On the roll of a 2, the bullet ricochets off the firearm and it will not fire for one round. On the roll of a 3, the bearer drops the firearm due to being hit and it will not fire for two rounds. On the roll of a 4, the bearer drops the firearm due to being hit. The firearm is damaged and will no longer fire.

# CHANGING A MAGAZINE OR RELOADING

A character cannot fire their firearm in the same round in which they reloaded it, but they can move as normal after the weapon has been reloaded. The following lists the amount of time it will take to perform the action of changing a magazine or reloading one firearm. Reloading a pistol (automatic) or (revolver with speed loaders) takes one round. Assault Rifles, Pistols (revolver with manual loading), rifles, shotguns and submachine guns take two rounds. The maximum rate at which the character can move while reloading a weapon is walking.

# BULLETPROOF ITEMS

You use bulletproof materials vest or in your car, you live longer. Bulletproof materials come in several different forms from glass, shields, vest, and various others. The following is a listing of the more common bulletproof materials.

## FULL BODY ARMOR

This is one of the most protective types of armor possible for a character. The armor provides cover for the character's head, neck, abdomen, chest, and both arms. Any characters wearing full body armor will reduce all Lethal damage into an equal amount of Concussive damage, no matter the type of ammunition or the firearm's caliber. While full body armor is quite protective to the wearer it is also quite restrictive. All wearing it will suffer an Average (-5) modifier to AGI and an Easy (-2) modifier to ACC and MV. Armor Piercing, Armor Piercing Explosive Tipped, Armor Piercing Incendiary rounds, and Pentrator slugs, due to their unique creation and structure, will ignore the use of bulletproof materials including vest and cause damage as normal.

## GLASS

Bulletproof glass is able to be used anywhere that regular glass can be used. This type of glass will provide protection from all types of attack except armor piercing rounds or shells, explosives, and cutting torches. This item is considered to have an AV of 12 when being shot at by firearms.

## HELMET

Any characters wearing a bulletproof helmet correctly will reduce all Lethal damage into an equal amount of Concussive damage to the head or neck with all types of ammunition and calibers.

## SHIELDS

Any characters holding a bulletproof shield correctly will reduce all Lethal damage into an equal amount of Concussive damage to any location covered by the shield with any type of firearm caliber. Bulletproof Shields are large enough to be carried and can cover an entire body if necessary.

## VEST

Any characters wearing a bulletproof vest correctly will reduce all Lethal damage into an equal amount of Concussive damage to the abdomen and chest with any caliber of .40 S&W or higher. With smaller caliber weapons, including the .380 or lower, the maximum amount of damage that a character can cause is one point of Concussive damage, no matter what the type of ammunition.

# EXAMPLE OF FIREARM COMBAT

The following is a typical example of combat in the Haven: City of Violence-The Action Adventure Role-Playing Game. Justice Walton versus Jack Cactus

| | Justice Walton | Jack Cactus |
|---|---|---|
| STR | 20 | 14 |
| WILL | 13 | 13 |
| AGI | 20 | 18 |
| STA | 10 | 14 |
| INT | 10 | 12 |
| PER | 17 | 19 |
| | | |
| INFL | 15 | 16 |
| MV | 15 | 14 |
| ACC | 19 | 19 |
| FV | 15 | 13 |
| SUB | 14 | 16 |
| CM | 15 | 15 |
| HEA | 14 | 14 |

Justice Walton is having a drink at his local bar, relaxing after a hard day of breaking legs and extorting money from people. As he is finishing up a cold one, a dark figure enters in through the bar room doors. Justice looks up at the dark figure. The figure walks into the light and their eyes meet. Then like a bolt of lighting, Justice realizes who the person is. It is Jack Cactus, hired killer from the Black Widow Crime Family. As quick as vipers, both of the men go for their weapons. Justice is armed with two .45 Colt 1991A1 with Hollow Point rounds holstered in two Shoulder Holsters. Jack is armed with a .50 AE Desert Eagle with Full Metal Jacket rounds holstered in a Waistband Holster.

## 1ST ROUND

Justice and Jack both draw their weapons. Justice's AGI is 20 minus his shoulder holsters an Average (-5) modifier and weapon type: pistol an Easy (-2) modifier for a final AGI of 13. Jack's AGI is 18 minus his waistband holster an Average (-5) modifier and weapon type: pistol an Easy (-2) modifier for a final AGI of 11. After comparing the AGI, Justice will shoot first, then Jack.

Justice decides to shoot and run for cover at the same time, hoping to dodge some of the bullet fire from Jack's attack. Jack has also decided to shoot and run for cover. Justice's ACC is 19 minus Short-Range (-

4), the Shooter's Movement: Running and Dodging an Average (-5) modifier, the Target's Movement: Running and Dodging an Average (-5) modifier, Shooting two weapons an Average (-5) modifier and Shooting with the wrong hand (for one of the shots) an Easy (-2) modifier. This comes to a total of 0 and −1, but in reality needing a 1 for each roll. Justice rolls a 12 and 16, missing both shots.

Jack's ACC is 19 minus Short-Range (-5), the Shooter's Movement: Running and Dodging an Average (-5) modifier, the Target's Movement: Running and Dodging an Average (-5) modifier. This comes to a total of 4. Jack rolls a 13 and misses the shot.

## 2ND ROUND

Justice has jumped behind the bar and is using it as a position of protection from where he can shoot, while Jack has found an overturned table that he uses as cover. Justice's AGI is 20 minus his weapon type: pistol an Easy (-2) modifier for a final AGI of 18. Jack's AGI is 18 minus his weapon type: pistol an Easy (-2) modifier for a final AGI of 16. After comparing the AGI, Justice will shoot first, then Jack.

Justice decides to shoot from this location at Jack, who is hiding behind the table. Jack has also found some fairly decent cover to shoot at Justice from. Justice's ACC is 19 minus Short Range (-4), the Shooter's Movement: Kneeling (0), the Target's Movement: Kneeling (0), Behind Soft Cover an Average (-5) modifier, Shooting two weapons an Average (-5) modifier, and Shooting with the wrong hand (for one of the shots) an Easy (-2) modifier. This comes to a total of 5 and 3. Justice rolls a 15 and 19, missing both shots.

Jack's ACC is 19 minus Short Range (-5), the Shooter's Movement: Kneeling (0), the Target's Movement: Standing (0), Behind Soft Cover an Easy (-2) modifier. This comes to a total of 12. Jack rolls a 6 and hits Justice. Jack rolls for the location and damage of the shot and rolls a 2 hitting him in the right leg. Since he is behind the bar, the bullet hits the bar and it protects him from taking any damage.

## 3RD ROUND

Justice decides that it is best if he tries to get one good shot off instead of two awful ones and shoots with one of his .45 Colts. Justice's AGI is 20 minus his weapon type: pistol an Easy (-2) modifier for a final AGI of 18. Jack's AGI is 18 minus his weapon type: pistol an Easy (-2) modifier for a final AGI of 16. After comparing the AGI, Justice will shoot first, then Jack.

After Justice decides to fire with one of his pistols, he fires from the protection of the bar, while Jack has become a little more confident after scoring and has started to move out of cover to get closer to Justice's position. Justice's ACC is 19 minus Short Range (-4), the Shooter's Movement: Standing (0) and the Target's Movement: Running, an Easy (-2) modifier. This comes to a total of 13. Justice rolls a 10 and hits. Justice rolls for the location and damage of the shot and rolls a 4, hitting him in the abdomen doing 1 Lethal HEA point of damage plus additional 2 Lethal HEA points for firearm caliber ammunition type, for a total of 3 Lethal HEA points. Jack's Lethal HEA is reduced to 11.

Jack's ACC is 19 minus Short Range (-5), the Shooter's Movement: Kneeling (0), the Target's Movement: Standing (0), Behind Soft Cover an Easy (-2) modifier. This comes to a total of 12. Jack rolls a 19 and misses Justice.

## 4TH ROUND

Justice decides that he is has better things to do then be shot at, and decides to get the hell out of this bar. Jack has decided to move even closer to Justice's position. Justice's AGI is 20 minus his weapon type: pistol an Easy (-2) modifier for a final AGI of 18. Jack's AGI is 18 minus his weapon type: pistol an Easy (-2) modifier for a final AGI of 16. After comparing the AGI, Justice will shoot first, then Jack.

Justice is running and dodging hoping that he will not be hit by any bullets and may even get lucky with a few of his shots. Justice's ACC is 19 minus Short-Range (-4), the Shooter's Movement: Running and Dodging an Average (-5) modifier, the Target's

Movement: Crawling (0) Shooting two weapons an Average (-5) modifier and Shooting with the wrong hand (for one of the shots) an Easy (-2) modifier. This comes to a total of 5 and 3. Justice rolls a 15 and 2, missing one shot and hitting with one shot.

Justice rolls for the location and damage of the shot and rolls a 10, hitting him in the head/neck doing 9 Lethal HEA points of damage plus an additional 2 Lethal HEA points for firearm caliber ammunition type, for a total of 11 Lethal HEA points. Jack's HEA is reduced to 0. The reaction to this hit causes Jack to stagger back 1'. He also shouts out in pain, screams out in agony, grasps his wound, and drops the pistol he is carrying in his hand. Jack slumps over dead. See you later Jack.

# EXPLOSIVES AND GRENADES

In the course of some role-playing it may be necessary for characters to use some type of explosive device. These devices are best used to damage or eliminate individuals or objects. The following is a list of the more common explosive devices and how they may be used effectively in the game.

## DYNAMITE

Dynamite is one of the most common industrial explosives used in the world. Dynamite is composed of Nitroglycerine and absorbent materials including kieselghur (porous, chalky earth), wood pulp, or starch. One stick of dynamite will do 12 Lethal HEA points of damage up to 10', 4 Lethal HEA points of damage from 11' to 20'.

## GRENADES

Grenades are small projectiles filled either with an explosive charge or with incendiary, smoke-producing, illuminating, or chemical devices. Grenades are used to attack enemy targets, vehicles, or fortified positions at close range and are thrown by hand or launched by rifles or by special grenade launchers. Grenades that are designed to be launched are more streamlined than hand-thrown grenades, and

| Material | Grenade | Dynamite | Plastic Explosive | Nitro-glycerine |
|---|---|---|---|---|
| Wood, up to 1' | 1 grenade | 1 stick | 1 oz. | 1 oz. |
| Wood and Plaster, 2' | 1 | 1 | 1 | 1 |
| Aluminum, ½" | 2 | 2 | 3 | 2 |
| Wood and Plaster, 3' | 2 | 3 | 3 | 3 |
| Brick, 6" | 3 | 4 | 5 | 4 |
| Concrete, 1' | 7 | 9 | 10 | 9 |
| Marble, 1' | 10 | 13 | 15 | 13 |
| Armor Plate, 2' | 14 | 18 | 20 | 18 |

occasionally have small propellant charges to increase their range. One fragmentary grenade will do 15 Lethal HEA points of damage up to 12', 5 Lethal HEA points of damage from 13' to 25'. Jumping on a live grenade results in the shielding character taking 20 Lethal HEA points of damage. Grenades will detonate at the end of the round which they were thrown.

## PLASTIC EXPLOSIVES

Plastic Explosives, also called RDX or C-4 in the military, is a mixture with TNT and wax called Composition B. One ounce of plastic explosive will do 10 Lethal HEA points of damage up to 10', 3 Lethal HEA points of damage from 11' to 20', 1 Lethal HEA point of damage from 21' to 40'. Plastic Explosives leave a very distinctive odor in the air after it has been detonated. Characters that possess the skill Military Science or Demolitions will be able to identify it with an INT roll.

## NITROGLYCERINE

Nitroglycerine is a powerful explosive derived from glycerin by treatment with a mixture of concentrated sulfuric and nitric acids. It is a heavy, oily, colorless or light-yellow liquid with a sweet, burning taste. Nitroglycerine burns quietly when heated in air, but it will explode when heated above 400° F or when heated in a closed vessel. Nitroglycerine is very sensitive to shock and therefore dangerous to transport for this reason. One ounce of nitroglycerine will do 12 Lethal HEA points of damage up to 20', 6 Lethal HEA points of damage from 21' to 40'.

The chart above is a chart listing the needed amount of explosives to pierce the listed material with a hole large enough for a person to crawl through.

## HAND-TO-HAND COMBAT

Hand-to-Hand combat is defined as any and all combat where either or both opponents are unarmed or armed with melee weapons. Melee weapons may be anything from just a fist, foot, knife, board, or even a broken bottle or chair leg. Off the streets and into the martial arts films, this can expand into swords and more exotic hand weapons.

## HAND-TO-HAND INITIATIVE

The first action when resolving a hand-to-hand combat situation is to figure out which group or person will make their attack first. This is called initiative. Initiative is determined by comparing the parties' PER with various modifiers to the PER. The character with the highest PER after all the modifiers goes first with one offensive action. The person with the second highest PER will go next with an offensive action. This will continue on until both opponents run out of actions or both choose to end the round. In each round of combat the characters will check for initiative to determine who will proceed first in that round of combat.

## HOW TO FIGHT HAND-TO-HAND

Unarmed combat is deadly in Haven. Like in real life, hand-to-hand fighting is simple, but a sharp mind and knowing your enemy can make all the difference. Once initiative is determined, the players secretly choose their fighting maneuver. Writing it down a piece of paper can keep people honest. A few things affect what maneuvers you can choose and how many you can get in a turn.

Both combatants reveal their maneuvers simultaneously and then compared on the Hand-to-Hand combat chart. The result will be a letter code that will detail how much damage was inflicted with a successful attack. Damage is dealt and then the next action or round starts the punishment again.

# FIGHTING VALUE

A character's FV determines the number of actions that allow a PC to either attack or defend during an unarmed combat. Characters that are extremely talented and skilled combatants with a high FV are able to perform more than a single action per round. Characters with multiple actions have their actions broken up in any way the player chooses. If the character can make four actions per round, they may choose to make three offensive actions and one defensive action. The character can also choose to break them down into two offensive actions and two defensive actions or just choose to make four offensive actions and no defensive actions. The player determines the amount of either. Players with a FV of 1 to 5 can perform one action. Players with a FV of 6 to 10 can perform two actions. Players with a FV of 11 to 15 can perform three actions. Players with a FV of 16 to 20 can perform four actions. Players with a FV of 21 or higher can perform five actions. When opponents both have multiple actions, they alternate between them. The opponent with the highest PER will go first, then the other opponent will go and this will continue till all the actions for the round are used.

## ACTION MANEUVER COST

The majority of the offensive combat maneuvers will cost only one action, but due to the complexity of certain hand-to-hand combat maneuvers, some attacks cost more than one action to perform. All Blunt, Hand, Edged, Elbow, Foot, and Knee Strikes cost one combat action. All defensive actions, except Clinch, Escape, and Reversal, cost one combat action. Arm Locks, Choke Holds, DDTs, Headlocks, Escapes, Leg Locks, Leg Sweeps, Shoulder Locks, Sleepers, Tackles and Wrist Locks cost two combat actions. Arm Throws, Bear Hugs, Body Slams, Guillotines, Hip Throws, Reversals, Rolling Throws and Suplexes cost three combat actions. Clinches cost the defender all of their combat actions for that round.

# HAND-TO-HAND DAMAGE

Hand-to-hand damage is handled differently than normal firearm Lethal HEA damage. A character's STR will determine the amount of damage that a character can cause to another. All damage that is done in hand-to-hand combat, except for edged weapons, is considered to be Concessive HEA damage. All Concessive HEA damage is normally only temporary damage. Characters that are reduced to zero Concussive HEA in this fashion are unconscious. After a character recovers from their unconsciousness, their Concussive HEA will be restored fully (See Unconsciousness). For each 15 points of Concussive HEA damage a character suffers, they will also lose 1 point from their Lethal HEA. This type of Lethal HEA damage will not be healed when the Concussive HEA damage is healed. The Lethal HEA damage acquired in this fashion is healed as normal (See Healing).

A person will kill another opponent in hand-to-hand combat when the loser's Concussive HEA is reduced to half of their normal Concussive HEA in negatives, the character dies. Characters with STR of 1 to 5 causes D4 points damage; STR of 6 to 10 causes D6 Concussive HEA points damage; STR of 11 to 15 causes D8 Concussive HEA points damage; STR of 16 to 20 causes D10 Concussive HEA points damage; and STR of 21 or more cause D12 Concussive HEA points damage. All melee weapons cause concessive damage in the same fashion as hand-to-hand combat attacks. A billy club causes STR damage plus D4 Concussive HEA points of damage; A fire axe cause D6 Lethal HEA points of damage; Knives cause D4 Lethal HEA points of damage; fire axe handle or baseball bat cause D8 Concussive HEA points of damage and Swords cause D10 Lethal HEA points of damage.

### Hand Strike

| Hand Strike | Block H | Block M | Block L | Up Parry | Down Sweep | Sweep | Escape | Reverse | Duck | Leap | Roll | Clinch | None |
|---|---|---|---|---|---|---|---|---|---|---|---|---|---|
| Chest | A | - | A | - | A | A | A | A | - | A | - | - | A |
| Groin | C | C | - | C | C | - | C | C | D | - | A | - | C |
| Head | - | B | B | B | - | B | B | B | - | C | - | - | B |
| Solar Plexus | A | - | A | - | A | A | A | A | A | A | A | - | A |
| Throat | - | C | C | - | - | C | C | C | - | D | - | - | C |

### Elbow Strike

| Elbow Strike | Block H | Block M | Block L | Up Parry | Down Sweep | Sweep | Escape | Reverse | Duck | Leap | Roll | Clinch | None |
|---|---|---|---|---|---|---|---|---|---|---|---|---|---|
| Chest | B | - | B | B | B | B | B | B | B | B | - | - | B |
| Groin | C | C | - | C | C | - | C | C | D | - | B | - | C |
| Head | - | B | B | B | - | B | B | B | - | C | - | - | B |
| Solar Plexus | B | - | B | - | B | B | B | B | B | B | B | - | B |
| Throat | - | C | C | - | - | C | C | C | - | C | - | - | C |

### Knee Strike

| Knee Strike | Block H | Block M | Block L | Up Parry | Down Sweep | Sweep | Escape | Reverse | Duck | Leap | Roll | Clinch | None |
|---|---|---|---|---|---|---|---|---|---|---|---|---|---|
| Chest | B | - | B | B | - | B | B | B | B | - | - | - | B |
| Groin | C | C | - | C | C | - | C | C | C | - | C | - | C |
| Head | - | B | B | B | - | B | B | B | - | B | - | - | B |
| Solar Plexus | B | - | B | - | - | B | B | B | B | - | B | - | B |
| Throat | - | C | C | - | - | C | C | C | - | C | - | - | C |

### Foot Strike

| Foot Strike | Block H | Block M | Block L | Up Parry | Down Sweep | Sweep | Escape | Reverse | Duck | Leap | Roll | Clinch | None |
|---|---|---|---|---|---|---|---|---|---|---|---|---|---|
| Chest | B | - | B | B | - | B | B | B | B | - | - | - | B |
| Groin | D | D | - | D | D | - | D | D | D | - | C | - | D |
| Head | - | B | B | B | - | B | B | B | - | B | - | - | B |
| Knee | F | F | - | F | F | - | F | F | F | - | - | - | F |
| Solar Plexus | B | - | B | B | - | B | B | B | B | - | B | - | B |
| Throat | - | C | C | - | - | C | C | C | - | C | - | - | C |

### Edged - Stab

| Edged - Stab | Block H | Block M | Block L | Up Parry | Down Sweep | Sweep | Escape | Reverse | Duck | Leap | Roll | Clinch | None |
|---|---|---|---|---|---|---|---|---|---|---|---|---|---|
| Arm | A | - | A | - | A | A | A | A | - | A | - | - | A |
| Chest | B | - | B | - | B | B | B | B | - | B | - | B | B |
| Neck | - | B | B | - | - | B | B | B | - | B | - | - | B |
| Head | - | C | C | - | - | C | C | C | - | C | - | - | C |
| Solar Plexus | D | - | D | - | D | D | D | D | - | D | - | D | D |
| Leg | A | A | - | A | A | - | A | A | A | - | A | - | A |

### Edged - Cut

| Edged - Cut | Block H | Block M | Block L | Up Parry | Down Sweep | Sweep | Escape | Reverse | Duck | Leap | Roll | Clinch | None |
|---|---|---|---|---|---|---|---|---|---|---|---|---|---|
| Arm | A | - | A | - | A | A | A | A | - | A | - | - | A |
| Chest | A | - | A | - | A | A | A | A | - | A | - | - | A |
| Head | - | B | B | - | - | B | B | B | - | B | - | - | B |
| Leg | A | A | - | A | A | - | A | A | A | - | - | - | A |
| Neck | - | C | C | - | - | C | C | C | - | C | C | - | C |

### Blunt Object

| Blunt Object | Block H | Block M | Block L | Up Parry | Down Sweep | Sweep | Escape | Reverse | Duck | Leap | Roll | Clinch | None |
|---|---|---|---|---|---|---|---|---|---|---|---|---|---|
| Chest | B | - | B | B | - | B | B | B | B | - | - | - | B |
| Groin | C | C | - | C | C | - | C | C | C | - | D | - | C |
| Head | - | A | A | A | - | A | A | A | - | A | - | - | A |
| Leg | A | A | - | - | A | - | A | A | A | - | A | - | A |
| Solar Plexus | B | - | B | - | - | B | B | B | B | - | - | - | B |
| Throat | - | C | C | - | - | C | C | C | - | C | - | - | C |

| Special Actions | H | M | L | Up Parry | Down Sweep | Sweep | Escape | Reverse | Duck | Leap | Roll | Clinch | None |
|---|---|---|---|---|---|---|---|---|---|---|---|---|---|
| Arm Lock | - | E | E | - | E | E | - | H | E | - | E | - | E |
| Arm Throw | - | F | F | - | F | F | - | H | F | - | - | - | F |
| Bear Hug | B | - | B | - | A | - | - | H | - | A | - | B | B |
| Body Slam | - | G | - | G | - | - | - | G | - | G | - | G | G |
| Chokehold | - | B | B | - | - | B | - | H | - | B | B | - | B |
| DDT | F | - | F | F | F | - | - | H | F | - | - | F | F |
| Guillotine | G | G | G | G | G | G | - | H | G | - | G | - | G |
| Headbutt | - | A | A | A | - | A | - | H | A | - | A | - | A |
| Headlock | - | A | A | A | - | A | - | H | - | A | - | - | G |
| Hip Throw | G | - | G | - | G | - | - | H | G | - | - | - | G |
| Leg Lock | E | E | - | E | E | - | - | H | E | - | E | - | E |
| Leg Sweep | F | F | - | F | F | - | - | H | F | - | - | - | G |
| Rolling Throw | G | G | G | - | G | - | - | H | G | - | - | - | G |
| Shoulder Lock | - | E | E | - | - | E | - | H | - | E | E | - | G |
| Suplex | G | - | G | - | G | G | - | H | G | G | - | G | G |
| Tackle | G | - | G | - | G | G | - | H | - | G | - | G | E |
| Wrist Lock | - | E | E | - | - | E | - | H | - | E | E | - | E |

The following chart lists the results and reactions to the effects of hand-to-hand combat.

**-:** No effect

**A:** This result is a Glancing Blow that does -3 Concussive or Lethal HEA points to STR or weapon damage. Any damage roll that causes the result to be zero or less is considered to have no effect.

**B:** This result is a Light Blow that does -1 Concussive or Lethal HEA points to STR or weapon damage and the target moves ½' back. Any damage roll that causes the result to be zero or less is considered to have no effect.

**C:** This result is a Moderate Blow that does Concussive or Lethal points to STR or weapon damage and the target moves 1' back.

**D:** This result is a Severe Blow that does +2 Concussive or Lethal HEA points to STR or weapon damage and the target moves 2' back.

**E:** This result is a Joint lock that does +1 Concussive or Lethal HEA points to STR or weapon damage. The defending character loses an action, defender's choice. At the end of their lost action, the character can recover from the attack and fight normally.

**F:** This result is a Partial takedown that does +2 Concussive or Lethal HEA points to STR or weapon damage. The defending character loses two actions, defender's choice. At the end of their lost actions, the character can recover from the attack and fight normally.

**G:** This result is a Full takedown that does +3 Concussive or Lethal HEA points to STR or weapon damage. The defending character loses three actions, defender's choice. At the end of their lost actions, the character can recover from the attack and fight normally.

**H:** This result is a Full Reversal. The attacker is on the receiving end of the attack and receives the damage from it.

# DEFINITION OF HAND-TO-HAND MANEUVERS

**Arm Lock:** This maneuver is when a character traps another person's arm in a joint lock. This action includes any type of specialized arm lock including the Arm Bar or Grapevine.

**Arm Throw:** With this type of throw, the attacker holds the opponent by the arm and tosses them on to their back by use of speed and momentum to throw the opponent. This action includes any type of specialized arm throw including the Arm Drag.

**Bear Hug:** With this maneuver, the character grapples the opponent trapping each of their arms by their side and squeezing to cause damage.

**Block:** A character will stop an attack by using whatever body part or object to stop it. An H block is a high block, an M block is a middle block, and L block is a low block.

**Blunt Object:** This action is defined as any attack with a blunt item or object. This may include any

type of stick, billy club, pole, 2" by 4" piece of wood, hammer, or mace.

**Body Slam:** This action is where the character picks up the opponent over their head and slams them down to the ground on their back. This action also includes any type of specialized body slam including the Power Bomb or Power Slam.

**Chokehold:** With this type of maneuver, the character tries to subdue an opponent by cutting off the target's air supply to the brain. This action includes any type of chokehold where the character is trying to use their arm or leg (or with the aid of an item) to choke the other person. This action includes any type of specialized chokehold including the Sleeper or Cobra Clutch.

**Clinch:** A very common boxing maneuver where one opponent grabs another, preventing either to attack. Even though this maneuver costs the attacker all of their actions, the defender can attack as normal.

**DDT:** This maneuver is when the opponent is caught with a reversed headlock and then the opponent's face is slammed into the ground. This action includes any type of specialized DDT including the inverted DDT, Bulldog, Pile Driver, and Neck Breaker

**Downsweep:** This action is when a character parries an attack downward. This maneuver can only be performed if the character has a weapon in their hand.

**Duck:** A character will avoid an attack by ducking below the source of the attack.

**Edged Object: Cut and Stab:** This action is defined as any type of attack with an edged weapon including a knife, shank, broken bottle, sword, and to an extreme, an ax.

**Elbow Strike:** This action includes any type of attack with the elbow. This action includes any type of specialized action including the Crossface and the European Uppercut.

**Escape:** A character will avoid an attack by escaping the attack. This maneuver is mostly used when one character has caught another in a lock or hold.

**Foot Strike:** This action is defined as any type of kick. This action does include any type of specialized kicks including a crescent kick, an ax kick, a round-house kick, or even a stomp.

**Guillotine:** The Guillotine is one of the most complex hand-to-hand combat maneuvers. The Guillotine maneuver is defined as a combination of an arm lock, headlock, and leg lock.

**Hand Strike:** This action is defined as any type of punch. This action includes specialized punches such as the ridge hand, karate chop, and even an old fashion thumb in the eye.

**Headbutt:** This action is defined as any type of slam of one's head in to another person.

**Headlock:** This maneuver is when a character traps another person's head in their arms or legs and squeezes like a vise. This action includes any type of specialized headlock including the Half Nelson or the Full Nelson.

**Hip Throw:** With this type of throw, the attacker holds the opponent around the waist and tosses them on to their back by use of speed and momentum to throw the opponent. This action includes any type of specialized hip throw including the Hip Toss.

**Knee Strike:** This action is defined as any type of attack with a knee.

**Leg Lock:** This maneuver is when a character traps another person's leg in a joint lock. This action includes any type of specialized leg lock including the Figure-Four Leg Lock, the Boston Crab, and the Texas Clover Leaf.

**Leap:** A character will avoid an attack by leaping above the attack.

**Leg Sweep:** With this action, the character will sweep, or take down, an opponent by tripping their legs from under them.

**Parry:** This maneuver can only be performed if the character has a weapon in their hand. This action is when a character blocks an attack by moving it to either side with the use of a weapon.

**Reverse:** A character will stop an attack by reversing the attack back on the attacker.

**Roll:** A character will avoid an attack by rolling out of the way.

**Rolling Throw:** With this type of throw, the attacker holds the opponent by the upper body as they roll on their back giving them enough speed and momentum to throw the opponent.

**Shoulder Lock:** This maneuver is when a character traps another person's shoulder in a joint lock. This action includes any type of specialized shoulder lock including the Chicken Wing.

**Suplex:** A suplex can be described as a combination of a bear hug then a hip throw. This action includes any type of specialized suplex including the Belly-to-Belly Suplex, German Suplex, and the Northern Lights Suplex.

**Upsweep:** This action is when a character parries an attack upward. This maneuver can only be performed if the character has a weapon in their hand.

# ITEM POSSESSION IN COMBAT

Item possession in combat will take place when two opponents are struggling over an item, whether it is a weapon or other such item. Characters must be within 5' of each other to initiate this type of combat. Either opponent can initiate this type of combat. Once the two opponents engage, they will compare their strengths with each other's and will roll against the specific number needed to succeed.

# THROWN WEAPONS

Often it is necessary for individuals to use weapons including throwing knives, shuriken, and throwing spikes. These types of weapons are usually thrown to be effective. When throwing a weapon, a character will use their ACC to determine if they are able to hit their target. All thrown weapons, like firearms, use modifiers to hit. But, their MV determines the

distance of these types of weapons. Use the grenade toss distance (see Movement Value Chart) for the maximum distance that these objects can be thrown. Damage for these weapons is worked out exactly the same as firearm damage.

| Range | Modifiers |
|---|---|
| Point Blank | Easy (-2) |
| Short | Average (-5) |
| Medium | Extreme (-14) |
| Long | Not Possible |

Since these types of weapons are smaller, they can be used at a faster rate than other larger weapons. A character can throw a throwing knife or shuriken equal to his AGI divided by seven per round, rounded down. A character with an AGI of 16 could throw up to two of these weapons per round.

# EXAMPLE OF HAND-TO-HAND COMBAT

The following is a typical example of hand-to-hand combat in the Haven: City of Violence-The Action Adventure Role-Playing Game.

| | Ace | Billy |
|---|---|---|
| STR | 19 | 16 |
| WILL | 18 | 20 |
| AGI | 12 | 14 |
| STA | 16 | 18 |
| INT | 12 | 13 |
| PER | 19 | 23 |
| | | |
| INFL | 19 | 22 |
| MV | 18 | 17 |
| ACC | 16 | 19 |
| FV | 16 | 15 |
| SUB | 16 | 18 |
| CM | 13 | 14 |
| HEA-C | 53 | 54 |
| HEA-L | 18 | 18 |

Ace, the local neighborhood leg breaker, is at the local bar doing his best to find the next notch on his bedpost. Billy, a noted woman beater and rapist, also happens to be in the same bar as Ace. Ace looks over to Billy's position and remembers that Billy has not made his weekly payment of $500 to the Carlucci Family. Ace decides to walk over to Billy and remind him what happens when you don't pay on time. Ace moves in, with Billy unaware that he is coming. Billy, with a drink in each hand and dancing around, finally sees Ace. Totally surprised, Bill drops his drinks and throws a punch to Ace's head.

## 1ST ROUND

Billy decides that it is best if he attacks twice and defends himself once. Billy is looking to take Ace out of action as quickly as possible. Ace knows that Billy is a lot more muscle than brains and decides to bring the fight to Billy. Ace chooses to take an equally offensive position and chooses to make two offensive and two defensive actions.

Both men compare their PER and discover Billy's PER is higher. This makes it possible for Billy to choose to attack first, which he does. Billy decides his offensive actions will be a hand strike to the head and an elbow strike to the chest, with Billy's defensive action consisting of a block to the middle. Ace concludes that his offensive actions will be a knee strike to Billy's solar plexus and a hand strike to the head. Ace's defensive actions will contain a duck and a block to the middle.

Billy attacks first with the hand strike to the head and Ace defends with a Duck. The result of the hand-to-hand combat is no effect, due to the fact that Ace ducked underneath the attack. Ace attacks with a knee strike to Billy's solar plexus, which Billy blocks with a block to the middle. Billy, then moves in with an elbow strike to Ace's chest, which is negated with Ace's block to the middle. With Ace's last attack coming Billy is most likely going to take some damage this round. Ace uses his last action with a good old-fashioned hand strike to Billy's head, and Billy with no defensive actions, takes the hit to the head.

The result is B, Light Blow, in the HTH Combat Chart, which does normal damage of D10-1 Concussive HEA pints. Ace rolls a 5 minus 1 and does a total of 4 Concussive HEA points of damage. Billy's Concussive HEA is reduced to 50.

## 2ND ROUND

Billy takes the punch like a veteran and barely shows any expression to the blow, except for a sinister smile. Billy, still with the higher PER, attacks first and decides to perform the actions of foot strike to Ace's knee and head and finishing his actions with a high block. Ace, feeling a little cocky after his success in the previous round, decides to get Billy under control by using a wrist lock and use two leap actions.

Billy moves in first with a foot strike against Ace's knee, which Ace easily leaps over. Ace attacks with an attempted wrist lock that is blocked by Billy's high block. Billy continues on with a follow up of a foot strike to Ace's head.

With this attack Billy's attack connects with Ace, due to his leap defense. The result is B, Light Blow, in the HTH Combat Chart, which does normal damage of D10 minus 1 Concussive HEA points. Billy rolls a 8 minus 1 and does a total of 7 Concussive HEA points of damage to Ace reducing his Concussive HEA to 46.

## 3RD ROUND

Billy grins like the proverbial cat that swallowed the canary, due to his success against Ace. Ace's face switches from an easy going state to one of focused control. Billy decides that Ace will want a little revenge, so it is now or never with his attacks. Bill decides to go all out with this attack with a foot strike to the groin, elbow strike to Ace's nose and finally defending with a low block. Ace's anger barely registers on his face. Ace chooses to get some payback against Billy. Ace attacks with a hand strike to the solar plexus and groin, in addition to his defensive actions of a low block and duck.

Billy continues his onslaught with a foot to the groin, which is blocked by Ace's low block. Smelling

blood, Ace moves in with a hand strike to Billy's solar plexus, which connects, avoiding Billy's low block. The result is A, Glancing Blow, in the HTH Combat Chart, which does normal damage of D10-3 Concussive HEA points. Ace rolls a 8 minus 3 and does a total of 5 Concussive HEA points of damage to Billy, reducing his Concussive HEA to 45.

Billy moves on to his elbow strike that misses Ace, due to him ducking. Ace follows up with a good old-fashioned hand strike to the groin that connects with no defense by Billy. The result is C, Moderate Blow, in the HTH Combat Chart which does normal damage of D10 Concussive HEA points and Ace rolls doing 6 Concussive HEA point of damage. Billy's Concussive HEA is reduced to 39 and is moved back 1'.

## 4TH ROUND

Billy decides this might be the right time to raise the action up a notch and decides to attack with an arm lock and defend with a high block. Ace is looking to go all out so he attacks with a foot strike to the head, solar plexus, and knee and defends with a duck.

Ace's duck fails to defend against Billy' arm lock. The result is E, Joint Lock, on the HTH Combat Chart. It does normal damage of D10+1 Concussive HEA points and Ace loses one action this round. Billy rolls a 6 plus an additional 1 for a total of 7 Concussive HEA points. Ace's Concussive HEA is reduced to 39. Due to the arm lock, Ace is forced to lose one of his actions, which he decides to lose the action of the foot to the solar plexus.

Ace attacks with the foot strike to the head, which is blocked by Billy's high block. Ace's final attack is a foot strike to Billy's knee, to which Billy has no defense. The result is an F, Partial Takedown, in the HTH Combat Chart, that does normal damage of D10+2 Concussive HEA points and Billy loses two actions. Ace rolls a 7 plus an additional 2 for a total of 9 Concussive HEA points. Billy's Concussive HEA is reduced to 30. Billy will lose two actions from next round due to the foot strike to the knee.

## 5TH ROUND

Both men are battered and bruised from each other's attacks. After the highly successful round by Ace, Billy has lost two actions from this round leaving him with one action. Billy, still with the higher PER, goes first and decides to be very careful and chooses to leap. Ace being a little more confident, decides to attack with a hip throw and then continue on to a hand strike to Billy's head.

Billy would normally attack first but since he has no offensive action, he defers first attack to Ace. Ace starts off his attack by going with the hip throw. Billy easily negates the attack with his leap. Now out of actions, Billy is at Ace's mercy with his next attack. Ace attacks with a hand strike that easily hits Billy with no defensive actions.

The result is B, Light Blow, in the HTH Combat Chart, which does normal damage of D10-1 Concussive HEA points. Ace rolls a 4 minus 1 and does a total of 3 Concussive HEA points of damage. Billy's Concussive HEA is reduced to 27.

## 6TH ROUND

Billy is in very bad shape. Ace is proving to be almost too much for him. Billy decides to go all out this round and put it all on the line. Billy, with the higher PER, goes first in this round of combat. He's going to attack with two foot strikes to the knee and a foot strike to Ace's head. Ace, sensing that Billy is on the "ropes", moves in to finish him off. Ace chooses to attack with a hand strike to the groin, two foot strikes to the groin, and one low block.

Billy starts off with one of his foot strikes to Ace's knee, which is blocked by Ace's low block. Ace then attacks with a foot strike to Billy's groin. Since Billy has no defensive action he must take the blow from this attack. The result is D, Severe Blow, in the HTH Combat Chart, which does normal damage of D10+2 Concussive HEA points. Ace rolls a 9 plus 2 points and does a total of 11 Concussive HEA points of damage. Billy's Concussive HEA is reduced to 16.

Billy, suffering horribly from that attack, comes back with a foot strike to Ace's knee. Like Billy, Ace is out of defensive actions and must take this blow. The result is F, Partial Takedown, in the HTH Combat Chart, that does normal damage of D10+2 Concussive HEA points and Ace loses two actions. Bill rolls a 5 plus an additional 2 for a total of 7 Concussive HEA points. Ace's Concussive HEA is reduced to 32. Ace loses his remaining two actions for this round due to the Billy's foot strike.

Billy continues on with a foot strike to Ace's head that easily connects. The result is B, Light Blow, in the HTH Combat Chart, which does normal damage of D10-1 Concussive HEA points. Ace rolls a 10 minus 1 and does a total of 9 Concussive HEA points of damage. Ace's Concussive HEA is reduced to 21.

## 7TH ROUND

At this point both of the combatants appear to be almost dead on their feet. Billy, with the higher PER, goes first in this round of combat. Billy wants to put Ace right out of the picture and attacks with an all out onslaught of a Rolling Throw. Ace knows that he cannot take much more of this type of punishment and plans to but Bill out of his misery. Ace decides on the offensive strategy of a DDT, foot strike to the knee and defensive leap.

Billy attacks first and is countered by Ace's defensive leap. Now at Ace's mercy Billy hopes it will all be over quick. Ace's first attack is with the DDT and Billy has no defense so it hits home. The result is F, Partial Takedown, in the HTH Combat Chart, which does normal damage of D10+2 Concussive HEA points and Billy loses two actions. Ace rolls a 6 plus an additional 2 and does a total of 8 Concussive HEA points of damage. Billy's Concussive HEA is reduced to 8.

Ace continues on with a foot strike to the knee, again Billy has no defense. The result is F, Partial Takedown, in the HTH Combat Chart, that does normal damage of D10+2 Concussive HEA points and Billy loses two actions. Ace rolls a 10 plus an additional 2 for a total of 12 Concussive HEA points. Billy Concussive HEA is reduced to –4 and he is knocked out.

Now that Billy is knocked out he is at Ace's tender mercies…

# DRIVING & VEHICLES

Driving is the most common way that people travel to other locations and places. The accuracy and ability of the characters driving is determined by the AGI minus any type of modifiers. Characters need not make AGI rolls when driving in normal and common road conditions. If the character encounters uncommon or hazardous road conditions it will be necessary to make an AGI roll to maintain control. The following chart consists of some of the more common and some extreme traveling obstacles that may occur when driving. A character must make an AGI roll every 10 rounds the character is under those types of driving conditions. Light Rain and Night Driving have an Easy (-2) modifier to driving. Flat Tires, Heavy Rain and Visual Deterrents have an Average (-5) modifier to driving. Burning Objects, Collision-Sized Objects, Flaming Oil Slicks and Oil Slicks have a Hard (-9) modifier to driving. Anti-Tire Devices and Smoke Screens have an Extreme (-14) modifier to driving. If more than one driving deterrent is present, the modifiers will be added together.

The chart contains the most common vehicles that can be found in Haven: COV RPG. The chart list the generic information of the vehicles:

**Type:** Whether the vehicle is land or sea based.

**Top Speed:** This is the maximum speed, in miles per hour, the vehicle can attain under normal situations.

**Range:** This is the maximum range, in miles, that the vehicle can attain under normal situations.

**Reliability:** This is the vehicle's ability to function at normal and beyond normal conditions.

**Turning:** This is the vehicle's ability to stay in control when turning.

**Cost:** This is the price in dollars for the vehicle.

**Body:** This in the Armor Value (AV) of the vehicle's body.

**Engine:** This in the Armor Value (AV) of the vehicle's engine.

**Tire:** This in the Armor Value (AV) of the vehicle's tire.

**Window:** This in the Armor Value (AV) of the vehicle's Window.

**Acceleration:** This is the vehicle's rate of acceleration.

## ACURA LEGEND

| Type | Top Speed | Range | Reliability | Turning | Cost |
|---|---|---|---|---|---|
| Land | 120 mph | 330 mi | 12 | 12 | $20,000 |

| Body | Engine | Tire | Window | Accel | Brake |
|---|---|---|---|---|---|
| 11 | 11 | 4 | 1 | 12 | 12 |

## BMW 528E

| Type | Top Speed | Range | Reliability | Turning | Cost |
|---|---|---|---|---|---|
| Land | 110 mph | 300 mi. | 12 | 12 | $28,000 |

| Body | Engine | Tire | Window | Accel | Brake |
|---|---|---|---|---|---|
| 11 | 11 | 4 | 2 | 13 | 15 |

## CHEVROLET CORVETTE

| Type | Top Speed | Range | Reliability | Turning | Cost |
|---|---|---|---|---|---|
| Land | 155 mph | 275 mi. | 12 | 12 | $27,500 |

| Body | Engine | Tire | Window | Accel | Brake |
|---|---|---|---|---|---|
| 10 | 12 | 4 | 2 | 15 | 15 |

## FERRARI MONDIAL

| Type | Top Speed | Range | Reliability | Turning | Cost |
|---|---|---|---|---|---|
| Land | 145 mph | 210 mi. | 12 | 12 | $40,000 |

| Body | Engine | Tire | Window | Accel | Brake |
|---|---|---|---|---|---|
| 9 | 12 | 4 | 2 | 18 | 14 |

## HARLEY DAVIDSON FXR SUPER GLIDE

| Type | Top Speed | Range | Reliability | Turning | Cost |
|---|---|---|---|---|---|
| Land | 105 mph | 525 | 12 | 12 | $10,000 |

| Body | Engine | Tire | Window | Accel | Brake |
|---|---|---|---|---|---|
| 8 | 10 | 4 | - | 17 | 12 |

**Brake:** This is the vehicle's ability to stay in control when braking.

## TURNING

All vehicles will normally travel in a straight line towards their goal. Any type of change in a vehicle's

### KAWASAKI ZX1000R NINJA

| Type | Top Speed | Range | Reliability | Turning | Cost |
|---|---|---|---|---|---|
| Land | 135 mph | 350 mi. | 12 | 12 | $8,000 |

| Body | Engine | Tire | Window | Accel | Brake |
|---|---|---|---|---|---|
| 8 | 10 | 3 | - | 17 | 16 |

### MAZDA RX-7

| Type | Top Speed | Range | Reliability | Turning | Cost |
|---|---|---|---|---|---|
| Land | 140 mph | 320 mi. | 12 | 12 | $21,000 |

| Body | Engine | Tire | Window | Accel | Brake |
|---|---|---|---|---|---|
| 11 | 11 | 4 | 2 | 14 | 11 |

### PONTIAC FIREBIRD TRANS AM

| Type | Top Speed | Range | Reliability | Turning | Cost |
|---|---|---|---|---|---|
| Land | 130 mph | 250 mi. | 12 | 12 | $19,000 |

| Body | Engine | Tire | Window | Accel | Brake |
|---|---|---|---|---|---|
| 9 | 10 | 5 | 1 | 13 | 16 |

### PORSCHE 911 TURBO

| Type | Top Speed | Range | Reliability | Turning | Cost |
|---|---|---|---|---|---|
| Land | 150 mph | 260 mi. | 12 | 12 | $35,000 |

| Body | Engine | Tire | Window | Accel | Brake |
|---|---|---|---|---|---|
| 10 | 11 | 5 | 2 | 15 | 15 |

### SUZUKI GSX-R 1100

| Type | Top Speed | Range | Reliability | Turning | Cost |
|---|---|---|---|---|---|
| Land | 140 mph | 300 mi. | 12 | 12 | $7,500 |

| Body | Engine | Tire | Window | Accel | Brake |
|---|---|---|---|---|---|
| 8 | 10 | 5 | - | 17 | 14 |

direction is made in 45-degree increments. A vehicle at its top speed can make only one turn up to 45-degrees during its move. This turn may be to the right or left and must be made at the beginning of the round. A vehicle traveling up to 25% of its top speed may make up to two turns per round. Each turn may be up to 45-degrees. The two turns may be combined into a single turn of 90-degrees, if that is necessary. A vehicle travelling up to 10% of its top speed may make up to any amount of turns. Each and any of these turns can be up to 360 degrees. For anything beyond the normal 45 degree turn at top speed, or pushing the normal limits of what the rules states while turning, roll a (Hard) -9 modifier against whatever the turning number of the car is, otherwise, roll on the out of control chart.

## ACCELERATING AND BREAKING

The two simplest driving maneuvers possible just place your foot on the accelerator or place it on the brake and that is it. In gaming terms, vehicles with higher acceleration are able to move quickly away from their targets, while those with lower acceleration numbers are not able to move as fast. When braking, a vehicle with a high number will stop sooner than those with lower numbers. A vehicle with an Acceleration of 1 to 7 can accelerate 10 feet. A vehicle with an Acceleration of 8 to 15 can accelerate 20 feet. A vehicle with an Acceleration of 16 to 20 can accelerate 35 feet. A vehicle with an Acceleration of 21 or higher can accelerate 50 feet. A vehicle with a Brake of 1 to 7 will take 100 feet to stop. A vehicle with a Brake of 8 to 15 will take 75 feet to stop. A vehicle with a Brake of 16 to 20 will take 50 feet to stop. A vehicle with a Brake of 21 or higher will take 35 feet to stop.

## DRIVING ACTIONS AND COMBAT

As with hand-to-hand combat, vehicle drivers possess a certain number of actions that can be performed in a round. A character's AGI will determine the amount of driving actions that they are able to perform in a round during a driving combat exchange. Characters that are extremely talented and skilled drivers with a high AGI are able to perform more than a single action per round. Characters with an AGI of 1 to 5 can perform one driving action. Characters with an AGI of 6 to 10 can perform two driving actions. Characters with an AGI of 11 to 15 can perform three driving actions. Characters with an AGI of 16 to 20 can perform four driving actions. Characters with an AGI of 21 or higher can perform five driving actions.

## RELIABILITY AND DRIVING ACTIONS

In addiction to driving actions derived from a characters AGI, a vehicles reliability allows the driver to coax more actions out of it.  The higher the vehicles reliability score, the more maneuvers the driver can get the vehicle to perform. Vehicles with a Reliability of 1 to 5 can perform one extra driving action. Vehicles with a Reliability of 6 to 10 can perform two extra driving actions. Vehicles with a Reliability of 11 to 15 can perform three extra driving actions. Vehicles with an AGI of 16 to 20 can perform four extra driving actions. Vehicles with a Reliability of 21 or higher can perform five extra driving actions.

## DRIVING MANEUVER COST

Basic driving maneuvers are quite easy to perform with little cost in actions. While more complex drive actions will cost more driving actions. Dodge, Hard Accelerate, Left or Right Turn and Quick Lane Shift cost one driving action. Bumping, Cutting Off and Hard Brake cost two driving actions.

The chart lists the results and reactions to the effects of driving:

**A:** Light bumping. AGI suffers an Average (-5) modifier for this round

**B:** Severe collision. AGI suffers an Extreme (-14) modifier for this round and the next round.

**C:** The vehicle moves past the other as many feet per round as equal to their Accel rating -10.

| MANUEVERS | A | Bu | CO | D | HA | HBr | LT | QLS | RT |
|---|---|---|---|---|---|---|---|---|---|
| Accelerate (A) | - | A | B | - | C | D | - | - | - |
| Bumping (Bu) | A | - | A | A | - | A | A | A | A |
| Cutting Off (CO) | B | A | - | - | B | A | B | B | B |
| Dodge (D) | - | A | - | - | - | - | - | - | - |
| Hard Accelerate (HA) | C | - | B | - | - | D | - | - | - |
| Hard Brake (HBr) | D | A | A | - | D | - | - | - | - |
| Left Turn (LT) | - | A | B | - | - | - | - | - | B |
| Quick Lane Shift (QLS) | - | A | B | - | - | - | - | - | - |
| Right Turn (RT) | - | A | B | - | - | - | B | - | - |

**D:** The vehicle flies past the other as many feet per round as equal to their Accel rating +20.

# DEFINITION OF DRIVING MANEUVERS

**Accelerate:** Just like the name states, the vehicle is trying to accelerate from the situation they are in. This is the simplest of all driving maneuvers.

**Bumping:** The technique of bumping is when one vehicle tries to force another vehicle off the road or out of control by hitting the side or rear of the vehicle. A vehicle may attempt to make a bump at any speed. All vehicles when involved with bumping must make an AGI roll to keep their vehicle under control. The driver who is bumping will make a normal AGI roll, while the person being bumped must make at AGI roll at an Average (-5) modifier. If both vehicles are trying to bump each other at the same time; each vehicle will suffer a Hard (−9)

modifier to their AGI roll. A vehicle can only bump another vehicle once per two rounds.

**Cutting Off:** A vehicle is attempting to "cut another vehicle off" by turning in front of it. This specific vehicle maneuver can normally be performed at any speed. The vehicle attempting the cut off must make an AGI roll to perform it. If the vehicle attempting the cut off fails their roll, the second vehicle is not cut off. If the vehicle attempting the cut off passes their roll, the second vehicle must then make an AGI roll at an Average (-5) modifier. If the second vehicle passes its roll, then they have not lost control of the vehicle. If the second vehicle fails their roll, then the driver has lost control of the vehicle (see Out of Control).

**Dodge:** This maneuver allows a driver to miss objects such as bullets, explosives and other such deadly objects and devices. This driving maneuver can be very dangerous not just for the most common reason but it is very common for the vehicle to go out of control. All person wishing to perform this driving maneuver must make an AGI roll with an Average (-5) modifier, then increasing by –1 for every dodge attempt thereafter. If a player fails their roll the vehicle is considered to be out of control (See Out of Control).

**Hard Accelerate:** Just like the name states, the vehicle is trying to accelerate as fast as possible. People with fast vehicles will normally find this technique quite impressive to run away from any type of pursuer. All persons wishing to perform this driving maneuver must make an AGI roll with an Easy (-2) modifier. If a player fails their roll the vehicle is considered to be out of control (See Out of Control).

**Hard Brake:** Just like the name states, the vehicle is trying to stop as quickly as humanly possible. Many times, vehicles trying this driving technique will lock up their brakes causing them to skid uncontrollably. All person wishing to perform this driving maneuver must make add an Average (-5) modifier to an AGI roll. If a player fails their roll the vehicle is considered to be out of control (See Out of Control).

**Left or Right Turn:** Just as the name implies, the driver of this vehicle is making a left or right turn. All persons wishing to perform this driving maneuver must make add an Easy (-2) modifier to an AGI roll. If a player fails their roll the vehicle is considered to be out of control (See Out of Control).

**Quick Lane Shift:** Just like the name states, the vehicle is trying to switch lanes at a high rate of speed. While it is not a very difficult driving technique it can be quite deadly if done incorrectly. All drivers wishing to perform this maneuver must make add an Easy (-2) modifier to an AGI roll. If a player fails their roll the vehicle is considered to be out of control (See Out of Control).

# SPECIAL VEHICLE DRIVING MANEUVERS

Most vehicles are created with one purpose in mind, to get you from one place to another. But some people always want to push the limits of their vehicle's capability and durability. The following are a list of some of the most common vehicle driving maneuvers that can be attempted or tried. Since this list is not complete, Players may create their own vehicle driving maneuvers, with G.O.D.'s approval.

## DOWNSHIFT

In this driving maneuver, a PC is attempting to shift a vehicle into a lower gear, reducing their braking distance. To attempt this maneuver, the PC must make an AGI with an Average (-5) modifier. If the PC succeeds, they will reduce their braking distance in half. If a PC fails their AGI, the vehicle is considered to be Out of Control (See Out of Control).

## RIDING ON ONE OR TWO WHEELS

In some cases it will be necessary for a driver of a vehicle to make their car or truck to ride on two wheels, or their motorcycle to ride on one wheel. This is very useful when trying to place a very large vehicle in to slightly smaller spaces. In gaming terms, all drivers wishing to perform this stunt must make an AGI roll with an Extreme (-14) modifier.

# CALLED SHOTS ON VEHICLES

Often there are times that a character will need to shoot at a particular location on a vehicle to stop the vehicle or injure the driver or passengers. The target of the shot could be anything from a wheel to the gas tank. Anyone attempting to shoot at the engine, propeller, windows, windshield and wing will suffer an Average (-5) modifier; tires will suffer an Hard (-9) modifier; and the rotor will suffer an Extreme (-14) modifier.

# BULLETS VERSUS VEHICLES

The most often employed way to stop a vehicle is the use of firearms. Characters will use the normal ACC modifiers to hit the vehicles. Unless stated by the character, all attacks on a vehicle will be considered to be attacks against the vehicle's Body. If the vehicle is hit, the firearm must be able to pierce the armor value of the vehicle. A character will roll using the firearm's armor penetration value to determine success. If the roll fails the firearm has not penetrated the armor value of the vehicle. If the roll succeeds, the character must roll off of the Out of Control chart listed below for the result of the shot.

## RAMMING

Ramming is defined as forcing a vehicle into another at an abnormally high rate of speed to cause damage. To ram another vehicle, the vehicle's driver must make an AGI roll. The following chart contains the ramming information that can be found in H: COV. The chart lists the information of the vehicles when they ram:

**MPH (Miles Per Hour):** The speed at which the ramming vehicle was traveling.

**Ramming Damage:** This is the amount of Lethal HEA damage that is done to a person if hit by a vehicle.

**AP (Armor Penetration):** This is the amount of AP the vehicle will do when ramming.

| MPH | Damage | AP | Ramming | Vehicle |
|-----|--------|----|---------|---------|
| 0 – 10 | D6 | D4 | A | A |
| 11 – 20 | D8 | D6 | B | A |
| 21 – 30 | D10 | D8 | C | B |
| 31 – 40 | D12 | D10 | D | C |
| 41 – 50 | D20 | D12 | E | D |
| 51+ | 2D12 | D20 | E | E |

**Ramming:** This is the amount of damage that the vehicle being rammed will take.

**Vehicle:** This is the amount of damage that the vehicle doing the ramming will take.

## RAMMING AND VEHICLE DAMAGE RESULTS

**A:** No Effect on the vehicle's ability to drive.

**B:** The vehicle's Armor Value is reduced by an Easy (-2) modifier, the top speed and feet/rounds is reduced by 25%.

**C:** The vehicle's Armor Value is reduced by an Average (-5) modifier, the top speed and feet/rounds is reduced by 50%.

**D:** The vehicle's Armor Value is reduced by a Hard (-9) modifier, the top speed and feet/rounds is reduced by 75%.

**E:** The vehicle is destroyed and is incapable of any type of movement.

## OUT OF CONTROL

One of the worse events that can happen while your character is driving is that the vehicle will go out of control. When this does happen, the only thing that you can really do is to hope and pray that you do not get hurt too badly and you that don't run anyone over. The following is a listing of the events that are possible when a vehicle is out of control. Roll and D6 and consult the chart for the result.

**D6    RESULT**

1    The vehicle suffers a minor skid. The driver will suffer an Easy (-2) modifier to AGI for the following round.

2    The vehicle suffers a skid. The car's tire has hit a slick area in the road. The vehicle will move off in a random direction (G.O.D.'s decision) for the following round. The driver will suffer an Average (-5) modifier to AGI for the following two rounds.

3    The vehicle begins to fishtail. The car will continue to fishtail back and forth for D4 turns. The driver will suffer a Hard (-9) modifier to AGI for the rounds the vehicle is fishtailing.

4    The vehicle careens on to two wheels. The driver will lose complete control of the vehicle for D6 turns. The driver will suffer an Extreme (-14) modifier to AGI for the rounds the vehicle is careening on two wheels.

5    The vehicle suffers a major fishtail. The vehicle continues to fishtail back and forth for D10 turns. The driver will suffer an Amazing (-19) modifier to AGI for the rounds the vehicle is suffering the major fishtail.

6    Tires catch on something in the roads, causing the car to flip over. Vehicle sustains heavy damage to its body, while the occupants suffer extraordinary injuries. All passengers aboard the vehicle suffer 2D12 points of Lethal HEA damage.

## GASES

All gases come in canisters. The canisters are cylindrical metal objects roughly 6" long by 2" in diameter. They are operated similarly to a grenade by pulling the pin and letting the release handle go. These canisters can also be fired from specially developed rifles.

All canisters of any type of gas; mace, smoke and tear gas; contain enough gas to affect a 25' by 25' by 10' area, a total of 6250 sq. ft. The effective radius of this would be halved to 3125 sq. ft. for well-ventilated or open area. Mace is a colorless gas or spray while smoke and tear gas are normally white and opaque. A lot of gases have odors, which can be identified by scent with an INT roll after they are detected.

For each tear gas canister released in an area, the character's affected will reduce their AGI temporarily by an Average (-5) modifier. Smoke Screen canisters, no matter the amount, will reduce the AGI of the character within the smoke by a Hard (-9) modifier. Gas masks and lights have no effect on a smoke screen canister.

Characters can choose to use a gas mask during a gassing attack. The character must notify the G.O.D. that the mask is on before the gassing or the character is still subject to the effects of the gas. A character attempting to put on a mask for protection during a gassing must make an AGI roll with an Average (-5) modifier.

## POISONS

On some rare occasions, characters will be affected with poisons. Poisons come in many different and unique forms from the simple old-fashioned Arsenic to Portuguese man-of-war venom. All poisons come in two specific forms, short term and long term. Short term poisoning works out similar to an attack; the character will take damage from the poison as if the character was being attacked for that moment. The character may resist the poison only if they have some type of antidote or protection from it. Most common short-term poisons do 3D10 points of Lethal HEA damage.

Long term poisoning will affect characters in a totally different way. Characters that have been exposed to poisons may initially be resistant to the poison but over time their resistance is worn down. All characters can resist the poison for as many turns as their STA. For each turn after the character's normal time limit, the character must make a STA roll each turn following at an Average (-5) modifier to their STA. If the character passes the roll, they are able to resist the long-term effects of the poison. This will continue on until the character either fails a roll or their STA reaches zero. After that the character's STA time limit has expired, the character will take the damage of poison per turn until a cure is found, death, or the poison becomes inert. Similar to short-term poison, most common long-term do 2D12 Lethal HEA points of damage per turn until a cure is used.

# CHAPTER:5

# THE GOLDEN RULES

*Judge not, that ye be not judged*

*Matthew 7:1*

It's tough being the one in charge. You have to be part leader, part entertainer and part foolish jester. The Game Operation Director, or G.O.D. as the illustrious position is better known, is completely responsible for anything that might go on and take place during a gaming session of Haven: COV. This section has been created to help all G.O.D.s, from beginners to experts, reaffirm the atmosphere of the environment, the ambiance of the scene, the impression of the surroundings and the proper lack of mercy.

In the setting of Haven, the G.O.D. must always try to make the players feel as though their fictional characters are really in Haven, the city where the smell of death is on the air and trouble lurks around every darkened street corner. The imaginary conflicts and resolutions of the game must be played out in a seriously intense atmosphere of realism. You must always know how to do that, but additionally must also keep it fun and entertaining for the players.

# THE GOLDEN RULES OF A GAME OPERATION DIRECTOR

There are several important rules that a G.O.D. must be aware of at all times. These "Golden Rules" are the most important codes that can be enforced on the game. These are not so much "Rules" as sage pieces of advice that will help you keep control of the action and with a little luck, be prepared for most eventualities.

## 1) KNOW WHAT YOU ARE DOING

If you are going to be the G.O.D., you must know the Haven: City of Violence game system. For some unknown reason several RPG rulebooks have become as thick as the New York City phone book and are more complex then figuring out the meaning of life. With all this you would think it would be silly for anyone to become a G.O.D. Well, yes and no. It is good to have a good grasp of the basic concepts and rules, but certain aspects such as character creation, combat, and movement should be understood with at least solid understanding. The rules are created to provide a springboard to help you figure out your own answers and solve problems that may arise during play.

## 2) WHEN IN DOUBT, MAKE IT UP

At some point when gaming, the players will do something that is not in any of the rulebooks, or perhaps something happens that will be totally new to your game that borders on the edge of confusing. At this point, a G.O.D. should do what feels natural to them. That is right; you should make up the rules. Now don't get me wrong, you shouldn't redesign the game so that your players always win with no sacrifice on their part. The situation should be something that the people designing this game did not think about.

Rules should also be improvised with some type of logical reasoning behind it. If a player does not like the ruling of a dice roll, they should not be able to make up the roll. But, if there is some type of conflict between not understanding a rule and the players, the G.O.D. must do their best to find some way to make it work. We have said it once and we will say it again, the object of this game is to have fun.

## 3) SUPERVISE CHARACTER CREATION

While it is important for players to control the conception of the character creation process, it's a wise G.O.D. will oversee that process and monitor each step. This will allow the G.O.D. to supply the players with any information and tidbits that would help flesh out characters and their relationships. Supervising character creation will also give you clues to what player are interested in as well as a

head start on coming up with challenges tailor made for your group's strengths … and weaknesses. This also ensure you can catch anyone trying to cheat or abuse the rules – trust us, there is one asshole in every crowd who is going to cheat and abuse the rules.

Some players will also acquire drawbacks just to get additional benefits without any thought to the consequences of drawback. Drawbacks should be just what they are: drawbacks. They are not created to make player's lives easier, drawbacks are meant to make life harder. Make sure that the players remain true to their character. If one of the characters or, for that matter, one of the players — is a dullard or a jerk, it's to your best advantage to find out early so you can make adjustments and help refine them to be more interesting and playable. Even if the G.O.D. is working with an experienced role-playing group they trust, it's still a good habit to be as involved as possible with players when they design characters. In fact, its best to have the whole group sit down and talk out their concept with everyone else. This cuts

down on duplicate PCs as well as allow players to create bonds for their PC group.

## 4) MOOD AND SETTING ARE EVERYTHING

Some persons believe that the setting and mood of a game are not really that necessary to help with the entire gaming experience. If you are one of these people, go rent of copy of you favorite action adventure film. We suggest John Woo's Bullet in the Head, Hard Boiled or the Killer. Now watch it during the middle of the day, adjust the television volume to mute and turn on all the lights or open the curtain to let the bright sun light stream in to the house, now watch your movie! If you don't think this destroys the atmosphere of your movie then you've rented a very bad movie, and role-playing games are just the same. Atmosphere may not be everything but it helps… a lot!

The accurate mood for Haven is created when a G.O.D. thinks about all the important aspects of the city of Haven. Haven is a soul crushing, dismal, and polluted environment for the characters. The people in Haven are not generally friendly or helpful. The sun rarely shines, or when it does its not warm, it seams to rain way to often and the sewers frequently overflow. The G.O.D. should always try to push the bleak hostile image of Haven, from the darkened rubbish cluttered alleyways with punks, shooters and chemical heads ready to take you're your life or your wallet to the pristine but no less dangerous boardrooms of Golden Heights.

## 5) GOOD COMBAT, SMART COMBAT

Who doesn't like to watch a good fight? What would you rather see, two old ladies hitting each other with handbags or Jackie Chan, Jet Li, and Bruce Lee go all out on each other with every type of kick and punch they can create or imagine. When the NPC first attacks, a solid strategy should be created for them as if they are real people who don't want to die and wouldn't brainlessly waltz through the players' kill zone. Have them use available cover, let them co-operate or use scenery against the players. Once you have created an initial combat tactic for the NPCs, just go with the flow. The following attacks by the NPCs will come natural. Remember that the NPCs will try to what ever is necessary to achieve their goals. If you really want to put the proverbial fear of God into the players have the enemy use real common sense strategy, like placing a sniper on the rooftop to cause some frustration.

## 6) ANYONE CAN DIE AT ANY TIME

This is one of the rules that keeps players always on their toes, keeps them thinking and completely aware of their surroundings. If a player thinks that there is truly a chance that their character could get killed or placed in some type of impending danger, they will think, re-think and think again all of their actions.

You must make the player feel that the character they are playing is their best friend. Anything that they do will affect the character, whether directly or indirectly. This will make all players remarkably paranoid of any of their actions. The feeling that a G.O.D. wants the players to experience is a combination of fear, anxiety and trepidation. Fear is always great at making the player focus more on what they are doing, while the anxiety will make them more apt to make careless simple mistakes. Just don't let them slow down a fast passed scene be analyzing every conservable angle, if a player is taking to long, just move along, they'll learn to think faster next time! Nature has a solution for the slow and stupid, - its called extinction.

Now after saying all of that, I must also tell you don't go remarkably out of your way to terminate a player character. This game is NOT about the players against you, but one where the G.O.D. helps and informs the players of the events and actions.

## 7) EVERYONE HAS THEIR OWN AGENDA!

If you looking for someone with a heart of gold in this little slice of hell, all you are going to get is Jack and Spit, and Jack left town two days ago. The setting of Haven is one where the people are said, "to live on the balls of their feet"; they are always expecting trouble and ready to react. Haven citizens have the street savvy and cunning of a 50 year-old veteran of living and surviving in New York City, East Los Angeles and Beirut all rolled into one.

Haven is a dangerous place and those perils exist everywhere. When you look down any street and see some of the common people, remember everyone you see has some type of story. Their story could be anything from how they may have been molested as a child and that caused them to become child molesters themselves, so PCs shouldn't be stupid or naïve.

## 8) EVERYONE MUST HAVE FUN

I cannot say this rule enough times. Haven: COV is a game. It is meant to help bring people together and enjoy each other's company. This game is there to help build friendship between the players and involve the more creative side of one's personality. If the people involved with the gaming sessions are not having fun, then you as the G.O.D. must discover what the problem is and how to amend or rectify it. Otherwise, you won't have any players very quickly.

# 9) KEEP PLAYERS IN CHARACTER

This rule will not only make it fun for the G.O.D. but it will help involves the players with their characters even more. If the character is crazy or mentally disturbed, make the player play that out completely while gaming. You might try instructing your players to arrive dressed like their characters, and to distinguish between out of game communications with the G.O.D. and in game chatter by changing accents. Not only is this a great way to get characters to interact with each other, it is a great way to help expand on the general atmosphere of the setting.

Another aspect that is important to the gaming session is the physical location of where the game is played. This can alter and directly boost the believability factor of the game. While a large kitchen table in the middle of the afternoon may be satisfactory to play the Haven: COV, it would be better to wait to begin playing after dark in a small room, perhaps a basement, with very dimmed lights, but not so dark that no one can see. There should be just enough to add an additional atmosphere of dread and apprehension to the game. The G.O.D. could have a radio plying the background with the sounds of aggressive music styles from hard-core rock to progressive techno. Play whatever styles the players like and helps with the believability of the game. None of these items alone will set the tone, but combine a few and things should be well on their way.

# CREATING AN ADVENTURE

The main purpose for gaming is to go on adventures. These adventures might be quick rides into the dark side that may only last a quick few hours of a gaming session. At other times, these adventures could last anywhere from a few months to a few years. This is all determined by the group of gamers, themselves, and specifically by the G.O.D.

First, the G.O.D. must create the adventure for the players to enjoy. An adventure can consist of anything from a simple everyday event to a long and drawn out worldwide conspiracy, that is all determine by the G.O.D. A G.O.D. can design these adventures completely from their own imagination, or use source materials likes books, television, and movies to help create the adventure.

The list of items that must be answered to create an adventure is known as the five W's and the one H:

**WHAT:** What is the basic concept, story idea and design for this adventure? What type of adventure will this be? Will this adventure focus on a vendetta, hit men on the run or be a good old fashioned "shoot out?" What is the reason for this adventure?

**WHO:** Who will be directly involved with this adventure? Who will be the villain of this adventure?

**WHERE:** Where will this adventure take place? Will the adventure take place on land, sea or air? Will it be a specific borough in Haven or all over the city in general?

**WHEN:** When, in a time frame, will this adventure take place? Will the adventure take place during the day or night? What season will be in swing, will gunfights ensue on slippery ice? Will you place your game in the current timeline or further back when the Coalition was clawing itself to death?

**WHY:** Why are the players involved with this adventure? Will the players stay together for the reason of business or fate and why is the villain doing what he is doing?

**HOW:** How do these players work together to accomplish their mission? Will the players work as a team or will they work in small groups or will the group work as individuals.

Now here are some sample ideas that G.O.D.s can use as simple adventure starters:

**Catching Bad Guys:** The PCs must find and capture thugs, mobsters or other such criminals.

**Information:** The PCs must search for a particular piece of information about a person, place or thing and return to their employer with the information.

**Stolen Item:** The PCs are ordered or hired to locate and bring back to their employer something that has been stolen, perhaps secret plans or an invention.

**Rescue Someone:** The PCs must locate and rescue someone who is being held prisoner, such as a hostage, a kidnap victim or a person in prison.

These few ideas will be easy way to start off a long term gaming adventure for the PC and the G.O.D. You may wish to even amalgamate several of these ideas and themes into one adventure. You could also create an adventure based on something discovered by the PCs in earlier gaming sessions. This will enhance the PC's enthusiasm and interest as gamers by using information and facts they have discovered in earlier adventures to solve the riddles in their current gaming sessions.

## SETTINGS

The most important thing to good adventuring is setting, setting, setting! The location, or setting as it is better known, of an adventure determine the events that can take place and people the PCs are likely to encounter. Your setting can be as large or small as the G.O.D. may wish. It is all determined by their imagination. An entire adventure could squeezed into a single room or spread across the whole city. The location created ought to have a rationale in the adventure. The PCs should complete some part of their purpose at each setting location. At each location, PCs can encounter a small clue to help move the adventure along. As you choose the settings you should record this information including any special bits and pieces about the setting.

Just as above, the five W's and the one H need to be addressed again:

**WHAT:** What is the setting's function? What does the setting look like? What person will be encountered in this setting?

**WHO:** Who will be directly involved with this setting? Who will be the villain in this setting?

**WHERE:** Where will this setting take place? Will the setting take place on land, sea or air? Will it be a specific area in Haven or all over the city in general?

**WHEN:** When, in a time frame, will this setting take place? Will the setting take place during the day or night? Will the setting take place during the summer or winter?

**WHY:** Why is this setting being used?

**HOW:** How will the setting affect the players ability to work together to accomplish their mission?

## EVENTS

Once the adventure purpose and settings for an adventure has been determined the G.O.D. must design the adventure's obstacles that the PCs will need to overcome to finish their adventure. Each of the events of the adventure will be placed in a specific setting.

When creating and crafting an adventure, events can be an impediment that the PCs need to overcome, an opportunity to gain something that will aid the characters in reaching their goal or even a simple lesson that can be learned for the PCs. Events should be stimulating or create a situational problem than must be solved before the PCs can progress further. The following are questions that should be answered to help create events:

- What is the purpose of this event? Will this event be a puzzle to resolve? Will it be a chance to acquire something useful?
- Determine the elements considered necessary in the event. Will the PCs encounter NPCs, animals, security systems or even other PCs.
- Determine how the NPCs will respond to the PCs and measures they will take to defend or work against the PCs.

## ARRANGING EVENTS

Once the events in an adventure are created, the decision of their order is determined by the G.O.D. Most events are built in a specific order in a "step-by-step" or linear situation, but this order of events is not set in stone and can be broken. These events should be "fluid" and "flexible". PCs should be able to reach their goal using several different methods in game play.

## CREATING THE SUPPORTING CAST

After the G.O.D. has determined the events that will direct your PCs to their goal, the GOD must create the supporting cast of minor characters called Non Player Characters, or NPCs, that will interact with the PCs. All significant information is recorded for the G.O.D.s easy access. The purpose and reactions of the NPCs will be recorded by the G.O.D. NPCs personalities can be from very peaceful and friendly to highly violent and psychotic. The NPCs will also be equipped according to their specific activity. All of these situations for the events will be determined by the G.O.D., of course having developed the basic idea of the overall story already you should have a fair idea of the type of adversaries you want the PC's to encounter.

## NPCS AND THEIR PURPOSE

The often forgotten and always neglected individual of role-playing is the Non-Player Character, better known as the NPC. NPCs will often hold a significant piece of information that will make it possible for the solving of the problem or situation that is plaguing the PCs on their adventure. Often forgotten by the G.O.D. is that the NPCs' make it possible for the game to be expanded and make it more enjoyable for all involved. The players will find NPCs with more active personalities easier to interact with and easier to expanded their PCs. The main reasons for a NPC and what they do for a gaming session are as follows:

- Enhance the Gaming Ambience and Setting
- Help move the Gaming Session Forward
- Sources of Information for the Players
- Additional Services for Players and PCs

## ENHANCE THE GAMING AMBIENCE AND SETTING

In this situation, a NPC will be able to give out information on the city of Haven, but they still hold back very important parts of information that will be revealed later. NPCs of this type also should not make more than one or at the most two appearances in a single gaming session. The NPC is there to relay information not "hog the stage time" of the game. Also, make the NPC fitting for the setting, if you are in Golden Heights, the type of mentoring NPC that you will run into will quite different from the NPC who you might encounter in the run down slums known as Rome Island.

## HELP MOVE THE GAMING SESSION FORWARD

NPCs can also be used to help, instruct, or even manipulate the PCs to accomplish the specific goals created for the group. NPCs often hold knowledge that is in need of being examined, or they may hold cryptic information that would expose jeopardy or fortune. There are several options that can be used when having an NPC as an adventure hook. The oldest, if not the best, adventure hook is an attack or kidnapping of someone close to the party. It does not matter if it is their mother, father, brother or sister, just as long as it is someone who has a direct personal connection to the PCs. Personal relations can be and should be exploited to the utmost.

Another method is to create an adversarial NPC for the PCs that they can directly interact with. If a PC is a gangster, then present an important NPC gangster from an opposing crime family that has their eye on the same prize. A character in this situation should not be revealed as a foe at first, it should take time. Ordinarily, the increased amount of time that passes between the introduction of the NPC and the divulgence of their true nature, the more climactic and exciting the end result will be. This tactic is one of the most common methods used in books and television and betrayal is a powerful motivator for PCs and most will want to get even.

The next method is to hire the PCs to undertake a very dangerous mission where there is a possibility of great wealth for the PCs. Often the local mob boss will need a little extra firepower, or some shop owner will want to stop people from robbing him every week. Using NPCs in this form often feels as if you are directly manipulating the situation and those involved with it. This method is very good, but can be easily overused and abused if used too often.

## SOURCES OF INFORMATION FOR THE PLAYERS

The best sources of information for the PCs will normally come from a NPC. There is a good chance there is some citizen in the City of Haven that could answer just about any question the players might want to ask. In the act of creating a NPC, an important question that should be asked is, how much information will this NPC have? How can this information either help or harm the PCs? What secrets might the NPC reveal or hold back for later use? Will the information that is given out be useful at the time it is revealed or sometime down the line?

Once you know who has the information that the PCs want you should ask how are they going to obtain it? Will the PCs have to force the information out of the NPC? Will the NPC give the information willingly? Does the NPC what to trade the information for something the PCs might have? If a NPC is giving out free information to the PCs make sure that this information is faint, almost non-existent. An off-handed comment is the best way to set something like this up. With this type of concept, hinting is king. Getting important information should be one part puzzle, one part pain and one part satisfaction.

## CREATING THE "GOOD" VILLAIN

Adolf Hitler, Genghis Khan, and Rasputin the Mad, these men are the true definition of the word, villain. As the G.O.D., it's your position to give birth to the villains your players will be speaking about for years

to come. After several minor appearances of the main villain, the players should finally get to meet with this the villain and actually discover how powerful he or she is.

## WHO AM I AND WHAT DO I DO

The first step in creating a memorable villain is giving him an identity. It's one thing to kill a small no name street corner drug dealer; it is totally another thing taking out Haven's most dangerous professional hit man-assassin at his home. The villain will become more realistic to players if you create a connection that makes the antagonist's motives personal to the players.

It is too easy to want to kill a person who has slaughtered hundreds of nameless crowds of individuals who have no direct connections to the players. The person who has killed a PCs best friend, brother or even their mother, however, is worse than a common killer. He has placed himself into a special category of villain. The hottest places in Hell are reserved for these types of criminals. Create this intimate bond between this important NPC and the characters, then let the players loose.

Give the arch-foe a personality and some personal goals to the adventure. All villains are not just evil for evil's sake. The villain must have some type of end goal. The end goal could be murder, assault, and just old-fashioned insanity. Sometimes the devil did make them do it, but most master criminals aspire to some type of empire or syndicate; perhaps simple material wealth is the lure or power.

## ALWAYS BE PREPARED AND HAVE A PLAN

Incompetent villains, even remarkably powerful ones, will try to prove themselves more powerful than the player characters. These types of villains are a dime a dozen and normally don't last more than fifteen minutes in the world of Haven. The more intelligent head villains will send their minions to strike out at the PCs first and then increase the level of threat.

This will normally continue until the villain has either no choice but to meet the PCs directly or has to escape to save him or herself.

All good heroes need to have great villains. Most people plan for the next move. Great villains plan not just for the next move, but the move after that, and the move after that, and the move after that. Planning is what makes a villain seem so powerful. The villain must always appear as if they are in complete control of each and every situation, even if they may not be. All good villains' plans are well thought out with several fallback contingences if a problem arises. Knowing what PCs are going to do next will also make the villain able to face the PCs at any time or at any contingency. Now the villain is not going to know every little thing that the PCs are planning, but they should never say, "I have no idea what to do next."

No major villain should be weaker than the PCs. Now this may not always be in physical abilities, but a villain should always be more sly and cunning then the PCs. The first meeting should be a painful experience for the PCs and a pleasurable one for the villain. The villain will be prepared to astound and surprise the PCs and make them worry about surviving their first encounter with the villain. After the first encounter with the PCs, the villain will be focusing on the weakness and deficiencies of the PCs and discovering ways to use those weaknesses as best the villain can.

## THERE CAN ONLY BE ONE

Sooner or later, the PCs will force the villain into direct combat, most likely to the death. The villain will wish to make the last conflict at the place of greatest strength, more often that naught, the villain's headquarters. These places are the greatest source of power and prestige for the villain. The final combat scene should be just as it says 'the final combat scene'. This is it. Either the PCs walk away alive and the villain lies defeated or dead at their feet, or the villain is victorious with the broken and battered bodies of the PCs at their feet. Somebody has to win and someone's got to lose. Ties do not really prove anything to anyone.

## SPECIAL SITUATIONS AND RULES

If any of your event situations created by the G.O.D. involve special circumstances or particulars that are not covered in the game rules, you should create them based on the rules of Haven: City of Violence before starting an adventure. G.O.D.s may wish to create special specific rules for unusual terrain, new equipment or devices, weather or various other items and situation that may come up. Make sure these rules are not very complex to keep the flow of game play going.

## CREATING MAPS FOR GAMING USE

After you have created the adventure, you should make corresponding maps of the areas that are needed during the game. The most common types of maps that are used in gaming are traditional gaming maps as well as combat maps. Game maps show the overall layout of the area being used in the adventure. These maps will reveal the adventure on a small scale. While the details of these maps are limited, they will denote large distances that may or may not be needed to travel during the adventure. The combat map is used when PCs are involved in any type of combat. Unlike traditional gaming maps, combat maps will be quite detailed showing such items as windows, doors, statues plus any other various other items and hazards that might occur. Map should list information about important encounter areas and situations that may happen during the event of the adventure. Often PCs will wish to create their own maps for their own use. The G.O.D. should prepare these maps himself, and let the players keep them, but it is often better for the PCs to create the maps for themselves. PC maps should have the general information of the area but nothing too specific. This will help add to the suspense of the gaming experience.

## REALISTIC GAMING ENVIROMENT

When doing an action that involves the use their imagination, it would be helpful to engage items that accent this experience. Engaging all five senses help make the event more 'real' to the players. The more realistic the event feels, the more naturally the players will react to the situations you place them in.

## WELL-DEVELOPED CHARACTERS

A well developed character, whether it is a player character or non-player character helps with game play. If all you design for a character is that they are a bodyguard who carries a gun, how much fun can that be? Above all else it is up to the players themselves to decide what type of character they will create. An informative G.O.D. will always help players in the most correct, most efficient way to create a positive character. Even though some of the players may be experienced in role-playing games, it is always best to have the G.O.D. around.

## STRANGE BUT FAMILIAR

The more familiar an item feels, the easier it is to pervert the original image and intent of the item to a hideous nightmare. Start it off with something that may be common to all the players like their first pet or first stuffed animal. Make the object cause the players to feel a particular way about it, make them feel that the object will provide them with support and trust. After the players believe totally in the object and trust it with no doubt, its true purpose should be revealed. The object should act in the most opposite way possible. If the childhood pet loved the player, then have it now attack the player when it sees them. Everything must seem as if it was colored white like new fallen snow but in reality it is darker than the darkest winter night.

## DETAILS

If you don't think details are important, compare the subsequent sentences describing the following person: He was a male who was tall. That was scary. Now read this one: His face was that of a grizzly scarred veteran, of several street gangs and several bloody wars with greasy jet-black hair and crimson red blood shot eyes, his body stood motionless like a granite statue rising to an enormous height. Now, of the two previous men, who are you more afraid of? A good G.O.D. will make the city of Haven come alive by closely interweaving it with everyday, common items that can be recognized by the players but slightly different.

## BUILDING DANGER

In the Haven: City of Violence setting, the advent of danger does not happen all at once. Many dangers should fall like dominos one by one, increasing the intensity with each successive fall. The area of right and wrong will be blurred with every second of playing the game. Any player may start off with good intention, but may end up at the front door to hell and not even notice how they got there. G.O.D.s must remember that fear and dread must start off as a simple, almost vague sensation that will build upon itself every second of gaming and to properly cause this effect will take time and should not be rushed.

In this event of building danger, being subtle is king. Quick blood drenched scenes of violence are easy to perform, but creating a scene when the action is constantly building is truly an art form. Hidden dice rolls always help to advance the idea of tension. Wait until the game has reached a quiet part and then make sure the players are watching you. Roll the dice secretly behind a screen, and then don't even mention anything about it to the players. Just continue with the game. They will then become suspicious of what you are doing and feel as though they are going to walk into a trap.

## FAMOUS LAST WORDS

There are no completely foolproof ways for being the G.O.D. in the Haven: COV or any other role-playing game. The best that is possible is that we provide you with examples and any guidance in how to run various circumstances from the simplest back alley conversation to the bloodiest blood bath and any thing in general during the course of a campaign.

Here are a few guidelines that can help all G.O.D.s in their own home grown campaigns.

# BE PREPARED

Players are an extremely sneaky bunch and can at any given time surprise you with something that is the last thing you would have thought of. Always plan the full adventure before the game actually starts, including contingency plans for everything that the players might do. This last bit is actually impossible, but if you know your players and how they think then you stand a chance of second-guessing how they will try to deal with certain situations. If the players throw you a curveball once in a while you must remember to be reasonable, sensible and somewhat aware of your options.

There is nothing worse than the players having to stop halfway through a game for the G.O.D. to plan the next part of an adventure. As well as being a waste of valuable gaming time, it also does not give the impression that they are playing an adventure that is of the highest quality. If the players are threatening to turn down an avenue that you had not planned for, you can subtly divert them, either with the threat of a powerful enemy or a greater reward in another direction.

# BE FAIR TO THE PLAYERS

This has been said before, and it applies always. The G.O.D. is in complete control of just about each and every situation involved in the game. They know what lies just ahead for the characters and what they will be running into in the very near future. Destroying the characters is not what this game is all about. It is about providing the players with a problem and giving them just enough information, like rope, where they can pull themselves out of trouble or hang themselves. Remember that the scenario is only as good as the G.O.D. and players.

# NO BUFFALOING

A buffalo is a player who tries to take over the game for his or her own personal spotlight on themselves.

This is a game that is built on the premise of people working together for a common goal. Not that somebody should lead all the time and not everyone else should follow all the time. It is a careful balance between give and take and the most important thing to remember is when you should give and when you should take.

# PATIENCE

Let the players make their own decision whether those decisions are good or bad. This is just like life; you have to live with the decision you make. Often in gaming there will always be a time where gamers will need to decide who will be in charge and who will follow, where they will be going, what they will be doing next. This all takes time so let the players have as much as is reasonably possible.

And most of all have fun.

# CHAPTER: 6

EMERALD HILL

# EMERALD HILL

*A Scenario for the Haven: City of Violence Roleplaying Game*

*By Steven S. Long*

## HERE'S THE SKINNY

When a skilled gang of independent thieves blows into Haven planning to take down a major score, they bring all sorts of trouble for the player characters along with them. Organized crime, rival gangs, and other enemies want to stop the newcomers, but the PCs can't just let the normal course of evolution in Haven take its course. The out-of-towners have information the characters desperately need, so the characters have to find a way to stop them without killing them — or letting anyone else kill them.

## SUMMARY

Known, at least by name, to law enforcement organizations on three continents, the Bryson Hill gang includes some of the world's most adept thieves among its ranks. Masters of high tech thieving skills, Hill and his partners have stolen from corporations, wealthy collectors, and governments. Their ability to evade or bypass alarms, infiltrate the target area, and get what they want despite security measures has become legendary. Sometimes they rely on sophistication and stealth, other times on brute force and a willingness to kill over the slightest of provocations — but they always get the job done.

Recently the characters got a tip that Hill and his partners have come to Haven for a "big job." Exactly what that job is they don't know — at first. A rash of unusual thefts soon has them running all over town, trying to figure out which ones might relate to Hill's job, and which simply belong to the normal Haven background noise.

As if this didn't give them enough to do, the characters soon learn they're not the only ones on the lookout for the Hill gang. Organized crime elements in Haven want to stop Hill and his partners because they don't pay the proper "respect" — or the tradi-tional cut of the take — to the right people. Corrupt businessmen, concerned their own organizations may be Hill's target, pressure the characters to "deal with the situation." And a quick-shooting bounty hunter from out of town has shown up looking to whack Hill in revenge for a murder from four years back.

Rest assured that if the PCs didn't get the Hill gang, one of these other organizations would. The problem is, the characters can't afford simply to let Hill and his partners die. First, there's a good possibility that innocent people (if such an animal exists in Haven) will get killed in the crossfire; it's happened with Hill before when people tried to capture or kill him. Second, and more importantly for many characters, Hill supposedly has knowledge about several major crimes and related incidents from the past three or four years, knowledge many prosecutors and cops would love to get their hands on. The characters want this information too, so gunning Hill down isn't an option. They have to do something even more dangerous than getting into a firefight with a known multiple murderer — they have to bring him in alive.

## BASIC INFORMATION FOR THE G.O.D.

### The Nature of the Player Characters

This scenario is written from the perspective of the player characters being police officers, vigilantes, or other characters fighting "the good fight," instead of simply participating in, and contributing to, the corruption, chaos, and crime plaguing Haven. If your campaign doesn't fit this model to a significant degree, you'll probably have to adapt the scenario slightly.

If your PCs are a gang of independent criminals themselves, you can turn the scenario on its head, making crooked cops and rival crooks the "bad guys." In this case, you get rid of the Hill gang completely (except perhaps as rivals for the characters). Then you present the characters with the main target — a large shipment of emeralds being sent to Rheingold Fine Gemstones — and let them figure out how to take it down and get away clean. They may not choose the methods described in this

scenario, but that's all right; you simply have to be prepared to deal with whatever they do think of. Meanwhile, corrupt detectives from the Haven Police Department, rival gangs, and organized crime groups seeking a "cut" of the action make trouble for the characters, and maybe even thwart their efforts altogether depending on how things turn out. You might even try to include some rare honest cops who are closing in. Better yet, think about how tough an honest cop would have to be in order to still be working on the force in razor sharp environment of Haven.

If your player characters belong to an organized crime group, the scenario runs much like it would if they were good cops, but from a slightly different slant. Rather than investigating the Hill gang themselves, they pay off corrupt cops for whatever information they can get, and use underworld contacts to dig up the dirt on Hill and his men. Instead of trying to arrest Hill and his men with a minimum of bloodshed, they'll probably look for an opportunity to kill

them, and then take it regardless of who else might get hurt. In other words, while they labor under a few restrictions cop characters don't suffer from, they have plenty of freedom to get the job done, and will probably do so in a much more violent fashion than the police would.

If your PCs are corrupt cops, they may not care much about what's going on in this scenario initially. To get them interested, you can use several levers. First, one of their superiors may be friends with someone who's involved (maybe even Abraham Rheingold), and put them on the case — if they don't do a good job, their boss will make their lives hell for months. Second, perhaps Rheingold pays them off to look into things, or the Hill gang refuses to bribe them (so they'll undoubtedly want revenge on the thieves). Third, perhaps an assistant district attorney to whom they owe a favor puts them on Hill's trail; he wants the publicity that he'll get from putting such a notorious criminal on trial, and is willing to risk the PCs in his efforts to catch Hill.

# INTEGRATING THIS SCENARIO INTO YOUR CAMPAIGN

Emerald Hill works best if you build up to it during the course of your campaign. Instead of springing the Hill gang, Rheingold Fine Gemstones, and the various crimes Bryson Hill and his men commit on your players all during the course of this one scenario, work them in gradually, over a couple of games, before the situation becomes sufficiently crucial to attract the characters' undivided attention. For example, find a way to mention Hill and his gang earlier in the campaign, perhaps as suspects in a particular case, or as rivals to the characters. Then, drop some hints the gang might be on its way to town. Over the course of the next couple of games, mention the precursor crimes described below — that many unusual thefts in so short a time period should get the characters interested in taking Hill down. This way the whole plot doesn't sound artificial, like something you've just thought up; instead, it unfolds like an actual series of dramatic events.

# BACKGROUND SUMMARY

Bryson Hill and his partners enjoy a reputation as one of the most skilled gangs of thieves in the world. They have pulled off multi-million dollar jobs in America, Europe, and Asia, confounding security devices and personnel with their ability to get in and out quickly, the wide variety of skills displayed while pulling off the jobs, and their willingness to use violence if necessary to accomplish their aims. Hill and his partners all have serious criminal records, having done time in prison earlier in their lives, but the authorities haven't come close to arresting them for many years now.

Hill and his partners specialize in high stakes, high-risk thefts. Their typical targets include museums, art galleries, jewelers, banks, commodities firms, and the like. They know how to defuse or avoid security systems, use computers, rewire electronic systems, pick or bypass locks, and forge documents. (See the end of this scenario for character sheets for them.) They live fast and well, spending their enormous earnings lavishly on the best hotels, women, food, drink, cars, entertainment, clothes, and equipment. (Hill, in particular, is known for his love of fast cars.) They have no known emotional attachments (wives, relatives they keep in touch with, or the like) and own no known property.

Through his contacts in the underworld and various industries, Hill has gotten word that Rheingold Fine Gemstones, a prestigious firm located on the four-teenth floor of the Burkhalter Building in Haven, will soon receive a large shipment of high-quality emer-alds from South America. Gem dealers and jewelry makers know Abraham Rheingold, the aged owner of the business, as a scrupulously honest professional who deals only in the best stones. Hill and his men estimate that if they time the robbery properly, they can get away with more than $20 million in emeralds that can easily be smuggled and transported— and they're right.

The issue of timing is an important one. They have to swoop in and snatch the emeralds after they're delivered, but before Rheingold sells them off. To make sure they don't miss their shot, they've been in Haven for some time now, casing the Burkhalter Building skyscraper, planning the heist, and obtaining all the supplies they need. Being thieves, they haven't exactly gone down to the Wal-Mart to buy their equipment, either. Some of it they've obtained on the black market, but some of it they've simply stolen. By investigating these crimes (described below), the player characters can track Hill and his men and – hopefully - stop them from robbing Rheingold Fine Gems.

Hill's basic plan is to approach Rheingold as a buyer, steal the gems, and then escape via the Burkhalter Building's elevator shaft and underground parking garage. To pull it off, he's going to steal some vehi-cles, and some equipment from a skydiving service. He's got a few other thefts to commit along the way.

# PART ONE: THE PRECURSOR THEFTS

## PRELUDE: RUMORS OF AN APPROACHING STORM

While a professional thief like Bryson Hill tries to maintain as low a profile as possible, inevitably he attracts a certain amount of attention from fellow denizens of the underworld, the police, security personnel, and the like. The player characters could find out he has come to Haven in any of the following ways:

## OFFICIAL CHANNELS

Interpol, the Department of Federal Investigation, or any other large law enforcement organization which tracks the movements of people like Hill and his gang might issue a bulletin describing Hill's last known whereabouts and activities. Characters with access to this sort of official information could use it to draw the conclusion that Hill has made his way to the City of Haven.

The most recent bulletins indicate Hill and his gang were present in either Paris, France or Lisbon, Portugal (or perhaps both). An Interpol confidential informant says Hill is on his way to "the eastern U.S." to pull "a big score." However, Interpol cannot confirm that report with anyone else, and lost track of Hill about five weeks ago; the organization assumes the gang is headed to New York City.

If the characters think to review security camera footage from major European airports during the period referenced in the Interpol report, and have access to that data, several days' worth of incredibly dull work will eventually yield results: about three weeks ago, Hill and his partners flew to Haven from Heathrow International Airport near London, England. They flew under assumed names, using falsified documents.

If the characters show Hill's picture to security personnel at the types of establishments the Hill gang targets such as one of the city's finest art galleries, then a guard at Golden Heights' Tre Uffizi Gallery recognizes him as a man who came in about ten days ago to look at paintings. Hill identified himself as "David Cahill" and spent most of his time examining a painting by the renowned modern Russian artist Kazurenkov. In the end he declined to purchase the work. (Characters who stake out the gallery, or have someone else do it, will come up empty-handed; Hill liked the painting, but not enough to waste time and resources stealing it.)

Characters with Connections at the Department of Federal Investigation can get a complete file on Hill and all of his partners, including photographs, known aliases, fingerprints, and criminal records.

## UNOFFICIAL CHANNELS

Some characters may prefer to dig around for information about Hill in the underworld instead of H.P.D. files. They probably won't have much luck, since Hill knows how to maintain a (reasonably) low profile, but they can learn a few things.

High-ranking members of one, if not both, of the Carlucci and Santucci families in Haven have "gotten word" that Hill arrived in town a few weeks ago. They won't say how they got this information, and they claim they have no idea why the Hill gang came to Haven. But they're convinced he plans to pull a job, and since he has not contacted them to pay his "respects" and offer them their fair share of the score, they want him stopped (permanently, if possible). They will cooperate with the authorities to get the Hill gang as long as they find it reasonable and beneficial to do so.

With some sufficiently low rolls on the relevant Skills (primarily Streetwise) the characters may make the acquaintance of one Jimmy Vertese, a fence working in Haven. Vertese is associated with the Carluccis and operates in the City of Haven at the family's sufferance, so his dealings with Hill have been very hush-hush — if the Carluccis found out he'd helped the renegade thief, Jimmy would die a messy death. If the player characters threaten to reveal his duplicity, apply other appropriate pressure, and/or make sufficiently low Interrogation rolls, Jimmy cracks. He reveals that he used his contacts in the garment district to obtain "some really nice clothes" for Hill and his gang — suits worth several

thousand dollars apiece. He also got them some briefcases, half a dozen Uzi submachine guns and plenty of ammunition, some 9mm handguns, and two handgun silencers. But that's all he knows. They picked up all the stuff from him; he has no idea where they're staying or what they have planned. He cannot identify Hill or his men from photographs; they looked nothing like the pictures in the files. (They were wearing simple disguises.)

Some of Hill's old underworld friends and partners live in or around Haven. One of them, a professional thief named Robert Brooks, is doing 10 to 20 at the Fullgate Penitentiary 120 miles from Haven for multiple thefts. If interrogated, Brooks will truthfully claim he hasn't seen or heard from Bryson Hill in close to a decade. The underworld grapevine tells him Hill has come to town for "a big score," but that's all he knows. If asked his opinion regarding Hill's potential targets, he'll respond, "Don't know. But he always had a thing for fancy stones and fancy art. Probably a museum or a jewelry store."

## OLD HABITS DIE HARD

Clever players may think to track the Hill gang through its extravagant, fast-living lifestyle. This could net them some information, but probably not enough to allow them to capture Hill et al. quickly.

## HOTELS

First, they can investigate the city's fancy hotels, mainly in the Golden Heights and Arcadia districts. They probably won't have much luck here, since the gang moves around every couple of days, changing names and disguises from hotel to hotel so as not to leave traces. So far they've stayed at the Haven Grande Resort, the Carshaw, the Haven Fritz-Barlton, and, most recently, the Wellington Arms.

If you want to inject a little excitement at this point in the scenario, you can throw in a chase and capture scene. As the characters check out the Wellington Arms (it's one of the city's finest hotels, they're bound to go there at some point during this part of their investigation), the spot a man crossing the

lobby — Greg Hamesley, a member of the Hill gang, and one of the gang's entry and weapons experts. He's carrying a small satchel. Of course, he's in disguise, so the characters have to make a Perception roll with a Hard (-9) modifier to realize who he is. At this point, they have two options: try to capture him; or try to follow him to the rest of the gang.

Hamesley, an extremely observant person himself (see his character sheet at the end of this scenario), almost certainly spots the characters if try to close in and take him. He runs for it, not hesitating to shoot innocent people, break things, take hostages, or steal cars in his effort to get away. If the characters choose to follow him, he gets into a car and drives away. Make rolls, pitting the characters' SUB against Hamesley's PER with the lower result the winner in a PER roll. If he losses to the tail, he uses his considerable driving skills to try to get away. If you orchestrate the scene properly, you can turn this into a rollicking, exciting car chase — albeit one that almost certainly ends up with Hamesley (if not some of the player characters) badly injured or dead.

If the characters kill Hamesley while trying to apprehend or follow him, so much for getting any information from him. If they capture him but he's badly injured, they'll have to wait until after he's had medical treatment to interrogate him. If they capture him relatively unharmed, they can try to pry information out of him right away. However, he stubbornly resists all forms of interrogation short of physical torture, and insist that the characters allow him to contact an attorney. Even if tortured, he tries to hold out for two hours — at which point the rest of the gang knows to evacuate their hotel because he's been compromised. After that, he has no problem telling where the gang is staying at present (the Arcadia Downs hotel), but he continues to hold back information about the gang's plans. The characters can only break him if they make extremely good Influence rolls.

## CALL GIRLS

Second, characters who examine the gang's records closely will note that Hill and his partners apparently make frequent use of high-priced call girls. If the characters have knowledge of, or can somehow gain access to, the most sophisticated, well-hidden parts of

Haven's demimonde, they may learn something useful.

Unless at least one of the characters has worked in Vice, or has friends there, or has Connections among Haven's flesh peddlers, the characters have to make Influence roll with an Extreme (-14) modifier to find the sort of people they need to talk to about this. One of the reasons Haven's best call girls command such high prices is that they, and the madams who control them, are very discrete. They service lots of men who dare not risk being associated with sex for hire — politicians, high-ranking police officials, religious figures, wealthy businessmen, prison wardens and the like. They get paid very, very well not to talk about their clients to anyone. To even get close enough to some of these "sex workers" to ask them questions requires the characters to talk to some unpleasant individuals and grease a few palms. Do your best to convey the essentially sordid nature of this situation to the characters, despite the fancy decor and polite manners they encounter.

Enough investigation and bribery finally brings them into contact with a Native American woman named Alicia Featherstone, who resides in a nice (not luxurious, but nice) penthouse apartment building in Arcadia. If they properly approach her, using the names of persons she trusts as references and not doing anything crude or rude, they can get her to admit, albeit somewhat obliquely, that she is the "madam" for a small group of expensive call girls. She doesn't know where her girls live; she contacts them by cell phone and pager to arrange jobs for them. She usually doesn't know the names of the clients, either, though she can recognize many of them on sight. (She can identify Bryson Hill and Jason Drake from their photographs.) Initially, Featherstone refuses to cooperate with the characters or answer any questions. However, properly applied pressure — such as threats to arrest or blackmail her and her girls — eventually breaks her resistance, provided the characters promise no harm will come to her or her "employees." If she trusts the characters to keep their promises, she puts them in touch with "Trudy" and "Amber," two of her girls who recently spent evenings with Bryson Hill and Mark Munroe. Both men let slip comments that struck the

girls as unusual. Munroe compared Trudy's pale green eyes to "emeralds," even though they're nowhere near that dark in hue; and Hill told Amber he was "thinking of taking up skydiving." Other than that, the girls know nothing; the men picked them up at designated locations (restaurants) and took them to apartments the girls maintain for their work. They have no idea where or how to find them. An examination of Featherstone's phone records shows that the call Hill and Munroe made to her was from a pay phone in Arcadia.

## PREVOTTI LAMBORGHINI

The following sections describe five different "precursor crimes" which take place in Haven in the two or three weeks leading up to the time the characters hear about the Hill gang and begin their investigation. The gang did not commit two of them (those crimes are "red herrings" designed to complicate the investigation).

About a week ago, two Lamborghinis, one red and one black, were stolen from Prevotti Lamborghini in Golden Heights. The thieves disabled two fairly sophisticated security systems, one on the back entrance to the dealership, and a second on a lockbox holding the keys to the dealership's cars. After obtaining the right sets of keys, the thieves simply opened the front gate and drove away with the vehicles. The Haven Police Department has investigated this theft, of course. Detective Charles Prentiss, who's in charge of the investigation, has determined relatively little other than that at least two thieves must have participated in the robbery. No fingerprints were left, and the tool marks obtained by the crime scene investigation unit have offered no help. Although he and his men have talked to several local fences who have enough "juice" to move this kind of loot, Detective Prentiss has not located any who worked with the car thieves. All of the fences vehemently deny any involvement with this crime.

If the player characters choose to visit the scene of the crime themselves, they won't find any additional evidence, for two reasons. First, the crime scene unit did a pretty good job; there really isn't anything left to find. Second, the Prevotti staff has already had all the cleaning done and repairs made; you could never tell a break-in occurred here recently. After all, Mr. Prevotti certainly doesn't want any bad publicity.

## PURPOSE OF THIS THEFT

Bryson Hill and Jason Drake committed this robbery for no real reasons other than greed and practice. Hill loves fast, powerful cars, and decided he wanted one to drive around town while planning the Rheingold theft. It's a foolish thing to do, and he knows it, but he just can't resist such sweet machines. He brought Drake along to steal the second car for sale to a fence in Washington, D.C. to bring in some extra cash in case they need any last-minute supplies. None of the local fences know anything about this deal because Hill arranged it directly himself.

Hill had the Lamborghini he kept re-sprayed gold. He has also switched the VIN (Vehicle Identification Number) plate on the dashboard for one he obtained from a junkyard, and used falsified papers to obtain a new license plate for the car. But he has not changed the serial numbers on any of the parts or the like; it wouldn't take long for a determined investigator who examined the car to ascertain that it's one of the stolen autos. However, while Hill was foolish enough to steal the car, he's not such a fool that he drives it recklessly or often. He takes care to obey all traffic laws, and most of the time leaves the car in the valet parking section of the parking deck at his current hotel. Unless the characters have the wherewithal to cast a citywide net in search of all Lamborghinis, they almost certainly cannot track Hill down through this theft... unless, of course, you feel like giving them a break or mixing a good car chase scene into this part of the scenario.

## SCHOOL BUS

A few days ago, an unknown person or persons broke into the School Bus Repair & Maintenance Yard operated by the Haven School District and stole a newly refurbished school bus. The thieves used bolt-cutters to cut the chain on the main gate leading into the lot, and knocked the guard dog out with a taser. Then they simply drove away with the bus they wanted.

The stolen bus recently underwent a thorough overhaul, including the installation of a replacement fuel pump. The interior was also redone, replacing the torn, ratty seats with unpadded backs for newer, safer models.

An investigation into this matter by the H.P.D. has turned up no leads. No one has reported seeing the stolen bus anywhere. The detectives suspect the thieves had the assistance of an "inside man," since they knew enough to steal a "new" bus instead of an old one in poor condition. While several of the yard's employees, who include student interns from a number of local high schools, have minor criminal records, none of them has ever involved himself in a crime of this magnitude (though two have joyriding convictions).

## PURPOSE OF THIS THEFT

This theft is a red herring — the Hill gang had nothing to do with it. The perpetrators belong to a gang from the Rome Island neighborhood, one of whom used to work at the Maintenance Yard and thus knew where to find the best buses. After taking the bus, they drove it to a deserted warehouse on their turf, repainted it white, and then covered the white paint with gang tag graffiti and other designs. Now it looks like the sort of beat-up old bus that run-down community centers and nursing homes use to ferry people around. An investigator would have to take a close look at the inside, or at the serial numbers, to determine it's the one stolen from the Yard. The gang hasn't figured out exactly what they're going to do with the bus yet.

Alternately, you can replace this explanation with one more tailored to your campaign. Perhaps the bus theft is part of a larger crime the player characters will have to deal with someday soon.

## RUPTURED DUCK SKY ADVENTURES

Just under two weeks ago, a skydiving company called Ruptured Duck Sky Adventures experienced an unusual break-in. During the night, while the company's hangar near one of the small regional airports was locked up and deserted, someone broke

in and stole ten parachutes, ten oxygen bottles, and the machine used to refill the oxygen bottles.

Ruptured Duck's facility doesn't have airtight security, but it has a good alarm system — after all, it has some valuable equipment, including a small airplane in the hangar. It wouldn't have taken a highly skilled burglar to get inside, though the detectives have noted that whoever did it disabled the alarm neatly and efficiently... the touch of a professional.

Two things about the robbery puzzle Haven Police Department investigators. First, why would anyone steal parachutes and oxygen equipment? Anyone can purchase such items fairly easily; they're not controlled and aren't that expensive, relatively speaking. Second, why not steal the other valuables in the place? There were computers, a stereo, and plenty of other things worth taking (not to mention the plane, though thieves might have trouble getting away with it).

## AN EXTRA CLUE

If the player characters visit Ruptured Duck to have a look around, they find the staff friendly and helpful, though troubled by the theft and confused about why anyone would commit it. Rich Drury, the owner and chief employee, has already replaced the stolen equipment. No one working for the company has a criminal record.

Have any characters at the hangar make Perception rolls. The character with the lowest result of 5 or below notices a small scrap of blue paper near where the company keeps its oxygen bottles. (If no one achieves a result of 5 or lower, the characters fail to notice the clue.) If the character retrieves the scrap, he finds it belongs to a blueprint — it's a corner torn off of one side of a larger piece of paper. It contains part of a registration number.

If the characters check with the appropriate offices (the register of deeds, building inspector, and so forth) and do some digging through old files (most of

which the departments have not computerized), they eventually discover that the blueprint fragment must have come from a copy of the plans for the Burkhalter Building skyscraper.

## PURPOSE OF THIS THEFT

The Hill gang committed this theft primarily to obtain parachute silk, which its members needs to prepare a "drop bag" to cushion them as they make their escape from the Burkhalter Building. The oxygen bottles and refilling pump were taken mainly to confuse investigators, though the gang does need some of the tubing and other parts from the pump. They stole the parachutes rather than buy them partly out of habit, and partly for practice.

The blueprint corner comes from the plans the gang obtained as part of their work "casing" the Burkhalter Building. One of them accidentally tore off a scrap, which got stuck to his clothes and came loose during the Ruptured Duck robbery.

## GOLD SHIELD SECURITY

Approximately one week ago, a security company called Gold Shield Security suffered a robbery. Gold Shield sells and installs specialized locks, alarm systems, and other security devices; it does not provide security guard services or the like. The thieves stole samples of several different security systems, including motion detectors, door keypad systems, various types of electronic locks, and so forth. They also took installation, programming, and user manuals for these and other systems.

Naturally, Gold Shield has dealt with this robbery very discretely; it will go out of business if its customers find out it suffered a break-in. The company's owner, Thomas Winchell, has made use of some of his Connections to bring in H.P.D. detectives who are friends of his to investigate the matter while keeping it as quiet as possible. Thus, the player characters may not hear about this theft initially (or at all). The most dramatic way to run this scene is to have one of the detectives working the case approach the PCs after hearing about how they're looking into "unusual thefts." Having made no progress on the case, he enlists their help —

provided he can trust them to keep their mouths shut about it.

An inspection of the crime scene probably won't reveal anything special or helpful to the characters. The thieves bypassed a sophisticated alarm system and other security measures; clearly they were professionals. The most likely explanation for the theft is that the perpetrators have another job in the works, and need the systems they stole to practice.

## PURPOSE OF THIS THEFT

And that's exactly what happened. Hill and his partners know that the safe at Rheingold Fine Gemstones has some of the systems they stole (it's got a security system custom-designed by Gold Shield using some stock systems). They want to practice getting it open quickly. They don't expect to have to go into the safe; if their plan works, Abraham Rheingold will already have taken the gems out for their inspection when they arrive at his office. But in case something goes wrong, they want to prepare.

If the characters have found evidence of a possible Burkhalter Building connection (such as the scrap of blueprint at Ruptured Duck Sky Adventures), and think to ask Thomas Winchell or the other Gold Shield employees about it, they learn the company has the following clients in that building: Sheerson, Feinman, Ross, and Carruthers (a law firm); Patrick Younce and Associates (an investment house); Rheingold Fine Gemstones; Taurus Financial (a stock brokerage); and Jeri's (the café in the lobby of the building). If they go one step further and examine the company's paper records for each of these clients, they find the thieves picked the lock on the file cabinet and stole all the technical installation data about each of them. The fact one of these places — Rheingold Fine Gemstones — has a vault and security system custom-designed by Gold Shield should definitely pique the characters' interest.

## BLACKBURN FURRIERS

Earlier this week, a group of six men wearing black clothes and black ski masks, and wielding Uzi submachine guns and handguns, entered Blackburn Furriers in Arcadia through its back entrance and robbed it. After disabling the alarm system and mercilessly beating a security guard into unconsciousness, the robbers lined the employees and three customers up against one wall, and then proceeded to steal hundreds of thousands of dollars worth of furs. They threw the furs in a panel truck with no license plates or other identifying marks. After cutting the phone lines, they fled in the truck. The robbery made all the papers and has led to a major Haven Police Department investigation, but so far the cops have made no arrests; in fact, they don't even have any major suspects. The security guard remains in a coma at Veteran's Memorial Hospital, and two employees and one customer have entered counseling to cope with post-traumatic stress disorder.

Blackburn's has remained closed since the robbery. The player characters may go to the store to conduct their own investigation, if they wish, but won't learn anything of value. One of the employees claims one of the robbers spoke with a distinct Russian accent, but none of the other witnesses can verify this. (No one in the Hill gang hails from Russia or any other part of Eastern Europe, but the characters may leap to the conclusion the robbers were disguising their voices.)

## PURPOSE OF THIS THEFT

This is another red herring. Although it sounds like some of the Hill gang's jobs, the resemblance is purely superficial. The perpetrators belong to some other gang, and committed the robbery as a single job solely for profit. If you wish, you can spin this out into another scenario, perhaps one relating to radical eco-terrorism, or have the group that committed this theft "lean on" the player characters to catch Hill.

## OTHER CRIMES OF NOTE

Besides the crimes described above, hundreds of criminal acts occur in Haven each and every day. In any given twenty-four hour period, the city experiences an average of 2.8 murders, 120.2 acts of robbery and assault, 4.3 rapes, 2.7 acts of arson, and 28.9 vehicle thefts. Any of these (particularly incidents of grand theft auto) might somehow attract the player characters' attention (after all, the thieves must have planned an escape from the scene of the crime, and it probably involves cars).

If the players seem to be tiring of the investigative aspects of this scenario, you can inject a little action at any time during this part of the scenario simply by dragging an everyday crime right across their path. Perhaps while they're on their way to check out one of the crime scenes described above, they witness a drive-by shooting, an assault, or a drug deal going down. For something more elaborate, maybe they have a run-in with the fur thieves as they try to rob a bank or a jeweler's. A short, sharp burst of action, particularly if it's an encounter the characters can win easily (thus boosting the players' morale), may be just the thing to shake the players up a little before you proceed with the rest of this scenario.

# DETERMINING HILL'S TARGET

One of the characters' potentially most difficult tasks during their investigation is trying to determine the Hill gang's target. After all, Haven contains many things of worth to highly skilled professional thieves. Several clues above — the mention of emeralds, the fragment of the Burkhalter Building blueprint, and the theft of all of Gold Shield's security plans relating to Burkhalter businesses — should point the characters towards Rheingold Fine Gemstones. If they approach Abraham Rheingold regarding a possible theft, he cooperates with them fully, with one exception: he will not reveal the names (or any other information) about any of his clients (or potential clients). Many, if not all, of them desire confidentiality, and as a professional with a longstanding reputation for ethical business practices, he cannot in good conscience even tell the Haven Police Department who his clients are. He would, however, allow undercover police officers to "work" in his offices for a reasonable period of time in an effort to protect him from thieves. (Of course, he requires more convincing if the characters lack official sanction; organized crime figures or other thieves can only enlist his cooperation via threats to his family.)

Of course, there's always a chance the characters will, through mistakes or rotten luck, overlook some or all of the clues regarding the Hill gang's intentions. In that case, you should mention some or all of the potential targets listed below to the players. In other words, give them a list of targets and let them figure out how to distribute their resources in an effort to stop Bryson Hill. If they guess wrong, you have two choices: re-arrange the scenario to give them a chance to defeat Hill (either by changing the target, or providing them with a last-second clue to correct them); or let the robbery proceed as planned. If you choose the latter option, the Hill gang almost certainly gets away scot-free. The characters have to wait for another chance to catch him (and be sure to give it to them).

# POTENTIAL TARGETS

Any one of the following locations, listed in alphabetical order, could be the target of the Hill gang's planned robbery:

**Chadwick Jewelers:** Located in the heart of Arcadia, in the famed "Money Mile" of fancy shops and restaurants, Chadwick's has served the wealthy of Haven, and indeed of the world, for over a century. Renowned for its custom-designed jewelry and watches, it also carries hundreds of thousands of dollars of jewelry from other designers. Jack Chadwick IV, the current owner, is a well-known "man about town" who spends lavishly and acts extravagantly. He has publicly boasted about the strength of his security system, which includes around-the-clock armed guards on the premises.

**Cochrane Museum of Natural History:** One of Haven's most prominent tourist attractions (indeed, one of its few tourist attractions), the Cochrane Museum of Natural History contains displays, samples, specimens, and creatures from all around the world and from every period of history and prehistory on Earth. From its fabulous Dinosaur Gallery, a favorite of children and adults alike, to its award-winning Petting Zoo, to its million-volume library, it contains something for everyone; thousands of visitors throng there every day. Among the many valuable items in its display cases: the Cullinan Gem Collection (unique gemstones gathered by the late Arthur Cullinan, worth many millions of dollars); a collection of moon rocks; and the Eflin Fossils (a group of paleoanthropological fossils collected in Africa by Thomas Eflin, with controversial implications for theories about the origin of man).

**Frederick DeLaVere:** Although many of Haven's richest citizens flaunt their wealth, Frederick DeLaVere is a noteworthy exception. Virtually a recluse in his secluded Golden Heights mansion (which has a high wall and thick gardens surrounding it), he devotes most of his time and attention to his collection of modern art. (Rumors that he has, or used to have, Mafia connections remain unproven; he earned his money in the stock market.) He has millions of dollars' worth of paintings, sculpture, and other works from the twentieth century from all over the world. While it wouldn't be easy for a gang of thieves to steal his entire collection, a carefully selected group of the most valuable pieces would make a rich prize.

**Haven Museum of Fine Art:** Endowed in the late nineteenth century by iron and steel magnate Abel Osterman, the Haven Museum of Fine Art has become one of the world's premiere institutions devoted to collecting and displaying great works of art from all places and periods. Many of its pieces, such as the Hanseatic Tapestries, the Blenheim Chalice, and several paintings by Monet, are world-famous; all of them are irreplaceable. Its current main exhibit, a retrospective on the works of Salvador Dali, displays valuable works of art borrowed from dozens of museums all over the world.

**Haven Federal Reserve Bank:** The branch of the Federal Reserve Bank located in Haven is one of the nation's largest and busiest. In addition to large quantities of cash, it also has some gold reserves. Naturally, it possesses tight security, including armed guards.

**Haven Customs Warehouse:** Haven serves as a point of entry into this country for thousands of people and millions of dollars' worth of goods every day. Most of the goods brought in pass through the Haven Customs Warehouse so that all the necessary paperwork gets processed and any necessary quarantine can take place. Many of the goods themselves, such as precious metals, make worthy targets for

thieves, and investigators should not overlook the possibility that some shipments contain even more valuable smuggled objects (such as drugs or art).

**Primerica Bank:** One of this country's largest financial institutions, Primerica Bank has provided fiscal security for businesses and individuals alike for over seventy years. Its headquarters, located in the Primerica Building in downtown Haven, controls tens (perhaps hundreds) of billions of dollars of assets. A clever thief with the proper timing could hit the bank when it has certain electronic passwords available, or has just received shipments of bearer bonds, or when it stockpiles cash for distribution to its many local branch banks, and get away with a king's ransom.

**Rheingold Fine Gemstones:** For over 120 years, the Rheingold family of Haven has served the gem and jewelry trade by providing the finest in precious stones. Diamonds, emeralds, rubies, sapphires, amethysts — whatever you want or need, Rheingold Fine Gemstones has it, or knows where to get it. Presidents, princes, and movie stars have come to Rheingold to choose the stones for engagement rings, crown jewels, and glittering necklaces. Located in the famed Burkhalter Building, the Rheingold offices typically contain millions of dollars' worth of loose stones, though the custom-designed security system keeps everything safe.

**Thomasin Numismatics:** Alfred Thomasin has been a numismatist (coin collector) and stamp collector all his life. Forty years ago, he took a chance and decided to make his hobby his job, and founded Thomasin Numismatics. His enthusiasm for and knowledge of the subject paid off, and he eventually became very successful, and very wealthy. Thomasin Numismatics, located in Golden Heights, has in stock a collection of rare coins and stamps worth millions to collectors. Though it has extensive security systems, a skilled team of thieves could probably penetrate them and make off with the easily-carried assets.

**Zelliger Gallery:** Private art collectors from all over America, Europe, and Asia come to the Zelliger Gallery every week to purchase the latest, trendiest, most fashionable art. From the old masters to the young turks of the twenty-first century art scene, the Zelliger Gallery carries it all. Located in Arcadia's "Money Mile," the Gallery remains open from 9:00 AM until midnight every day except Sunday.

### Complications

At any point during this scenario, you can complicate matters by throwing another player into the mix. Organized crime elements or rival gangs, both of whom have reason to hate the Hill gang and want to stop to them themselves, may put in an appearance. They could threaten the characters ("Back off — this guy's ours. We'll take care of him our own way... and you, too, if you don't butt out"), or perhaps try to form an alliance with them (a deal with the devil if there ever was one).

Furthermore, there's another person in town hunting for Bryson Hill. His name is Jackson Booth; he's a private investigator and bounty hunter from New York City (use the "Bounty Hunter" sample character sheet in the Haven core rulebook for him). Four years ago, the Hill gang robbed a jewelry store in the Big Apple, in the process killing three people — one of whom was Booth's wife. Crazed with hatred and anger, he's been hunting Hill ever since. Although he seems calm and professional, in truth he's virtually obsessed with killing Hill, and won't hesitate to sacrifice his own life — or kill one of the player characters — to accomplish that goal.

## THE ROBBERY

Once the characters have completed their investigation, or you feel it's time for the scenario to proceed, the Hill gang stages its robbery.

## THE GANG'S PLAN

The theft, as planned by Bryson Hill and his men, should go as follows: Hill and his partners, using false names, have scheduled a meeting with Abraham Rheingold and his staff for 2:00 PM on a particular day. Earlier that morning, one member of the gang, Lawrence Mavretic, drives a small delivery truck into the underground delivery area and parking garage beneath the Burkhalter Building. The truck actually contains some of the equipment the gang will use in its getaway. He will back it into an out of the way parking space.

Mavretic has several jobs to perform while he waits for his partners to arrive. First, he has to pick out a dozen cars in the parking garage that the thieves can use as part of their escape. If possible, he should choose cars backed into their spaces, so the gang can leave quickly. If he can do so without being observed, he will go ahead and pick the locks on the car doors (also disabling alarms, if necessary). Second, wearing a workman's uniform, he has to sneak into the bowels of the building and use his laptop and other computer equipment to tap into the computer servers that controls the building's elevators, security systems, and the like. Third, he has to prepare the escape equipment — the "drop bag" assembled from the stolen parachutes and oxygen equipment. He hooks the hoses up to the building's ventilation system and then hides everything else.

Shortly before 2:00 PM, the rest of the gang arrives via rented helicopter, landing on the helipad on the building's roof. Dressed in the suits obtained for them by Jimmy Vertese, and wearing disguises (complete with forged identity papers), each thief carries a briefcase containing several items: an Uzi submachine gun; small velvet drawstring bags, a small backpack, some climbing equipment, and jimmies and tools for defeating locks and security systems. Additionally, each carries on his person a handgun (fully loaded, with one extra clip), a fiberglass knife, a digital phone, and a small selection of easily concealed thief tools. A couple of them also carry tasers.

As the gang proceeds down the stairs to the elevators, and then to the Rheingold Fine Gemstones offices on the 16th floor, Hill calls Mavretic on his digital phone and orders him to proceed. Mavretic activates the programs he's inserted into the building computers, causing the central elevator to go all the way to the top floor and shut down. Then he finishes setting up the drop bag by putting it at the bottom of the central elevator shaft and attaching the hoses so the ventilation system inflates the bag. If anyone discovers him while he's doing this, he will knock them out with his taser and stuff them in a closet or, if necessary, kill them. While waiting for his partners, he does anything else he can to prepare the possible getaway cars, including turning them around so they can drive out of their spaces (if necessary), parking them as close to the elevator well as possible, and marking them with large Post-It™ notes on the windshields.

Once in the presence of Abraham Rheingold, his staff, and the emeralds they have supposedly come to buy, Hill and his men pull their Uzis and steal the emeralds, shooting or tasering anyone who tries to stop them. After quickly dividing the emeralds up among themselves, they put them in their drawstring velvet bags, and then put the bags and any tools they want to keep in the small backpacks. Concealing their guns beneath their suit jackets, they then proceed to the elevators on the 16th floor, pry open the doors on the central elevator, and use their climbing equipment to carefully slide down the elevator cable to the bottom of the shaft, where the drop bag allows them to land safely. It takes about 30-60 seconds for each thief to get down and out of the shaft, assuming all goes well. In the event a problem arises, they can take the much slower route of using the ladder built into the side of the shaft, or even have Mavretic call the elevator (they don't want to use the elevator car if they can avoid it, since they feel they could easily get trapped inside it).

As each thief gets out of the elevator shaft, he quickly moves into the parking garage, takes one of the cars marked by Mavretic (breaking into it if Mavretic has not yet opened it), and drives out as calmly as possible. Mavretic waits until everyone has made it down the elevator shaft before he leaves. If necessary, he uses his access to the building's computer to interfere with security's efforts to stop the robbery; he can even blow the whole system and

shut down the building entirely if he has to. After all members of the gang have exited the building, they proceed by separate routes to a pre-arranged rendezvous point outside of the city — a small country hotel called the Chanticleer. Their routes contain double-backs, long open stretches of highway, and other means to detect people following

**Why Not Parachute?**
Given the theft of the parachutes, the characters may assume the Hill gang either plans to parachute onto the target of the theft, or intends to use the parachutes as part of their escape. Several considerations dictate against the Hill gang doing this, however, and smart characters may realize this at some point.

First, not all of the members of the gang are skilled parachutists. They have all skydived before, but only Mark Munroe is truly experienced at it.

Second, even if they were skilled skydivers, it's very difficult to hit a target as small as the roof of a building.

Third, even skilled BASE jumpers would hesitate to jump off something as relatively short as the 16th story of a building (or even a 25-story building). The odds do not favor a problem-free jump.

As you know, the gang uses the parachutes for its "drop bag," not for skydiving. However, if the characters fixate on this aspect of the scenario, you may not want to disappoint them. In this case, you can have the thieves leave the parachutes on the helicopter which brings them to the building, use the helicopter for the first part of their getaway, then parachute out of the chopper somewhere in the rural areas outside of Haven.

them and evade pursuit. If a member cannot shake his pursuers, he does not go to the rendezvous; instead he keeps trying to escape and meet up with his partners at the secondary rendezvous point in Chicago one week after the robbery.

If someone tries to stop them, the gang doesn't hesitate to respond with deadly force, if appropriate. They prefer to get away quickly and cleanly, without bloodshed, but they'll kill if they have to. If necessary they can alter their plan, perhaps using the helicopter to escape, taking hostages, or pulling a fire alarm and trying to mingle with the office workers as they flee the building.

## THE BURKHALTER BUILDING

Construction began a few years after World War II and completed in 1953, the Burkhalter Building has become a landmark of downtown Haven. Its distinctive profile and grey-green glass windows make it easy to detect in the City of Violence's skyline. It has twenty-five stories, with a helipad on the very top.

Unlike so many buildings in Haven, the Burkhalter is solidly constructed, with sturdy interior walls and columns that could actually provide some cover from gunfire (as opposed to most modern buildings, whose cheap plaster walls can't stop a bullet). Although it shows its age a bit on the inside, it remains a favorite of many Havenites, and thanks to several infrastructure upgrades still qualifies as Class A office space.

The bottom three floors of the building form a vast, airy lobby with marble floors. The lobby includes an elegant waiting area for people visiting the building, a directory of the offices upstairs, and various service businesses catering to the thousands of people who work here (a card store, a drycleaner's, a copy shop, a mailing store, and so forth). Chief among these facilities are Jeri's (a nice but not too expensive restaurant on the ground floor) and the Mezzanine (a bar and lounge on the mezzanine overlooking the lobby).

The twenty-two floors above the lobby contain offices for dozens of businesses, ranging from law firms, to financial firms, to advertising agencies, to small "boutique" companies like Rheingold Fine

Gemstones. The building's management has its offices on the fourth floor.

The Burkhalter also has two underground levels. The basement (Level A) includes the main offices of the security staff (which maintains a watch desk in the lobby) and the janitorial staff. The sub-basement (Level B) contains the building's heating, ventilation, and air conditioning equipment, phone switching stations, computer servers, and the like; it also leads into the first level of the five-level underground parking garage.

A bank of three elevators runs through the entire length of the building, as do two flights of stairs. The building also has a separate service elevator.

## ENTER THE PLAYER CHARACTERS

Where and how the player characters enter into this part of the scenario depends entirely on how well they do with their investigation. If they figured things out early enough, they may be waiting for the Hill gang when the thieves arrive. Otherwise they're either going to have to wait to see what the Hill gang does, and try to react accordingly, or show up late and desperately attempt to prevent the gang's escape.

If the players have completely overlooked or misinterpreted the clues pointing towards Rheingold Fine Gemstones, you can create a plot device to bring them back into the scenario. Perhaps a security guard at the Burkhalter Building thinks he recognizes one of the thieves and calls the cops, or maybe the theft goes bad and becomes a hostage situation to which the characters can respond. Only if the characters have completely blown things should the Hill gang get away, in which case you might want to drop a few clues to give the chance a characters to pursue them (perhaps leading to a dramatic confrontation at the gang's first rendezvous point).

## THE HILL GANG

Here are game statistics and profiles of the members of the Hill gang. Feel free to discard some of them if you have a small group of player characters, or to duplicate one or two if you have a large group requiring more opposition.

# BRYSON HILL

STR: 14  INFL: 16
WILL: 16  MV: 15
AGI: 18  ACC: 17
STA: 15  FV: 15
INT: 16  SUB: 16
PER: 15  CM: 17
HEA-C: 45  HEA-L: 15

**Skills:** Acrobatics +1, Actor +2, Computers +1, Demolitions +3, Disguise +1, Driving +2, Electronics +1, Espionage +1, First Aid +1, Forgery +2, Gambling +1, Streetwise +2, Thievery +4

**Languages:** English – United Kingdom (Native) 19, German 13, French 11, Spanish 10

**Benefits:** Ambidextrous, Area Knowledge (London), Authority Figure, Connections (underworld), Perfect Timing, Wealthy

**Drawbacks:** Pursued (various police forces), Rivalry (other top thieves)

**Starting Equipment:** Nice clothing, expensive car, various firearms and thieves' tools

**Background:** The authorities know relatively little about Bryson Hill's background. He was born in London in roughly 45 years ago and grew up there, though his family moved to New York City when he was 17. His good looks, winning manner, and quick wit allowed him to make friends easily, and his outgoing personality and strong will made him a natural leader. Though he could have succeeded at virtually anything he set his mind to, he never seemed inclined to follow the rules or do what was expected of him. An adolescence marked by convictions for committing petty crimes soon grew into a young adulthood of serious criminal behavior. After being imprisoned with the legendary thief Leo O'Toole, he redirected his career toward major thefts, and soon developed a reputation for his skill, daring, and successfulness. And it's all gotten better and better for him since then.

**Quote:** "Let's do this quick and do it right, boys. If everything goes as planned, we'll be a whole lot richer a couple of hours from now."

# GREG HAMESLEY

STR: 12  INFL: 15
WILL: 14  MV: 13
AGI: 15  ACC: 15
STA: 14  FV: 13
INT: 13  SUB: 14
PER: 15  CM: 15
HEA-C: 40  HEA-L: 13

**Skills:** Acrobatics +2, Actor +1, Artist +1, Chemistry +1, Civil Engineering +1, Computers +1, Demolitions +1, Electronics +2, Espionage +2, Forgery +3, Streetwise +1, Thievery +3

**Languages:** English (Native) 17, Italian 9, Spanish 7

**Benefits:** Connections (Underworld), Eagle Eyes, Lucky, Sex Appeal, Wealthy

**Drawbacks:** Braggart, Pursued (Various police forces), Rivalry (Other top thieves)

**Starting Equipment:** Nice clothing, various firearms and thieves' tools

**Background:** Greg Hamesley met Bryson Hill in prison while they were both serving time for theft. The two hit it off immediately, and when Hill got out and decided to form his own gang of thieves, he asked Hamesley (who had earned his release a year previously) to join him. Hamesley, eager for a way to use his electronics and thieving skills, not to mention his abilities as a forger, to make money, was glad to team up with his friend. They have prospered ever since, though Hamesley's loose tongue and tendency to brag about his exploits (especially to women) have landed the gang in hot water more than once.

Quote: "Oh, that was nothing. Let me tell you about the time we...."

## JASON DRAKE

| | | | |
|---|---|---|---|
| STR: | 18 | INFL: | 14 |
| WILL: | 13 | MV: | 18 |
| AGI: | 16 | ACC: | 16 |
| STA: | 18 | FV: | 17 |
| INT: | 15 | SUB: | 15 |
| PER: | 15 | CM: | 16 |
| HEA-C: | 49 | HEA-L: | 16 |

Skills: Aeronautical Engineering +1, Agriculture +1, Demolitions +1, Driver +3, First Aid +1, Military Science +1, Piloting +3, Streetwise +2, Thievery +1, Tracking +1

Languages: English (Native) 16, Spanish 11, Arabic 6

Benefits: Gifted Fighter, Wealthy

Drawbacks: Foolhardy, Pursued (various police forces), Rivalry (other top thieves)

Special Abilities: Tough As Nails

Starting Equipment: Nice clothing, several cars, various firearms and thieves' tools

Background: Jason Drake grew up on a farm in Wyoming. As a young man he enlisted in the Army, was trained as a helicopter pilot, and served in Operation Desert Storm. He was dishonorably discharged for operating a smuggling ring while in Saudi Arabia, and soon drifted into the underworld. His skills as a driver and pilot, not to mention his natural ability as a fist-fighter, soon brought him to Bryson Hill's attention. After observing Drake carefully for several months, Hill decided the young man had what it took to be a contributing member of the Hill gang, and invited him to join. Drake accepted, and has been a part of the gang ever since.

Quote: "Look, you guys just worry about getting the stones. I'll worry about getting us out of here."

## MARK MUNROE

| | | | |
|---|---|---|---|
| STR: | 16 | INFL: | 16 |
| WILL: | 15 | MV: | 17 |
| AGI: | 17 | ACC: | 17 |
| STA: | 17 | FV: | 16 |
| INT: | 16 | SUB: | 33 |
| PER: | 17 | CM: | 17 |
| HEA-C: | 48 | HEA-L: | 16 |

Skills: Actor +1, Climbing +3, Computers +4, Demolitions +1, Disguise +1, Driving +1, Electronics +3, Espionage +3, Gambling +2, Military Science +1, Parachuting +3, Streetwise +2, Thievery +3

Languages: English (Native) 18, Russian 15, Arabic 14, Chinese (Mandarin) 9

Benefits: Connections (underworld; espionage world), Natural Athlete, Wealthy

**Drawbacks:** Pursued (various police forces), Rivalry (other top thieves)

**Special Abilities:** Sixth Sense

**Starting Equipment:** Nice clothing, high-end laptop computer tricked out for hacking, various firearms and thieves' tools

**Background:** After being convicted of breaking into his college's computer to change his grades (and those of other students who paid him), Mark Munroe was recruited by the Central Intelligence Agency. He spent several years working for the "Company" as a computer warfare and security expert, and also on occasion as a field agent (though he usually proved too unpredictable and violent for sensitive missions). When he finally decided he was wasting his time working for peanuts for the government, he contacted Bryson Hill, whom he'd had some contact with during his espionage career, and offered his services. Delighted at the prospect of having a highly skilled hacker in his gang, Hill brought him into the fold.

**Quote:** "Okay, once I take down the security systems, you guys are gonna have only about ten minutes to get the job done, so don't screw it up."

## VINCE GILDER

| | | | |
|---|---|---|---|
| STR: | 14 | INFL: | 17 |
| WILL: | 15 | MV: | 15 |
| AGI: | 18 | ACC: | 18 |
| STA: | 16 | FV: | 16 |
| INT: | 17 | SUB: | 18 |
| PER: | 18 | CM: | 18 |
| HEA-C: | 45 | HEA-L: | 15 |

**Skills:** Accounting +1, Computers +2, Demolitions +1, Driving +2, Electronics +3, Espionage +1, Gambling +1, Military Science +2, Streetwise +3, Thievery +2

**Languages:** English (Native) 12

**Benefits:** Ambidextrous, Fast Draw, Iron Will, Marksman, Rapid Fire

**Drawbacks:** Psychological Disorder (anti-social personality disorder), Pursued (various police forces), Rivalry (other top thieves)

**Special Abilities:** Predator

**Starting Equipment:** Nice clothing, various firearms and thieves' tools, two knives

**Background:** No one in the Hill gang knows much about Vince — where he comes from, how he learned his mixed bag of skills, or why he's so violent. Though the diversity and breadth of his skills, particularly his uncanny accuracy with firearms and knives, makes him a valuable member of the group, unlike the others he's inclined to use force to get things done. He seems to enjoy it, and in fact Munroe and Mavretic both know he's killed several prostitutes with no discernible provocation. Sooner or later his psychopathic tendencies will outweigh his value to the gang, and Hill will kill him.

**Quote:** "Look, why bother with all this sneaking around? We can just shoot them and walk right in."

## LAWRENCE MAVRETIC

STR: 10　　　　INFL: 18
WILL: 17　　　MV: 12
AGI: 15　　　　ACC: 17
STA: 13　　　　FV: 14
INT: 18　　　　SUB: 18
PER: 18　　　　CM: 17
HEA-C: 40　　　HEA-L: 13

**Skills:** Accounting +2, Computers +2, Electronics +2, Espionage +2, Finance +3, Forgery +1, History +1, Philosophy +1, Social Science +1, Streetwise +1, Thievery +3

**Languages:** English (Native) 20, German 15, French 13, Russian 9

**Benefits:** Area Knowledge (NYC), Connections (Underworld), Eidetic Memory, Wealthy

**Drawbacks:** Pursued (various police forces), Rivalry (other top thieves)

**Starting Equipment:** Nice clothing, high-end laptop computer tricked out for hacking, various firearms and thieves' tools

**Background:** Small and scrawny since he was a child, Lawrence Mavretic was gifted with an immense intellect and intellectual curiosity to make up for his physical deficiencies. Soaking up knowledge like a sponge with his photographic memory, he quickly earned a reputation as a "brain" and a "geek." To look "cool" in the eyes of his peers, he got involved in computer hacking and petty crime. He dropped out of high school in his junior year, convinced he could learn more, and make more money, on his own than he could if he went to college. A stint working for a major computer firm ended quickly, since his renegade personality and tendency to break rules for his own benefit clashed with the corporate culture. He gradually drifted more and more into the underworld, eventually earning himself a place in Hill's prestigious gang with his security and hacking talents. Although his sarcastic personality doesn't endear him to his partners, he more than makes up for it with skills at his disposal.

**Quote:** "Go in through the front? Why don't you just go ahead and shoot yourself now to save time? If you want to do this right, let me hack their security and find a better way in."

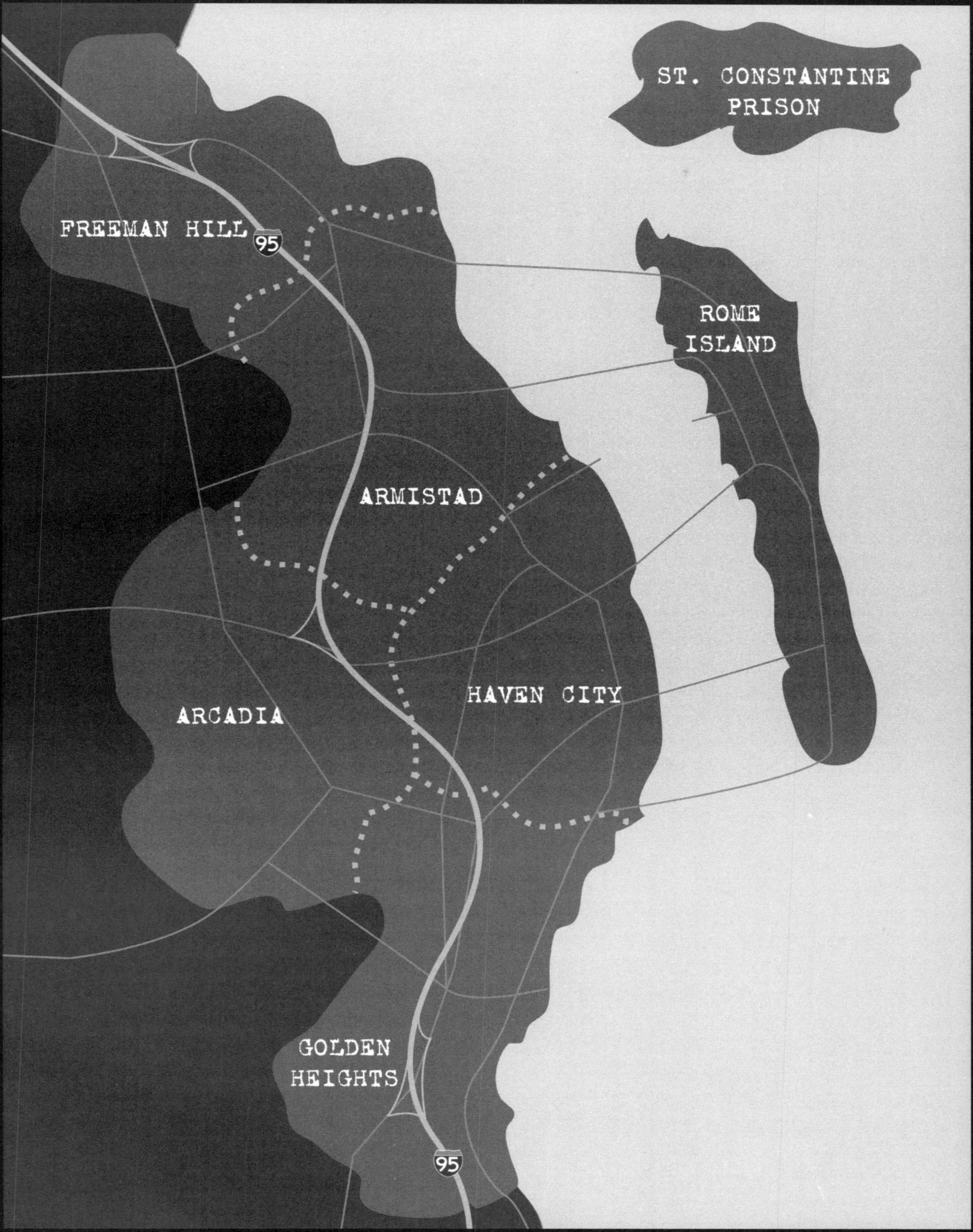
ST. CONSTANTINE
PRISON
FREEMAN HILL
95
ROME
ISLAND
ARMISTAD
HAVEN CITY
ARCADIA
GOLDEN
HEIGHTS
95

# The Home of
# Haven: City of Violence

I know who you are

# www.lpjdesign.com

# COMINING SOON...

# BULLETPROOF SCREEN

## GAME OPERATIONS DIRECTOR SCREEN
## AVAILABLE JUNE 2003

# COMINING SOON...

# PATH OF RAGE

## CITY OF HAVEN SOURCEBOOK
### AVAILABLE JULY 2003

# COMINING SOON...

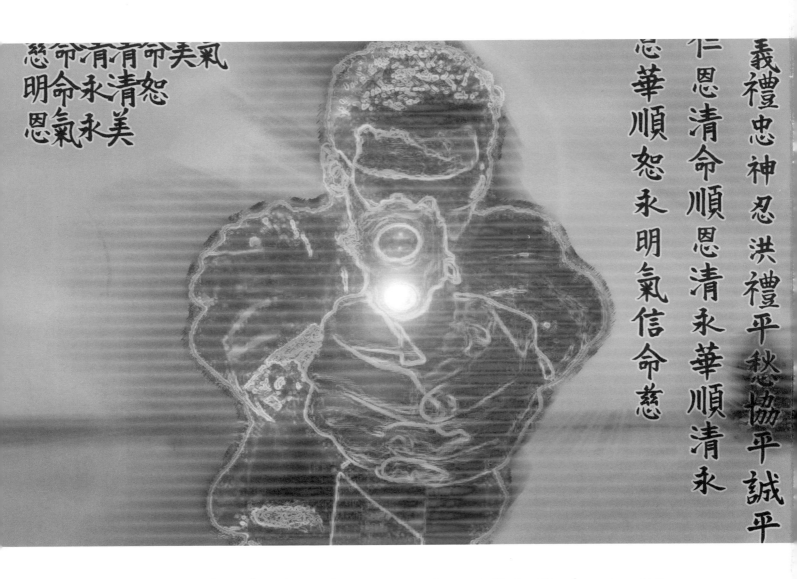

# KILLING FIELDS

## MARTIAL ARTS & FIREARMS SOURCEBOOK
## AVAILABLE JULY 2003